Crime as Play

Crime as Play:

Delinquency in a Middle Class Suburb

Pamela Richards
The University of Florida

Richard A Berk
The University of California
Santa Barbara

Brenda Forster
Elmhurst College

Ballinger Publishing Company • **Cambridge, Massachusetts**
A Subsidiary of Harper & Row, Publishers, Inc.

This book is printed on recycled paper.

International Standard Book Number: 0-88410-798-1

Library of Congress Catalog Card Number: 79-12772

Printed in the United States of America

fM

Library of Congress Cataloging in Publication Data

Richards, Pamela.
   Crime as play.

   Bibliography: p.
   Includes index.
   1. Juvenile delinquents—United States. 2. Middle classes—United States. 3. Suburban crimes—United States. I. Berk, Richard A., joint author. II. Forster, Brenda, joint author. III. Title.
HV9104.R52   364.36   79-12772
ISBN 0-88410-798-1

Contents

v

List of Tables

Preface

We began this research with an interest in middle class delinquency, welcoming the opportunity to analyze self-report data from a group of affluent adolescents. Middle class adolescents are seldom the subject of detailed delinquency research, and there is relatively little available data on the topic. In the process of our work it became clear that many of the most familiar explanations of middle class delinquency did little to help us understand the patterns in our data. We found ourselves turning to alternative perspectives for additional insight; the product of this reorientation is the leisure decisionmaking framework that guides this analysis. It is a somewhat unusual approach to the issue, emphasizing both the leisure character of middle class delinquency and the decisionmaking process by which individuals make leisure choices. It has been useful for a number of reasons, particularly for the way it has forced us to examine many assumptions about the character of middle class delinquency.

We are grateful to many people for their help throughout this work. Financial support for data collection was provided by a citizen's youth council in the community studied, and members of the council were generous with their criticism, feedback, and encouragement during the initial stages of the research. Early analyses were read by Gary Albrecht, Howard Becker, Remi Clignet, Fred DuBow, and Robert Winch. Lengthy discussions with Sarah Berk, Michael Hennessy, Angela O'Rand, and Charles Wood helped clarify the issues involved in extending a leisure framework to middle class delinquency. To them we owe special thanks for their support and encouragement. Advice from Chip Hay and Debbie Anderson simplified the mechanics of data manipulation considerably. Habib Al-Moussallie helped prepare the manuscript, which Trina Miller and Adelle Gold typed with constant patience and good humor.

Most of all we wish to thank the students who generously agreed to share their experiences with us. Their candor and insight are deeply appreciated.

P.R.
R.A.B.
B.F.
April, 1979

Chapter One

Class Issues in the Study of Delinquency

INTRODUCTION

Delinquency is usually thought to be a lower class phenomenon, largely confined to the urban poor. While no one would deny that middle class children are occasionally delinquent, their activities are seldom considered to be as serious as those of lower class adolescents. Yet a quick glance through news reports and popular magazines reveals a growing public concern over middle class delinquency. Newspaper editors allude to a "rise" in crime among middle class youths and delinquency is becoming a major issue in some affluent suburbs. While people debate the causes of middle class delinquency most agree that it is a problem, and youth programs, anti-delinquency campaigns, and counseling services have been instituted in efforts to curb its growth.

Middle class delinquency is becoming an issue of academic interest as well. Social scientists have also assumed that delinquency is concentrated among lower strata groups and often focus their research on lower class populations. The majority of theories explain delinquency in ways requiring large and systematic differences in its class distribution. Middle class adolescents are assumed to be less delinquent than their lower class peers, and auxiliary theories of middle class delinquency are constructed to explain the delinquency that affluent adolescents do report. However, researchers who examine the class distribution of delinquency seldom find the differences that most theories predict. Self-report studies show little systematic variation along traditional class lines, and the limited data

available from middle class groups suggest that patterns of delinquency among affluent adolescents parallel those found in other
populations.

Still, relatively little is known about patterns in middle class
delinquency. Information is limited, and theories of the middle class
case are usually modifications of those originally formulated for
lower class adolescents. Our goal in this book is to present extensive
data on the "delinquent" activities of middle class adolescents and to
construct an account of these experiences that provides a theoretical
alternative to the most familiar explanations. Our empirical analysis
will rest on self-report data from a survey of nearly 3,000 students
living in an affluent suburb of a large midwestern city. Respondents
were asked about recent "delinquent" activities including vandalism,
drug use, minor theft, serious delinquency, and what we will call
"noncrime" delinquency. Each of these topics is examined in detail
in the chapters that follow. Our theoretical perspective on middle
class delinquency will stress its leisure character and the role that
individual decisionmaking can play in structuring the activity. Before
proceeding, however, it may be helpful to review more traditional
approaches.

THE IMPORTANCE OF CLASS
IN DELINQUENCY THEORY

There are few issues more central to the study of delinquency than
that of class. Assumptions about the class distribution of delinquency are at least implicit in most theories, and these alleged
differences are also crucial components of most *ad hoc* explanations.
There are, of course, several types of class theories, each with a
slightly different view of the role that class plays in delinquency. One
set focuses on the way life chances are structured by class position,
arguing that deviant behavior can be traced to the experience of class
inequality. A second set of theories focuses on the way in which
lifestyles (particularly culture and values or attitudes) are presumed
to vary by class. These differences in cultural patterns are alleged to
produce differential propensities toward deviance.

Both schools have their roots in early ecological theories of
delinquency. Ecologists noted that disadvantaged city neighborhoods
had consistently higher delinquency rates than more affluent areas
and proposed explanations based on the concept of "social disorganization."[1] Forces such as family breakdown, mental illness, or
cultural conflict were thought to lead to a general decay of
conventional social order, disrupting the normal functioning of social

control mechanisms. Since these forces were differentially distributed by social class, disorganization was most likely to occur in lower
class neighborhoods. Thus, class differences in the degree of social
disorganization were held responsible for high delinquency rates in
lower class urban environments.

There are several components of ecological theory that can be
traced to later delinquency perspectives. Subcultural theorists have
extended the concepts of cultural conflict and normative ambiguity
to an explanation that stresses value differences. Since subcultural
theories were originally meant to explain the delinquent activities of
lower class gang members, their theoretical class assumptions are
quite explicit.[2] Lower class groups are presumed to have different
values from those of the middle class. "Unique" values produce
"unique" behavior, which in turn tends to be labeled deviant.
Sometimes "subculture" is used to refer to a general lower class
culture that predisposes members to deviant behavior (for example,
Miller, 1958). Other times a more narrow meaning of the term is
employed to describe the culture of delinquent adolescents whose
"negativistic" or "nonutilitarian" values lead to negativistic and
nonutilitarian (delinquent) activities (for example, A.K. Cohen,
1955; Cloward and Ohlin, 1960).

Subcultural theorists often disagree about the source of the
cultural variation that occurs along class lines. Socialization theories
are among the most popular amounts of cultural differences, since
child-raising strategies are generally presumed to vary by class. Lower
class value systems that apparently endorse violence and encourage
minimal conformity to legal codes are explained by reference to the
allegedly corporal nature of punishment in lower class families or an
emphasis on avoiding sanctions rather than observing the spirit of
rules.[3] Other subcultural theorists rely on a model of individual
adaptation to stress in an effort to explain class variation in cultural
patterns. Here subcultural values are formed in response to individual
perceptions of the futility of conforming to middle class values and
codes. Lower class boys know that they have little to gain by
conformity; frustration leads them to rebel against middle class
authority and to espouse oppositional values (for the clearest
example of this perspective, see A.K. Cohen, 1955).

Whatever the source of value differences, subcultural theories
assume that class variation in cultural patterns can be used to explain
delinquency. There is, however, another component of ecological
reasoning that has been developed in delinquency theory—the notion
of structural "breakdown." Theories in this tradition emphasize the
ways in which the organization of social relationships can break

down or, as components of the larger order, can fall out of phase. For example, strain theorists argue that structural disjunctions between goals and opportunities for achievement can produce systemic pressures toward deviance.[4] Since opportunities for success are differentially distributed along class lines, structural strains should be strongest among lower class groups. They have the fewest resources and least access to opportunities, and deviant or delinquent adaptations could be one response to strain. Structural pressures toward deviance are also given a causal role in conflict theories that see delinquency as an adaptation to class exploitation.[5] Lower class groups are thought to develop distinctive behavior styles in response to social inequality. This should increase their chances of law-breaking (and delinquency) and should lead to more deviance among members of lower classes. One can note similar assumptions implicit in many control theories of delinquency. Control theorists argue that delinquency can be deterred by bonds or ties to conventional social order. Stakes in conformity, or what one stands to lose if deviance is discovered, are presumed to be a powerful element in this bond. Such stakes should vary by class. Lower class individuals have less to lose by deviance than middle or upper class individuals since they have less invested in the conventional order. Thus, stakes in conformity should be a weaker delinquency deterrent among lower class adolescents and should lead to a higher incidence of delinquency than in the middle class.[6]

Despite these predictions, research routinely fails to uncover consistent class differences in delinquent behavior. Comprehensive reviews of the literature produce mixed evidence about the class distribution of delinquency (for reviews of the class differences literature see Tittle and Villamez, 1977; and Box and Ford, 1971), and researchers who analyze class differences in a single data set with a representative class range seldom find meaningful differences along conventional class lines.[7] This failure has been explained in both theoretical and methodological terms. Several of these issues are particularly important in understanding the problems involved in studying middle class delinquency.

EMPIRICAL EVIDENCE FOR CLASS DIFFERENCES IN DELINQUENCY

Most of the evidence used to support predictions of class differences in delinquency is drawn from official statistics. The delinquency rates that were analyzed by Chicago ecologists were gathered by official law enforcement agencies; studies of officially labeled delinquents or incarcerated offenders also tend to show class distributions of the kind predicted by familiar perspectives. However, there are class biases inherent in official statistics, and most authors agree that they offer little information about the class distribution of delinquent behavior itself.[8]

Researchers have turned to self-report delinquency measures in an effort to remedy some of these problems, and it is in self-report studies that class differences often fail to appear. Time after time, self-report researchers are forced to conclude that there are few differences in the delinquent activity of lower and middle class respondents (see reviews by Tittle and Villamez, 1977, and Box and Ford, 1971, for a comprehensive discussion of this issue). Both qualitative and quantitative differences seem minimal, the direction of differences fluctuates, and patterns in the predicted direction are often substantively unimportant. Yet the logic of class differences remains firmly entrenched in the delinquency literature. In part this has to do with the way class is usually conceptualized and, in part, with the variety of ways in which class is measured.

DEFINITIONS OF CLASS IN DELINQUENCY THEORY

There are two major issues involved in relating class to delinquency—the way in which class should be defined and the way in which adolescents should be placed within a class structure. Delinquency theorists have tended to rely on a socioeconomic (SES) model of class similar to that which underlies most deviance theory. Most often, class is used as a descriptive category that denotes lifestyle characteristics. Class is seen as a continuum that can be quantified along dimensions such as education, occupation, and income. Upper middle, and lower classes are identified by rather arbitrary high, medium, and low cutoff points along this composite range.

This is not the only way that class can be conceptualized. Other class theorists employ the term as an analytic category that specifies the nature of economic relationships between different social groups. This more marxian view links the concept directly to participation in the productive process. The class division between workers and owners sets up an inequality between these groups that places them in opposition. Here class is not a continuum of status or lifestyle characteristics, nor does it refer to strata grouped in descriptive terms. To identify classes according to productive roles is to recognize the potential conflicts between classes and to anticipate the way in which workplace inequality extends to social relationships outside strictly economic spheres.

SES models of class are the most popular of these two perspectives used in the study of delinquency. Status models are obviously more consistent with popular subcultural theories or socialization perspectives: strata variation in child-raising patterns, cultural values, or world views can be termed class differences only when groups are identified according to status or lifestyle rather than conflict inherent in productive roles. Status models are also implicit in structural explanations that concentrate on the problem of status achievement and blocked mobility (e.g., strain theory). Disjunction between aspirations and expectations is often phrased in terms of a ladder model of stratification that presumes that movement between contiguous status categories is or should be possible.

The development of class models of delinquency has lagged behind that of status models. In part this may be due to the difficulty in fitting adolescents into a framework that places primary emphasis on economically productive roles. To study the class distribution of delinquency one must be able to assign adolescents a class position. However, adolescents are seldom fully active members of the work force. Thus, they do not participate directly in production. Their role is mediated by institutions such as the family or the school, and they do not occupy clear class positions themselves. Consequently, a class analysis of adolescent deviance is difficult. At the very least, it requires some modification of the concept of class and a reevaluation of traditional assumptions about the relationship between class position and deviance. Given the complexity of these issues, it is not surprising that there is little delinquency research from this class tradition.

SES models do not escape problems inherent in assigning adolescents a class position, but their focus on lifestyle considerations rather than productive roles makes it easier for them to skirt the issue. Just as adolescents are classless, so they possess no socioeconomic status of their own. Analysts are forced to assign adolescents a SES position that reflects (1) attributes of other actors who are thought to exert a causal impact on their behavior or (2) predictions about adolescents' future class positions. Either strategy relies on a theorists' ability to relate these class categories to adolescent deviance.

Most delinquency researchers specify adolescents' SES according to the occupational or educational characteristics of their parents (usually their father). A theory tying parental status to child deviance is required to explain any anticipated class differences. Subcultural theories that focus on intergenerational transmission of values offer one such explanation. Cultures are presumed to vary by SES, with the status position of parents determining the type of culture they pass on to their children. The unique values of lower class cultures are assumed to create greater propensities toward deviance among their members. This should produce class differences in delinquency when class is measured by parents' socioeconomic status. A similar line of reasoning underlies other value theories that emphasize child-rearing practices.[9]

Researchers occasionally assign socioeconomic status to adolescents in another way. Information on parental SES is supplemented with data on the class position that an adolescent is likely to assume upon entrance into the work force. Again, a theoretical link between future status and current behavior is required if this definition of class is to be meaningfully related to delinquency. Strain theories are among the most likely to attempt this link. Measures of an adolescent's educational and occupational expectations are used as indicators of future status, and "strain" is identified on the basis of inconsistencies between these expectations and an individual's aspirations. A boy who expects a blue collar job is categorized as working class. If he simultaneously aspires to be a doctor, he is presumed to be in a position of strain with its attendant risk of deviant adaptations. Since lower strata groups are more likely to experience this strain, delinquency should be differentially distributed by socioeconomic status.[10]

Like class theories, these SES models assume that class or status is not experienced by children in the same fashion as by adults. Status inequalities are mediated by the family, the peer group, or the school, and these mediating institutions are crucial in relating class to adolescent deviance. Obviously, general status models of deviance have been extensively modified in order to make them applicable to children. Yet even under these conditions, delinquency research fails to uncover the patterns predicted by most theories. Parental occupations seldom differentiate between types or degrees of delinquency; apparent strains fail to predict systematic deviant responses. There are two obvious explanations for these null findings. Either status models of delinquency are inaccurate, or status (class) is so poorly measured in delinquency research that true class differences are obscured. Some theorists choose the first of these options and reject class or status theories in favor of explanations that focus on some other dimension of inequality. However, most attribute the absence of class differences to methodological problems in delinquency research. Until these problems can be solved, most delinquency researchers prefer to withhold final judgment on the validity of class- or status-based theories.

METHODOLOGICAL ISSUES IN ANALYZING
THE CLASS DISTRIBUTION OF DELINQUENCY

Many of the methodological problems involved in studying the class distribution of delinquency stem from difficulties in operationalizing an adolescent's class position. Others are related to general methodological weaknesses in delinquency research. There seem to be three main problem areas in research on class differences: (1) those related to the measurement of class or status position, (2) those involved in the measurement of delinquency itself, and (3) those reflecting weaknesses in research design or techniques of analysis.[11]

Delinquency researchers generally rely on familiar SES measures of social class. Most argue that these measures are a common sociological convention and that items such as father's occupation are as good an indicator of social status as most others. The theoretical utility of this approach to adolescent status has been discussed above, but it also has some methodological problems worth noting. One of the most important is that of cross-study comparability. SES measures differ from study to study. Some researchers focus on one dimension of status (e.g., occupation) while others concentrate on another (e.g., education). Yet class differences in delinquency may vary with the status dimension used in an analysis. Differences may also vary with the degree of detail used in assigning status position. Some researchers employ rather broad measures of class (e.g., lower class versus middle class) that may not adequately differentiate between individuals who occupy different statuses. Null findings could be one result.[12] It is also difficult to compare analyses that use broad status categories with those that use finer distinctions. Without comparable status measures, it is difficult to know whether findings reflect methodological decisions or actual behavior patterns.

Different levels of analysis also make it difficult to compare studies of class and delinquency. For example, ecological data come in aggregate geographical units (usually arrest rates). Since most delinquency theories are phrased at the individual level, the relationship between ecological distributions and class differences in actual behavior is difficult to establish. There is always a temptation to conclude that variation in area rates reflects differences in the behavior of individuals, but to do so means running the risk of the ecological fallacy. These difficulties are most obvious in studies that use individual level delinquency data but have no individual measures of social status (see for example, Wolfgang, Figlio, and Sellin, 1972). In such cases, researchers reluctantly substitute information about the class characteristics of an individual's neighborhood (e.g., census tract) for individual level data on class or status. The assumption that an individual's class position is the same as that of most families living within his or her census tract is sometimes a risky one, and it is difficult to prove that any apparent class patterns reflect individual level class differences. Research using other types of official statistics can also encounter problems with levels of analysis. Since the most popular delinquency theories are theories of individual behavior, aggregate data are not likely to offer fully valid tests no matter what the apparent class distribution.

These methodological problems are often compounded by the way delinquency itself is measured. Some researchers measure delinquency with additive scales; others prefer cumulative indexes. The same items are seldom used as scale components from study to study. There are also authors who prefer to analyze delinquency without combining their measures into any sort of composite index at all. We will have more to say about these measurement issues in Chapter 3, but it is clear that this makes it difficult to reach firm conclusions about the class distribution of delinquency. The lack of consistent findings about class differences could be due to different measures of delinquency as well as different theoretical perspectives on the nature and proper measurement of class.

General design weaknesses also make it difficult to study the class distribution of delinquency. For example, delinquency research is plagued by the use of limited samples. Often these samples lack sufficient class variation to test class assumptions or establish class differences in delinquent behavior. Other researchers artificially limit the class range in their data when they exclude categories of respondents assumed to be theoretically irrelevant along some other dimension. Often this is done for practical reasons. The rather limited analytic techniques used by many delinquency researchers (e.g., crosstabulation) make comprehensive statistical controls difficult. To circumvent this problem, analysts exclude girls or blacks in order to avoid controlling for sex or race. This may reduce the adequacy of a class analysis, since any resulting class patterns may not apply to data gathered from unconstrained populations.

There are other methodological problems related to this issue of statistical controls. In order to isolate true class patterns, an analyst must be able to control for factors that may obscure class differences. However, comprehensive controls are difficult to exert with tabular techniques since cross tabulation and its variant require large samples. In addition, control via cross tabulation produces almost innumerable tables in any complex analysis. This makes it difficult to summarize overall patterns. Frequently analysts lack the required sample sizes or concise summary techniques that are needed to draw a clear picture of class differences in delinquency.[13]

Earlier we noted that official statistics are often used to demonstrate class differences in delinquency. Research design problems as well as measurement issues are related to this strategy. Studies that compare groups of incarcerated delinquent populations to matched groups of unincarcerated nondelinquents are likely to discover class differences in delinquency by virtue of class biases in official treatment strategies.[14] Research comparing official delinquents with general populations is likely to uncover class differences for many of the same reasons. Since much of the class difference literature is based on designs that use officially identified delinquents, conclusions about the class distribution of delinquency are somewhat risky.

These are some of the methodological issues that make class-based theories of delinquency difficult to falsify. Yet the theories predict differences that should be far too large to be completely masked by methodological artifacts, and forty years of research should have uncovered some systematic class differences if these explanations are useful. Nonetheless, literature review after literature review fails to uncover any clear relationship between class or status and delinquent behavior. The absence of these predicted differences seems more than a methodological artifact. Either there are no class differences in delinquency as conventionally defined, or the differences that do exist are much smaller than most theories predict. In either case, the utility of these familiar explanations is clearly suspect.

Authors convinced by this argument have responded in two ways. Some construct theories that do not necessarily assume that delinquency is differentially distributed by class. Others modify familiar theories in an effort to account for the absence of class differences. Among the most interesting of the latter are theories of middle class delinquency. Most such theories attempt to explain how middle class children could be as delinquent as those from lower strata and are an effort to adjust for the wealth of equivocal findings about the class distribution of delinquency.

THEORIES OF MIDDLE CLASS DELINQUENCY

Theories of middle class delinquency are usually extensions of perspectives originally developed to explain lower class delinquency. Subculture, strain, and socialization theories have all been applied to middle class delinquency, although they have undergone some changes in the process. Modifications are necessary because they originally located the causes of delinquency in the conditions of lower class life. Since middle class life is presumed to be quite different, the theories must be altered if they are to explain the behavior of middle class adolescents.

Most theories of middle class delinquency are a response to apparent increases in the rate of middle class delinquency during the 1950s and 1960s. This gives them several foci, and makes it difficult to know precisely what theories of middle class delinquency are meant to explain. Some perspectives seem designed to account for differences between middle class and lower class delinquency; others, to explain variation in delinquent behavior among middle class adolescents themselves; still others, to account for an alleged increase in middle class delinquency over time. The last of these is perhaps the most frequent concern found in the literature, leading to theories that are phrased in a language of change. Changes in either middle class lifestyles or postwar stratification systems are assumed to have narrowed differences between lower and middle class experiences and increased the probability of middle class delinquency. Some authors argue that middle class youths are beginning to experience mobility constraints similar to those that are traditionally encountered by members of the working class. This leads to (deviant) responses analogous to the delinquent behavior of working class adolescents. Other authors suggest that lower class youths are assuming apparently middle class lifestyles while retaining much of their lower class heritage. The growth of middle class delinquency is thus a product of lower class mobility into middle class strata. Uniting both perspectives is the assumption that middle class adolescents have come to resemble working class adolescents and thus encounter many of the problems traditionally thought limited to the working class.

Subcultural perspectives were among the first delinquency theories to be extended directly to the middle class case. They have traditionally relied on the concept of delinquent working class subcultures to explain adolescent deviance, hypothesizing that oppositional subcultural values motivate delinquent behavior. Several versions of this reasoning have been applied to middle class delinquency, but the most popular are "youth culture" theories.[15] Affluence is thought to be the catalyst for the growth of youth cultures. Since middle class life requires little personal sacrifice, the lifestyle encourages an essentially purposeless, affluent consumerism. Adolescents perceive the futility of this and respond in several characteristic ways. Some reject the moral bankruptcy of the middle class and join countercultures or become politically active. Both student radicalism and the phenomenon of "dropping out" have been explained in these terms (see for example, Goodman, 1960; Flacks, 1970; Friedenberg, 1971; Kenniston, 1968a). However, the bulk of middle class adolescents respond to the meaninglessness of life by constructing a peer alternative—a youth culture centered on conspicuous consumption and characterized by the pursuit of artificial excitement.

Theories of lower class delinquent subcultures have stressed the importance of peer groups in developing alternative values; peers are also the focal point of youth culture perspectives. However, lower class delinquent subcultures are presumed to be an inversion of middle class morality, created in angry response at being denied a chance for middle class success. By contrast, youth cultures are a somewhat amorphous response to affluence. Ennui rather than rage characterizes the youth culture; adolescents turn to peers in an effort to relieve boredom and anxiety. Pursuit of pleasure is their overriding concern, while clothing, cars, or precocious sexuality are attempts to give meaning to an otherwise meaningless existence. Delinquency provides a kick missing from the easy homogeneous consumerism of daily life.

In this way, middle class adolescents develop a different world view from that of their more conventional parents. This redefinition supports a variety of activities that are inconsistent with traditional middle class values. The new youth culture ethic emphasizes hedonism rather than sacrifice, immediacy rather than deferred gratification, resignation rather than optimism. In short, youth culture values are similar to those usually thought to characterize lower strata groups. The more middle class adolescents adopt these values, the more they resemble lower strata adolescents and the more they increase their chances of delinquent behavior. Delinquency is thus the logical outgrowth of youth culture values.

A second extension of subcultural reasoning to middle class delinquency focuses on changes in stratification systems and their implications for status mobility. Movement between the working and middle classes has never been easy despite the Horatio Alger myth. Most subcultural perspectives explain this difficulty in terms of value differences between the two groups. Members of the working class are presumed to lack the Calvinist virtues of deferred gratification and self-sacrifice that make mobility possible. Without these characteristically middle class values, movement into the middle class is thought to be unlikely. Since values serve as mobility barriers, to be mobile one must first undergo a value transformation.[16]

Postwar affluence has changed all of this. Blue collar workers can now afford the affluent middle class lifestyles once thought to be limited to white collar workers. Because they can buy their way into the middle class, they no longer need to acquire the attitudes thought to underlie mobility. Blue collar groups can retain their lower class values even while affluent and thus may still harbor the attitudes that are assumed to promote delinquency. If this is the case, much of the apparent increase in middle class delinquency can be attributed to the activities of affluent youths who are really lower class in values and outlook. In short, middle class delinquency is seen as the work of lower class adolescents who only appear middle class to the causal observer. (Perhaps the clearest presentation of this line of reasoning is to be found in Bohlke, 1961).

Socialization theories are especially popular accounts of middle class delinquency. One familiar explanation of lower class delinquency identifies child-raising strategies that presumably lead to deviance among lower strata groups. Obviously this must be modified if socialization techniques are to explain middle class delinquency. Most modifications begin by arguing that there have been fundamental changes in middle class socialization practices in the years since World War II. Increased "permissiveness" is often cited as a cause of greater delinquency among middle class children. Parents no longer train their children in the traditional middle class virtues of self-control and deferred gratification that serve as barriers to delinquency. Instead, indulgence and an emphasis on individual development has produced a generation that lives for the here and now and that demands immediate gratification. Again, these are presumed to be new values among the affluent that bear a marked resemblance to those attributed to the lower class. They are thought to lead to delinquency for many of the same reasons.[17]

In point of fact, the literature on socialization and delinquency can lead to a number of predictions about class differences in propensities to deviate. Popular "permissiveness" explanations attribute increases in middle class delinquency to changes in socialization strategies over time. Other perspectives focus on the ties between socialization styles and the behavior required in lower versus middle strata occupations. Unlike traditional views, which predict greater delinquency among lower class groups, these predict potentially greater amounts of delinquency in the middle class. For example, Kohn (1969) argues that white collar jobs are more likely to require independent decisionmaking and autonomy than are most lower strata occupations. This means that middle class parents must foster independent thinking in their children while lower strata parents must emphasize direct obedience and conformity to rules. Socialization styles reflect these needs: lower class parents are thought to punish children on the basis of demands for simple rule observance while middle class parents evaluate their children's misdeeds in light of numerous extenuating circumstances. Rules can be circumvented provided there is good reason. This leads to lower class behavior styles that stress conformity to rules in and of themselves, but to middle class styles that permit or even encourage occasional deviation. Thus, the training for independence and autonomy stressed in a middle class context could create greater potential for delinquency among middle class children than among those from the lower class.

Subcultural and socialization theories of middle class delinquency are based on assumed parallels between the values of affluent adolescents and those held by lower strata groups. In contrast, strain theories of middle class delinquency focus on similarities in the mobility constraints encountered by both classes. Meaningful status mobility is assumed to be a problem for middle class adolescents with the growth of the middle income sector of the population. For the first time they find themselves in a structural position that is similar to that of lower class youths. Their responses to strain and status anxiety may take on many of the same potentially deviant forms. One of the most popular strain explanations again emphasizes the importance of general affluence.[18] Middle class lifestyles are readily available, and presumably this has made it difficult for middle class adolescents to achieve meaningful increases in status over that of their parents. They know that significant changes in their status position are unlikely no matter how much effort they invest in mobility. Yet middle class culture still stresses an achievement ideology. As a result, affluent adolescents experience strain. In a sense, they now face mobility anxieties similar to those that have always been a part of lower class life. Of course, the character of middle class status anxiety is somewhat unique. The anxiety of lower class adolescents stems from perceptions that structural barriers (including active discrimination) make upward mobility virtually impossible. Regardless of effort, lower class status and its attendant inequalities are virtually assured. The injustice of this situation can lead to passive acquiescence, but it can also lead to angry retaliation in the form of negativistic delinquency.

The status anxiety experienced by middle class adolescents is somewhat different. It is the product of a perception that significant increments in status are unlikely and that one will be middle class no matter what. The objective experience of this injustice is not as marked. Instead, achievement ideology is no longer functional for middle class adolescents. Since achievement is unlikely, activities that traditionally foster achievement (educational success, civic participation, hard work) no longer make sense. Some middle class adolescents may be angry, but most are expected to acquiesce and substitute the pursuit of pleasure for the pursuit of success. This pursuit of pleasure can take the form of "delinquency."[1][9]

IMAGES IMPLICIT IN THEORIES
OF MIDDLE CLASS DELINQUENCY

Although these theories differ in some respects, they share several themes that produce a consistent picture of middle class delinquency. There are two components of this picture worth noting—the model of the delinquent actor implicit in these explanations and the model of middle class delinquency itself. Theories of middle class delinquency carry a distinctive image of the delinquent actor that draws its inspiration from assumptions about the relationship between affluence and deviance. Middle class delinquents are caught in an affluent but essentially meaningless lifestyle. This experience seems beyond their control; the actors only dimly perceive the forces operating in their lives. In this context, middle class delinquents appear as basically passive individuals who respond to the vagaries of affluence in ways they do not fully understand. Because they are seldom conscious of the pressures of their situation, their responses are not deliberately "chosen" in the classic (and economic) sense of the term. Instead, their actions appear constrained by either unconscious individual mechanisms (e.g., frustration or world views bred by permissive child-rearing) or external pressures that they cannot easily manipulate (e.g., barriers to status mobility). The middle class delinquent is disaffected and withdrawn from the adult world, often rejecting conventional (albeit meaningless) activity in favor of a poorly articulated pursuit of pleasure. Occasionally the frustrations of middle class affluence can become too great, and the adolescent may lash out at these constraints. However, such outbreaks (usually identified as delinquency) are primarily expressive and are not deliberately designed to alter the adolescent's situation.

This purposeless, expressive image of the middle class delinquent has had a major impact on the way in which middle class delinquency is understood. It leads theorists to search for causes of delinquency in motivations internal to the individual. This has meant a preoccupation with individual pathology or individual values that might be associated with middle class delinquency. Like general delinquency theory, more attention is given to the characteristics of the individuals involved in the activity than in their actual delinquent behavior. In line with this interest, middle class delinquency theories have tended to focus on individual coping strategies to the neglect of structural factors that could be related to deviance. This is perhaps most obvious in the case of subcultural or socialization theories that emphasize the impact of internalized values. Strain theories also lose much of their structural character when applied to the middle class case. Since status anxiety, an individual fear, is the key element in the translation of strain into delinquent action, strain perspectives on middle class delinquency are generally phrased in terms of individual coping strategies.

Not only do images of the middle class delinquent focus on individual pathology, they rely on a general causal model that assumes that delinquent behavior is more evoked then chosen. This is an emphasis that they share with many general delinquency theories, one that has had substantial impact on the meaning attributed to middle class delinquency. Individual pathology, youth culture values, or inability to cope with affluence are all phrased in terms that imply that middle class delinquents do not fully comprehend their situation or their reactions to it. Given this lack of understanding, their reactions cannot be entirely conscious or volitional. Delinquency may be a poorly articulated expression of problems, but it is not a deliberately chosen attempt to redress grievances or alter life situations. As such it has little meaning for the actor him or herself, and to the analyst it is meaningful primarily as a symptom of some underlying problem of individual adjustment.

This individualistic view of delinquency has channeled research in familiar ways. In particular, we know little about the delinquent *behavior* of middle class adolescents. This is partly due to the strong class assumptions in general delinquency theory that are used to justify neglect of middle class populations. It is also due to the tendency for researchers to gather more data on personality or background characteristics of individual delinquents than on what they actually do. Since middle class delinquency is seen as a symptom of some other "true" problem, there is little motivation to study its patterns in detail.

IMAGES OF MIDDLE CLASS DELINQUENCY

Although there is relatively little research available on middle class delinquency, theories and their attendant image of the actor lead to some predictions about its typical patterns. Implicit in most theories are general expectations about the type, persistence, and frequency of middle class delinquency. However, precise predictions are difficult to make, because theories often provide several explanations for the same behavior. For example, youth culture perspectives assume that adolescents use delinquency as a relief from the ills of affluence. This relief can take a number of forms. Some individuals may withdraw, using drugs and alcohol to block out anxiety and ambiguity. Others may seek artificial thrills through drugs, drinking, sexual promiscuity, shoplifting, joyriding, or vandalism. Still others may find themselves caught in a consumption-oriented youth culture, while lacking the resources to participate on an equal footing with peers. In this situation they could turn to delinquency (e.g., shoplifting) in order to have the clothes, records, or other possessions crucial to successful participation in the youth culture. In short, activities such as drug use can be the product of "withdrawal" or "risk taking"; shoplifting can be motivated by a need to compete or by a search for thrills.

Socialization theories offer another example of multiple explanations for the same behavior. They attribute middle class delinquency to permissive child-raising strategies and look for its causes in self-indulgence, immediacy, and poor self-control. Drug use, sexual promiscuity, or alcohol use may be the mark of self-indulgence; they may also be the result of a search for immediate gratification or the outgrowth of poorly developed individual controls. Strain theories can also lead to a variety of predictions about activities which should characterize middle class delinquency. Mobility anxiety may lead some people to withdraw from competition via alcohol and drugs; others may turn to peers in an effort to construct alternative status systems. The intricacies of life in this alternative can produce competition that takes the form of delinquent activities that demonstrate autonomy (i.e., drinking, smoking, truancy, running away).

In short, theories of middle class delinquency predict a wide range of delinquent activities, although the justifications for these predictions are diffuse and sometimes contradictory. Despite this diversity, these predictions have one unifying theme. Almost all theories of middle class delinquency assume that it is "minor" deviance. Images of middle class delinquency seldom include more serious activities such as rape, gang fighting, assult, or armed robbery. This seems to stem from assumptions about the relationship between affluence and deviance. Theories that focus on lower class delinquency assume that adolescents' responses to the deprivation and discrimination of lower class life are angry and frequently retalitory. This is consistent with an image of lower class delinquency as serious, violent, and predatory. Theories of middle class delinquency stress the ease and monotony of affluent living. Instead of defining themselves as deprived, middle class delinquents see themselves as players in a pointless game. Since middle class delinquency expresses amorphous alienation rather than rage, it should be minor and generally nonviolent.

The image of the middle class delinquent also leads to expectations about patterns in middle-class delinquency. The acquiescent nature of the middle class delinquent leads one to expect him or her to be inordinately sensitive to external influences, particularly group pressures. Thus, middle class delinquency should be group oriented and have a strong social character. This image is consistent with stereotypic middle class forms of delinquency such as drug and alcohol use, vandalism, or joyriding. The presumably unconscious, reactive, and purposeless character of the middle class delinquent also fits well with popular views of the types of people who vandalize, drink to excess, use drugs, shoplift, or steal cars for kicks. These activities seem mysterious to those who wonder why children from "good families" turn to delinquency. External constraints working on an unconscious and arational actor offer a somewhat reassuring explanation for this puzzling phenomenon.

In general, theories of middle class delinquency predict that it should take a variety of minor forms. The limited empirical work available is largely consistent with these expectations. Middle class students are likely to report minor rather than major law infractions, and they seem to favor activities such as shoplifting, drug or alcohol use, vandalism, and auto theft. For example, Casparis and Vaz (1974) note that gambling, drinking, vandalism, and petty theft characterize the delinquent activities of their upper middle class Canadian respondents. Wise (1967) finds that fist fighting, truancy, drinking, petty theft, vandalism, and auto-related offenses are popular among her sample of middle class students, while serious infractions are much less common. Overall, middle class delinquency appears to be rather minor, as most theories predict. However, it is worth noting that this differential weighting of offense seriousness is true of all social strata, and that the vast bulk of lower class delinquency is also rather minor.

So far we have discussed only the *types* of delinquency predicted by theories of the middle class case. These theories also lead to some general predictions about the frequency or persistence of delinquent behavior. Central to these expectations is the assumption that middle class delinquents are more or less trapped into delinquency by factors beyond their control. This assumption is also common in general delinquency theory and has been criticized by authors who wish to to restore an element of individual choice to images of the delinquent actor. Following David Matza's lead, they argue that the image of the evoked delinquent leads one to predict far more delinquency than actually occurs. It also leaves an analyst hard pressed to explain why delinquents spend most of their time behaving in conventional ways (see Matza, 1964, for a fuller exposition of this argument—as well as Platt, 1969, and Hirschi, 1969). Most theories of middle class delinquency suffer from these same limitations. The overwhelming anomie of middle class life and the all-pervasiveness of the youth culture are invoked in such strong terms that one might expect middle class youths to be consistently delinquent. Permissive child rearing should similarly support persistent delinquency. Even status anxiety, if it is as prevalent as authors imply, should lead to frequent delinquent innovations.

Yet these theories appear to overpredict the amount and consistency of middle class delinquency. By focusing on the deviant potential of modern middle class lifestyles they often neglect the overwhelmingly mundane and conventional character of most things middle class adolescents do. Affluent adolescents are highly conventional people (as are youths from lower social strata), participating in school and sports activities, innocuous leisure pursuits, and just plain living. Theories of middle class delinquency tend to overlook this fact. In doing so, they may misrepresent crucial characteristics both of middle class adolescence and of middle class delinquency. Middle class students are involved in delinquency, but the nature of their involvement is likely to be more fluid than is implied by popular theories. The available self-report research, although limited, indicates that middle class teenagers are not strongly committed to delinquency and that they report delinquent activities with more or less the same frequency as other adolescents. Some revision of popular middle class theories seems necessary if middle class delinquency is to be understood on its own terms as well as within a wider class context. Such a revision requires a closer examination both of causal assumptions underlying popular theories, and of assumptions about the nature of delinquency itself.

NOTES

1. Among the most important of these early ecological works are those of Shaw (1931), Shaw and McKay (1942), Shaw et al. (1929), and other Chicago ecologists. For a comprehensive review of ecological perspectives on deviance and delinquency see Taylor, Walton, and Young 1973.

2. For a general review of subcultural approaches to delinquency see Matza (1964), Hirschi (1969), or Downes (1966).

3. There is a large literature on class differences in child-rearing

techniques. The classic works, such as those by Sears, Maccoby and Levin (1957), Davis and Havighurst (1946), and Bronfenbrenner (1968), attempt to document differences, while other authors attempt to link these differences to probabilities of deviance in a more direct fashion. Among the more provocative are those provided by Kohn (1969), Cohen (1955), Nye (1958), and Glueck and Glueck, (1960). However, the relationships between socialization and deviance or delinquency have been the topic of much debate. For a review of this issue see Erlanger (1974).

4. Merton (1957) provides the classic discussion of "strain" and general deviance, which has been modified and extended by delinquency theorists such as Cloward and Ohlin (1960), Cloward (1959), S. Cohen (1972), and A.K. Cohen (1965) or, for the middle class case, by England (1964) and Bohlke (1961). There are numerous empirical tests of strain perspectives. Among the most comprehensive are the works of Stinchcombe (1964) and Hirschi (1969).

5. Most work in the area of conflict theory focuses on adult deviance (i.e., crime) and the way in which official treatment strategies reinforce basic social inequalities. They have paid relatively less attention to the etiology of individual behavior patterns, although some conflict theorists have attempted to link individual adaptations to large-scale structural inequalities (see, for example, Quinney, 1965, 1975). Readers interested in general issues in conflict theory will find representative discussions in Turk (1966, 1969), Vold (1958), and Quinney (1970, 1975). Direct applications to juvenile delinquency can be found in Turk (1966), Quinney (1975), and the work of other radical criminologists interested in official definition, identification, and treatment of delinquents (e.g., Platt, 1969; Schwendinger and Schwendinger, 1978).

6. "Control" theory is a rather broad category, and some control theorists are more explicit about class variation in delinquency than others. For example, Hirschi (1969) discusses class differences in detail and operationalizes several tests for class differences in self-reported delinquency, discovering few differences. Still, he does not elaborate on the implications for presumed variation in overall "stakes" in conformity between classes. Matza (1964) focuses on subcultural delinquency in his analysis, generally ignoring the issue of delinquent activity on the part of adolescents (in the middle class) who are not members of such a subculture.

7. Numerous studies have examined class differences in both official and self-report delinquency. In addition to the general literature reviews of Tittle and Villamez (1977) and Box and Ford (1971) mentioned above, readers may find the following works of

interest: Akers (1964), Clark and Wenninger (1962), Dentler and Monroe (1961), Empey and Erickson (1966), Garrett and Short (1975), Harry (1974), Hirschi (1969), Kelley (1975), Kvaraceus (1944), Nye, Short, and Olsen (1958), Reiss and Rhodes (1961), Stinchcombe (1964), Vaz (1965), Voss (1966), and Williams and Gold (1972).

8. Studies of official delinquency have been criticized as unrepresentative of general patterns in delinquency, particularly in terms of the class differences that often appear. For useful general critiques of official statistics see Kitsuse and Cicourel (1963), Hirschi and Selvin, (1967), Hirschi (1969), Williams and Gold (1972), and Black (1970), among others.

9. Since this is the most common operationalization of "class" in delinquency research, there are numerous studies that take this approach. Among the most interesting examples are Nye (1958), Hirschi (1969), Nye, Short, and Olsen (1958), Empey and Erickson (1966), and Clark and Wenninger (1962).

10. There is less empirical work in this tradition than in that of fathers' SES. For perhaps the most comprehensive example see Stinchcombe (1964).

11. These problems are discussed in greater detail in Tittle and Villamez (1977), to whom we are indebted for many of the points that follow.

12. Hirschi (1969) makes this point by comparing an SES distribution of self-report delinquency to a class distribution in his analysis. He finds no meaningful SES differences when respondents are categorized according to traditional measures of fathers' SES but modest differences in the predicted direction when he compares respondents whose fathers are unemployed or on welfare to those whose fathers have a consistent work history.

13. One must also keep in mind that even if proper controls are applied in principle, inevitable measurement error in these controls results in biased and inconsistent estimates of real class differences. In effect, differences other than class are not held fully constant. While this is a problem in virtually all multivariate models used by sociologists (and other social scientists), it further complicates any assessment of the role of social class in delinquency. Recent advances in techniques for models with imperfectly measured exogenous variables promise some improvement in this situation.

14. Like multivariate statistical controls, matching is also unlikely to fully adjust for factors confounded with social class.

15. There is a somewhat diffuse literature on youth cultures, including classic works by authors such as Coleman (1960), Ken-

niston (1962, 1968b), Flacks (1970, 1971), Goodman (1960), and Friedenberg (1965). Empirical work on delinquency from a youth culture perspective is represented by authors such as Coleman (1960), Vaz (1965), and Casparis and Vaz (1974) among others. For an overview of youth culture theory applicable to the middle class case see Vaz (1967) and England (1967).

16. The literature on social mobility and subcultural values is quite extensive. For one of the most comprehensive presentations of a general subcultural view see Gans (1964).

17. Discussions of this type vary from popularized indictments of "permissive" parents like those found in Shalloo (1952), Madison (1970), and Hendin (1975) to more specific discussions of the impact of child-rearing practices by more academically oriented researchers such as those cited in note 3, *supra*.

18. For a comprehensive discussion of many of these assumptions see the readings in Vaz (1967).

19. Only a few authors (most notably Stinchcombe, 1964) devote detailed attention to anxiety about downward mobility, particularly in terms of middle class adolescents' fears of falling back into the working class. Instead, the major emphasis has been on the futility of striving for success within an amorphous middle class context.

20. There are relatively few studies of middle class delinquency *per se*, although information about middle class delinquency can be gleaned from a number of studies that report delinquency data broken down by class categories (see note 7, *supra*). Readers interested in other data drawn from middle class populations may find the work of Vaz (1965), Wise (1967), and Myerhoff and Myerhoff (1964) of interest.

Chapter Two

Delinquency as a Leisure Activity

INTRODUCTION

Crime is a favorite metaphor in delinquency research. The identification of delinquency as precriminal behavior underlies much popular concern with the issue, and early researchers defined delinquency in terms of a wide range of troublesome behavior that they assumed led to crime. Most recent work relies on a narrower quasi-legal definition of delinquency. Instead of general "problem behavior," current images are more likely to concentrate on strictly illegal activities. This is largely a response to the work of societal reaction theorists and sociologists of law who argue that illegality or infraction is the only characteristic that all "delinquent" activities share. But whether a "problem behavior" or "infraction" definition of delinquency is imposed, a picture of delinquency as child crime is implicit in most delinquency work.[1]

This crime image fits certain theoretical approaches better than others and channels explanations of delinquency in subtle ways. First of all it assumes that delinquency is "deviance" of a particularly serious sort (crime or precrime). Consistent with this assumption is the tendency to extend theories of adult crime to adolescent delinquency. This is not a problem in and of itself. However, crime theories are attempts to explain allegedly serious deviance. As a result, they are likely to rely on strongly phrased causal models that assume that individual deviance is motivated by powerful forces often beyond individual control. Within such models, criminals (and delinquents) appear radically different from the law abiding. Their

23

behavior is governed by forces that push them toward serious deviance; these forces are not experienced by members of the conventional population.

However, these strongly phrased theories of deviance produce a picture of delinquency that is at odds with many of the readily observable patterns in delinquent behavior. Models of strong motivation predict radical differences between delinquents and nondelinquents that self-report research seldom finds. Since virtually all adolescents report delinquent behavior, it is difficult to maintain the clear distinctions between delinquents and nondelinquents that are required by most crime perspectives based on models of serious deviance. It is also difficult to argue that delinquency is serious crime. The most popular forms of delinquency are quite minor (e.g., underage drinking, minor property damage, small-scale shoplifting) and the bulk of even official delinquency consists of activities that are illegal only for children (e.g., status offenses such as running away and incorrigibility). In light of these difficulties, there is seldom a close fit between models of crime or serious deviance and patterns in common forms of delinquency.

The most serious problem with these perspectives lies in the causal model they typically impose on the delinquent actor. Serious deviance (crime) should require strong motivation; strong motivation implies that there are powerful factors virtually forcing individuals to deviate. The accuracy of this sort of reasoning has been challenged repeatedly by theorists who argue that it is far too limiting as an explanation because it neglects the role of individual choice in delinquency or crime. Behaviors, particularly of the mundane or commonplace sort that comprise the bulk of delinquency, are obviously not completely determined by forces beyond individual control. Delinquents and criminals are not naive actors; they choose much of their behavior in light of reasoned assessments of the situation. This assessment involves a wide range of considerations. Some individuals have a greater range of choices than others, but there is still a degree of choice in any activity. If one is to understand patterns in deviance, one must examine ways in which decisions are made within the life situations of individuals.[2] Theories that see delinquency in more everyday terms than implicit in "crime" and that allow the individual a role in fashioning his or her own behavior move in this direction.

While models of choice are not unknown in the sociological literature on delinquency,[3] one must turn to microeconomics to find parsimonious perspectives embedded in a larger theoretical framework (see for example, Ehrlich, 1974, and Becker, 1974, among others).[4] In essence, economists argue that people invest time and other resources in a wide range of activities based in part on expected returns. Much like the activity of firms, the investment process is governed by efforts to maximize total returns (i.e., utility), subject to constraints reflecting the total amount of resources available for investment (i.e., a budget constraint) and extant investment options (i.e., opportunity costs). At the margin (i.e., at the point of maximum total returns), resources are optimally allocated so that any other allocation would produce lower returns.

It is critical to acknowledge that such models of human behavior are deliberate simplifications of reality and, in addition, that they consciously neglect other determinants of people's actions. Among the most important of these are what economists identify as taste or individual preference. Economists assume that taste is a given and leave the explanation of taste or preference to other social science disciplines. In other words, economic models are not meant to account for the fact that particular teenagers may obtain more satisfaction from smoking marijuana than from drinking beer. Instead, taking this preference as given, economic models might focus on the relative amounts of marijuana and beer purchased (and therefore consumed), subject to the prices for both and the amount of money (or other resources such as time) that individuals are prepared to invest in these purchases.

It is also important to recognize that economic models of individual choice are often misrepresented. They do not necessarily assume that individuals have perfect knowledge of the factors affecting decisionmaking or that choice involves lightening fast calculation. Indeed, some of the most interesting and important of these models examine decisionmaking processes under conditions of uncertainty. Nor do economic models automatically assume that individuals are consciously aware of all components of the decision-making process. Economists would argue that as long as people behave as their decisionmaking models predict, individual awareness of these principles is of little concern. Equally important is an understanding that economic models are "ideal-typical" characterizations meant to reflect processes that are at best approximated in the real world. They are most useful as models of general aggregate tendencies that can be seen clearly only once individual aberrations cancel out.

This is not to say that microeconomic models of choice are not without serious problems (see for example, Berk and Jurik, 1979). Among the most important of these are the demands that they place on the nature of human rationality. Even as ideal typifications, there is considerable debate about the extent to which they represent real world processes. However, as imperfect as they are, economic models of choice do provide a useful vehicle for examining patterns in juvenile delinquency, one that changes familiar theoretical foci in a number of intriguing ways.

While formal microeconomic models have been applied to crime, few direct extensions have been made to adolescent deviance. Delinquency is a particularly interesting issue to examine in light of microeconomic assumptions about choice, and we will extract several general (and tentative) premises from microeconomic models to guide our analysis of middle class delinquency. We will not attempt to derive a formal theoretical model of delinquency in this volume. Considerable controversy exists about the details of such efforts even among economists broadly sympathetic to the work of Becker, Ehrlich, and others. Instead we will use basic microeconomic principles of decisionmaking to gain some broad insights into patterns in middle class delinquency.

First, we will hypothesize that for the vast majority of middle class adolescents (and perhaps all adolescents), the decisionmaking processes of those who participate heavily in delinquency are not different from the decisionmaking processes of those who do not participate heavily in delinquency. By implication, delinquents are not automatically more hedonistic, impulsive, or neurotic than nondelinquents and their behavior is not necessarily the product of some fundamental individual pathology.

Second, we postulate that the mix of legitimate and illegitimate activities that middle class adolescents undertake can be at least partially explained by the utility they provide. Time and other resources (such as money) are invested in a variety of activities, based in part on the expected marginal returns (i.e., the returns per unit of value invested) from that investment. Both anticipated benefits and costs are considered in that investment.

Third, we assume that middle class adolescents (and others) attempt to maximize the total returns of their investments. That is, they invest varying amounts of resources in different activities (both legitimate and illegitimate) so that in principle an optimal allocation results (subject to "budget constraints," of course).

Fourth, these investments require information, since returns are contingent on the consequences of investing in one or another activity. Therefore, some of the activities in which adolescents engage are not undertaken solely for their returns, but also to obtain data on the likely outcomes from various investments. In other words, some resources are invested in learning the costs and benefits that can be obtained from unfamiliar activities. We will refer to such learning as "experimentation," which is, of course, a common characterization of initial involvement in various forms of deviance (and of non deviant activities as well). We will provide some examples shortly.

Fifth, experimentation provides not only information about the likely consequences of one's actions but both information and skills that enhance one's ability to negotiate complex social situations. An initial exposure to delinquent activities is in some sense on the job training for future delinquent (and nondelinquent) activities. Similarly, experience with the tensions of risky situations may produce greater poise and composure in the future. We will discuss some examples of this shortly, but it is important to keep in mind that much the same sort of learning is needed for nondelinquent activities such as taking standardized tests, playing competitive sports, or getting along with members of the opposite sex.

Finally, even after considerable experimentation with a range of legitimate and illegitimate activities, investment decisions will still rest in part on uncertain outcomes. It is often impossible to accurately gauge the results of potentially deviant activities. For example, one never knows for sure whether or not one will be arrested for stealing a car or caught while shoplifting. (Analogously, one never knows for sure whether one will win a sandlot baseball game, no matter how skilled one may be or how much prior experiences one has.)[5]

At this point it is important to reemphasize that we will be using these premises as initial statements of the principles by which middle class adolescents choose to undertake both legitimate and illegitimate activities. With the exception of the maximization hypothesis (which is not really central in any case), our analysis will be devoted to assessing the fit between these assumptions and the patterns observable in our data. With this as groundwork, we now turn to a more general discussion of the kind of resources that middle class adolescents have to invest in various activities. We will argue that the bulk of these resources consist of time and that leisure time is a particularly important resource in adolescence.

LEISURE IN ADOLESCENCE

Leisure has a complex character, particularly in adolescence, since the formal meaning of leisure is not at all clear even for adults. Economists have traditionally relied on a simple distinction between paid work and everything else; the everything else is then called leisure. Recent microeconomic work makes much finer distinctions, but in the process, leisure sometimes connotes little more than consumption. For example, making a meal is a form of household production; eating a meal is consumption and therefore (loosely speaking) leisure. Obviously this ignores the various social realities along which people define leisure. This is a problem, since these can have an important impact on decisionmaking. The reader will soon see that we have no simple answers to such difficulties. Still, for purposes of initial discussion, we will use leisure to refer to activities that (1) do not involve jobs in the market sector, (2) do not involve the production of household commodities (e.g., cutting the grass, clearing the table, babysitting for siblings), and (3) do not involve formal "investment" in human capital (e.g., the acquisition of instrumental marketable skills in an institutional context such as school).[6] This is clearly not a formal definition, but is sufficiently precise to allow us to separate investments into four main categories:

1. Employment in the market sector,
2. Production of household commodities,
3. Investment in marketable human capital, and
4. Leisure.

As long as we are defining leisure in terms of what is is not, it might be helpful to discuss several other uses of the term. Leisure often implies recreation, entertainment, or other sorts of enjoyable distractions. While these may be one component of the leisure activities we have identified here, recreation is not synonymous with leisure. In addition, we will argue that leisure is not solely devoted to consumption in the strict sense of the term.

It should be obvious that the proportion of activities individuals allocate to each investment category varies by age. Adolescents are seldom fully employed nor are they likely to have household responsibilities as heavy as those of female adults. Instead they are likely to be investing in human capital (school). This suggests that they may have relatively more "leisure" available than most adults and that a good portion of their activities are either human capital or leisure oriented. In short, adolescence is a life stage where the relative mix of daily activities is concentrated in investment in human capital and "leisure."[7]

THE INVESTMENT OF LEISURE TIME

Given a desire to optimally invest leisure time (a resource) and our characterization of adolescent time as heavily leisure based, it is important to discuss the ways in which this resource can be allocated.[8] For our purposes, the allocation of leisure time can be divided into three major categories: (1) consumption from which utility is directly obtained, (2) production in which labor and market goods are combined to generate commodities, and (3) capital accumulation in which information and other skills (including non-market skills, which will be our main focus) are gained. Satisfactions and dissatisfactions can only be derived from consumption, although commodities can be viewed as "stored" utility that can be consumed at a later point. Capital accumulation alters the "quality" of the labor employed in commodity production, and is an important aspect of adolescent leisure.

Perhaps a brief example will clarify how "deviant" investments of leisure time can be made. Assume that a teenager invests leisure time in shoplifting a portable radio. At the beginning, a prospective shoplifter may learn something about how one pockets small consumer goods while avoiding detection. He or she also gains knowledge about the chances of getting caught and the likely consequences of success or failure. Much of this information may be gathered from more sophisticated friends, past experience in roughly similar situations (e.g., stealing food in the school cafeteria), or observation of the layout of the targeted store (or other similar stores). Note that there is no assumption that this information is complete or free of error, and that we have only partially described this data-gathering process. Still, one can think of this learning process as capital formation where necessary information is gained and necessary skills are learned.

One can view the initial shoplifting itself solely as commodity production. The teenager combines his or her time and perhaps a large coat with big pockets (a market good) to steal a portable radio. The stolen radio is the commodity produced by shoplifting. However, in the process of stealing the radio, psychic rewards (e.g., excitement, fun) and costs (e.g., fear, guilt) are also generated. These are necessarily consumed on the spot, so that in practice, the production of most commodities involves both production and consumption.[9]

At this point an important complication surfaces. The net returns to shoplifting a radio depend on whether or not the thief is caught. That is, the balance of rewards and costs depends on one or two "states of the world"—apprehension (and what follows) or nonapprehension. Neither can be anticipated with certainty. *A priori* the best that the potential thief can do is act on the (Bayesian) probabilities that one state or the other will occur. In other words, the net returns are conditional on one or more uncertain outcomes. For instance, if the thief is caught, the radio will have to be returned, and a range of additional costs will no doubt be incurred (e.g., embarrassment and formal and informal sanction from friends, parents, and law enforcement agents). An efficient allocation of time between legal and illegal (or any other kind) of activities must take such uncertain outcomes into account before resources are allocated.

At this point, capital formation and commodity production are over, and leisure time may be invested more directly in consumption. The successful thief may spend additional time listening to the radio and basking in the glories heaped on him or her by admiring (perhaps) friends. On the other hand, there may be some guilt involved, and for many adolescents shoplifting clearly has some consumatory costs (disutility). The unsuccessful thief, of course, suffers a wide range of penalties that are not likely to be experienced as rewards.

Finally, the entire cycle may well be repeated, especially if the net returns are sufficiently positive and capital investment (i.e., acquiring necessary skills) is sufficiently beneficial. Thus, shoplifting provides not only opportunities to consume (gain utility) but information that channels the next investment decision. The shoplifter may learn that crime does not pay; he or she may also learn that crime does pay. Whatever the lesson, it can affect subsequent investment of leisure time.

So far we have argued that basic economic principles can be used to describe the ways that adolescents can invest their leisure time, and that these investments can be made in both legitimate and illegitimate leisure activities. The example outlined above is consistent with basic assumptions of microeconomic models of choice and also has a number of ties to more general sociological perspectives on leisure. Leisure theorists argue that leisure time can be used for individual development (personal growth), the repair of psychic stress (relaxation), and socialization.[10] This socialization function is assumed to be particularly important in the case of children since it gives them opportunities to learn rules for behavior and to experiment with a variety of social roles. For these theorists, games serve as a metaphor for life on a broader scale, and leisure serves as a relatively safe arena for testing the limits of proper behavior and for learning which actions are allowed and which are not.[11]

Most literature on moral development through leisure concentrates on young children. However, leisure can operate in a similar fashion for adolescents. Young children may learn basic social rules through game playing, but there are subtleties that remain to be decoded. Rules are often rules in name only, and one must understand more than the exact content of rules if one is to know how to behave. One must also know which rules are enforced and which are not; which are to be given lip service and which are to be strictly observed; which may be broken with impunity, which can be circumvented, and under what conditions. Adolescents may face these subtleties during leisure hours. Since the choice of leisure activities is a relatively wide one, it may be a useful time to put rules to a behavioral test. This is analogous to the experimentation and capital accumulation outlined above.

In essence, the socialization literature adds an important dimension to economic perspectives on adolescent deviance. Not only do adolescents enhance their nonmarket human capital through the learning that takes place during leisure experimentation, their preferences ("tastes") may be altered as well. Hence, the process of choosing between different behavioral options rests in part on a synthesis of earlier experiences that makes leisure activities differentially attractive. For example, similar sorts of pleasure (utility) may be obtained both by drinking beer and by smoking marijuana. To some extent, choosing one over the other may be affected by previous exposure that helps determine which of these is more "acceptable."

This issue of taste is a complicated one for any perspective that focuses on decisionmaking. "Tastes" are basically individual preferences, holding costs and opportunities constant. To assert that tastes differ among individuals admittedly says little about why peoples' tastes differ or what these differences might be. These are useful questions, and in fact, much delinquency research has focused on tastes (i.e., stable propensities to deviate) and their impact on delinquency. The problem is that tastes or preferences operate within *situations* where other factors (i.e., costs, purposes) are also important considerations in decisionmaking. By restricting attention to what one might broadly identify as tastes, past research has tended to construct deterministic causal models with few links to the situations in which delinquency occurs. Study of these situational characteristics as well as individual tastes can offer insight into the context of decisionmaking and round out an understanding of how delinquent activities are selected.

Obviously the process of refining tastes and learning which behaviors are "right" and which are "wrong" is quite complex. Moral prohibitions are attached to some behavior, moral imperatives to others, but there is often considerable ambiguity about the moral character of any particular action. Activities are not inherently moral or immoral; such attributes are necessarily situational and the same activity can be acceptable or unacceptable depending on its context. Under some conditions, Halloween pranks are "just good fun"; under others, they qualify as vandalism. Sexual behavior can be a "healthy expression of one's feelings," or it can be evidence of "promiscuity." Fighting can be a legitimate act of self-defense, but it can also be seen as "bullying." One can begin to learn the difference by experimenting, but since the moral character of activities shifts with the situation, it is impossible to establish their deviant character once and for all. Through experience one learns an increasingly complicated set of contextually based preferences that are still somewhat fluid. Since the deviant or nondeviant character of activities shifts in ways that cannot be anticipated with complete certainty, each situation must be in part negotiated anew.

In short, we would argue that leisure time can be invested in three major ways—direct consumption, production of commodities, and experimentation that results in capital accumulation. This experimentation may also shape preferences. Leisure time can be invested in both legitimate and illegitimate activities, and the relative mix of choices depends on anticipated (marginal) costs and benefits. There are a number of actors who can provide both information and instruction in leisure skills as well as direct costs and benefits for leisure choices. This makes them important components in the investment of leisure time. One can sketch the process of leisure decisionmaking in greater detail by assessing their potential impact on decisionmaking. We will devote the remainder of this chapter to this issue.

LEISURE, PEERS, AND DELINQUENCY

Peers are one set of actors who can influence the investment of leisure time. Delinquency theorists are well aware of this and generally give them an important role in theories of adolescent deviance. In fact, the most popular delinquency theories are those that make peers the focal point of their explanations. Some theories stress the pressures that peers can exert as deviant role models (e.g., differential association, subcultural theories); others, the importance of peer-based status systems that offer an alternative to adult status systems (e.g., strain theories); and still others stress the importance of peer contexts in which alternative prodelinquent value systems and lifestyles can develop (e.g., subcultural theories). Most perspectives seem to assume that peers are important factors in delinquency because for one reason or another they encourage deviance. Theories seldom imply that peers can also be "conventional", exerting influence in nondeviant directions. (For an important exception, see control theories such as the one proposed by Hirschi, 1969.)

Instead of assuming that peers exert a basically prodeviant influence on one another, our perspective indicates that peers and peer reactions are important components of benefits and costs attached to leisure choices. They also contribute to the process by which skills and information are learned. Many leisure activities are group activities and by definition they cannot be done alone. One cannot play a basketball game alone; neither can one have a drunken party by oneself. This means that peers are a crucial structural component in many leisure activities and that they are likely to figure importantly in leisure choices. Indeed, within the decisionmaking framework outlined above, peers may serve at least five functions. First, in some sense peers are part of the environment that defines many leisure activities. As we have already noted, peer involvement is necessary by definition for much of what takes place during leisure. Second, peers are important components of leisure situations that individuals must learn to master. The many awkward moments adolescents experience at parties, during dates, and in a host of other settings should be ample testimony to the need to acquire mastery over new and unfamiliar settings. In part this involves learning how to manipulate peers, anticipate their responses, and navigate complex social interaction. Much leisure activity includes gaining experience and skill in handling these situations (both legitimate, as in going to the movies with a date, and illegitimate, as in having a beer party) where peers are an important element to be manipulated. Third, peers are a critical source of information about the world. For example, much of what teenagers know about sexuality comes from peers; peers can provide similar information about other leisure activities. They can "instruct" one in proper techniques for drinking beer or smoking marijuana; they can also give lessons on how to dance or what kind of clothing is "proper." Fourth, peers provide myriad sanctions (both positive and negative) for almost every visible activity in which adolescents invest. This, of course, comes closest to the "peer pressure" that has been the focal concern of most delinquency theory. However, it is important to note that peers deliver costs *and* benefits for both legitimate and illegitimate activities, and there is no reason to assume *a priori* that friends always endorse deviant choices and belittle an individuals' conventional behavior. Finally, peers also shape the preferences (tastes) that adolescents bring to leisure opportunities. By whatever mechanism, teenagers (like adults) come to incorporate many of the likes and dislikes of their peers, which in turn help to determine the ways in which leisure opportunities are differentially evaluated. Note that the shaping of tastes is rather different from the shaping of choice

through direct sanctions. The former involves more stable preferences between different activities that are brought to the decisionmaking situation. The latter involves the rewards and costs peers
actually deliver for any one choice.[1][2]

All of this suggests that peers should figure prominently in any
analysis of adolescent leisure (and by extension, leisure-based deviance). A leisure framework leads one to expect strong associations
between the leisure choices of an individual and those of his or her
friends. Adolescents who report experience with leisure-based delinquency should have friends with similar experiences. Indeed, this sort
of association is perhaps the most common finding in delinquency
research. However, the meaning of such an association is the topic of
extensive debate. It could be due to peer pressure where friends
"force" individuals into delinquent activities; it could also be an
essentially spurious byproduct of some third set of factors that
promote both individual delinquency and the formation of like-
minded (delinquent) peer groups. Delinquency theorists tend to take
sides on this issue, some arguing that the association between
individual and peer deviance is the product of peer pressure (e.g.,
subcultural theories, theories of differential association, some versions of strain theories), others arguing that already delinquent
individuals tend to congregate for mutual support (e.g., control
theory). Within a leisure decisionmaking framework, both of these
alternatives are possible. The fact that peers influence tastes suggests
that like-minded individuals seek out one another, producing an
association between individual and peer deviance. If one wishes to
play basketball, one must find others who also want to play; if one
wishes to have a beer party, one must find others who wish to join.
At the same time, peers can provide costs and benefits for leisure
choices that influence the probability of delinquent choices more
directly. Still, it is important to note that this cost-benefit approach
does not assume that peers pressure one another in a rigid fashion.
Peer influence is not automatically prodeviant, and the costs and
benefits that peers supply channel rather than force both deviant and
nondeviant decisions.

There is a third way in which associations between peers' and
individuals' delinquency might be explained within a leisure framework of the sort we propose. Peers are an important structural
component of many leisure activities, including delinquency. In such
cases there should be strong associations between individual and peer
deviance quite apart from causal theories of peer influence. If, for
example, beer parties are necessarily group events, a relationship
between an individual's drinking patterns and the alcohol use of
peers should appear automatically.

Given our perspective on leisure decisionmaking, we expect to find important correlations between individual's and peers' experiences in our analysis of middle class delinquency. Our data on peers consist primarily of respondents' estimates of the number of their friends involved in selected delinquent activities. (For a detailed presentation of these friends' items see Appendix B.) We will use these estimates as reflections of an individual's chance to observe and, by implication, to learn from the potentially deviant leisure experiences of others. They will also serve as a rough guide to the potential costs and benefits that peers may provide for various delinquent choices. For example, friends who have shoplifted may give information about its risk and proper technique (hence, reducing risks for the learner); they may also provide some information about how friends are likely to value the activity (positively or negatively). Obviously, there is no absolute assurance that friends with delinquent experiences will reward that behavior in others. However, we will assume that friends with delinquent experiences are more likely to positively reinforce such choices than are friends without such experiences.

LEISURE, FAMILY, AND DELINQUENCY

Family members can affect the nature of leisure choices in many of the ways that we have noted for peers. However, because adolescent leisure time is more likely to be spent with peers than with family members, the relative impact of these influences is likely to be somewhat different. Family members, primarily parents, provide obvious costs and benefits for leisure activities. Punishment for incorrect choices can be formal (i.e., grounding, taking away privileges, etc.) or informal (e.g., expressions of disapproval); both formal and informal rewards can be given for proper leisure choices. Family members can also shape an individual's preferences and tastes (one of the byproducts of socialization) and provide important information about a wide range of leisure options. In fact, parents often make explicit attempts to impart such information, instructing children in the "facts of life," the likely outcomes of drug use, or in the responsible use of alcohol.

However, family members are less likely than peers to be important structural elements of adolescent leisure. They are necessary prerequisites for some potentially delinquent leisure activities (it is difficult to run away from home unless one has a home from which to run), but the bulk of adolescent leisure takes place in situations where parents are not likely to be directly involved. Similarly, family members are less likely than peers to take an important role in leisure activities over which mastery must be learned. While adolescents obviously learn to manipulate parents and to anticipate their responses to choices, parents are less likely to participate in adolescents' leisure pursuits than are peers.

This suggests that some family factors should be more important than others in an adolescent's leisure choices. The direct costs and benefits that parents provide may be reflected in family rules and methods of rule enforcement. Rules and rule enforcement techniques are a common topic in delinquency research, generally because they are assumed to affect individual adjustment and subsequent propensities to deviate. Rules and rule enforcement may be important issues within a leisure framework, although not necessarily because of their impact on individual adjustment. Instead, they can affect the relative balance of costs and benefits to be derived from deviant and nondeviant choices. Stringent rules and strong enforcement can increase the costs of forbidden leisure activities, reducing the likelihood that they will be chosen.

Many delinquency theories stress the importance of affective ties between parents and children, generally under the assumption (1) that parent-child conflict alienates children from parents and drives them to essentially expressive delinquent outbursts or (2) that conflict reduces the effectiveness of parents as conventional role models. While affective ties can function as informal costs and benefits within a leisure framework, there is no need to assume that negative affect (as expressed, for example, by parent-child conflict), automatically leads to delinquency. All other things being equal (which they seldom are) negative affect seems as likely to deter delinquency through more direct and rigid rule imposition as to promote it through alienation or active rebellion. The causal connection between leisure decisions and the affective ties of parents and children is quite complex. Conflict may be a product of disagreement about earlier leisure choices as much as a precipitant for future delinquency. In other words, conflict may alter the balance of costs and benefits of leisure choices in a dynamic way, reflecting disagreement over earlier choices while structuring future options. Since nonfamily actors (especially peers) also affect the overall balance of costs and benefits that accrue to leisure choices, it is difficult to know when conflict between parents and children is likely to raise the costs of adolescent deviance and when it is likely to increase the benefits. Still, affective ties can shape both formal and informal costs and benefits for deviant activity and for this reason should have a role to play in the way that potentially delinquent choices are made.

In an effort to unravel some of these relationships, our analysis of middle class delinquency will include traditional measures of family structure (e.g., broken homes, maternal employment), measures of family rules and rule enforcement, and assessments of parent-child conflict (see Appendix B for the exact wording of these items). We will use these items as indicators of potential costs and benefits that family situations can provide for deviant choices and our analysis will focus on potential links between family conflict and adolescent deviance.

LEISURE, SCHOOL, AND DELINQUENCY

Since adolescents spend so much time in school, school experiences are generally expected to have an important role to play in juvenile delinquency. School variables are commonly included in analyses for reasons ranging from assumptions about status frustration engendered by school performance (e.g., strain theories) to those about the deterrent role of school as a conventional or supervisory influence (e.g., control theories). A leisure decisionmaking model leads to somewhat different expectations about the role of school, and these differences are worth spelling out in some detail.

Schools structure the leisure options available to adolescents in several ways. Like other institutions, schools can provide the necessary prerequisites for a variety of leisure choices. In fact, many school-related activities are specifically designed to limit and channel adolescent leisure. Extracurricular clubs, school-related sporting events, and school projects of various kinds all provide leisure options that are presumably conventional and that adults hope will keep adolescents occupied in "healthy" ways. Obviously one cannot invest leisure resources in after school recreation without school programs that function as a prerequisite for this choice. Similarly, potentially delinquent activities such as school vandalism require that school property be available; delinquent activity designed to make life difficult for school authorities requires that there be school authority figures.

While such assertions are obvious, it is surprisingly easy to overlook their potential impact on leisure choices. Unless school property is readily available, it is difficult to vandalize school buildings no matter how much one may want to; without teachers around, it is difficult to devise effective ways to torment them. This should underscore the fact that these prerequisites are quite similar to those that schools provide for conventional leisure pursuits (sports, clubs) and that school structures both deviant and non-deviant leisure options. It is interesting to note that although schools attempt to channel adolescent leisure choices in presumably healthy directions, they are often ineffective in doing so. There is little assurance that students will participate in the conventional leisure activities schools provide, or that these activities will function in the healthy manner desired. Conventional time fillers can increase the probability of other more deviant-leisure activities. For example, students may attend a football game, but what they do afterward is difficult to anticipate. The game brings adolescents together, and peer groups can continue to structure leisure choices throughout the evening.

Schools structure potentially deviant leisure activities in another interesting way. Market-related job skills are not all that adolescents learn in school. Lessons are also given in character development in order to make students tempermentally suited to future occupations (for a detailed discussion see Bowles and Gintis, 1976). In other words, students learn "proper" behavior and the costs and benefits attached to proper and improper choices. Within school this learning can take place in a way that parallels the learning process during general leisure. Much of the school day consists of waiting or killing time (e.g., study halls, lunch hours, periods between classes, even some classes themselves). Since schooling involves learning proper attitudes and behavior, the subtleties of rules and roles can be refined during odd hours of the school day. Educators are often concerned about the delinquency that occurs during these hours—activities that range from smoking cigarettes in the restrooms to violent assaults on teachers. When seen in a decisionmaking framework, these activities appear quite similar to potentially deviant leisure options. While waiting for school to start one may have the chance to try out some new skill (e.g., smoking on the school grounds); during study hall one may be able to test the limits of adult authority and discover the costs and benefits attached to challenging authority figures. Peers are an important audience during school hours and are likely to structure school-based deviance in much the same way that they influence more general leisure choices. In short, much of what passes for school delinquency may occur through a process quite similar to that of leisure.

School actors also provide direct rewards and sanctions for leisure choices. School authorities can apply both formal and informal sanctions to students who make wrong choices; they can also provide positive feedback to those who learn and follow the rules. Still, it may be difficult to know what these costs and benefits are without actively testing the limits of proper behavior. For example, someone caught smoking in the lavatory may receive a stern warning; he or she may also be expelled from school, depending on extenuating circumstances. Decoding those extenuating circumstances can be a complex process which requires a good deal of information. Informal sanctions are also available to school authorities, and students who care what their teachers think of them are likely to fashion choices in ways consistent with teachers' expectations. School authorities offer benefits as well as costs for potentially deviant activities. If something is to be gained from challenging school authorities, teachers' responses may constitute part of the benefit derived from smarting off in the classroom. School officials also provide costs and benefits for more conventional leisure pursuits. Being a successful basketball star may bring reinforcement from teachers; at the same time, the risk of failure could keep students who care what their teachers think from even trying out for the team.

However, peers are perhaps the most important set of school actors who provide negative and positive sanctions for leisure choices. School is a major arena in which peer groups are formed and friendships established. This may have an important impact on peer group structure and thus affect leisure choices. As noted earlier, school experiences that foster peer group formation (e.g., clubs, sports) may increase the probability of choosing deviant leisure activities even while serving as conventional time fillers. In fact, it is often difficult to tell exactly what impact school experiences might have on deviant choices net of their effect on peer group formation. This is one issue we will examine in our analysis.

Our data on school experiences include measures of school performance, participation in school activities, attitudes about school experiences, and affective responses to school authorities. We will use school performance measures as a rough estimate of the costs and benefits involved in deviant behavior (students performing well have more to lose through deviant activities than those performing poorly). Performance and satisfaction may also serve as indicators of dimensions along which peer groups may form. Attitudes toward school and school actors may also affect the costs and benefits involved in various leisure activities, either by altering the sanctions that others are likely to impose or by altering the degree to which those sanctions are likely to be meaningful to the individual. In this way they should be related to leisure choices. (The exact wording of school variables can be found in Appendix B.)

SUMMARY AND MEASUREMENT IMPLICATIONS

So far we have outlined the basic premises of a leisure decision-making perspective on delinquency and identified important considerations that can affect this decisionmaking process. This perspective is a useful one for several reasons. It moves away from explanations of delinquency that presume individual pathology and toward a more mundane image that does not assume delinquency is inherently abnormal or pathological. Instead, delinquent activities are chosen in ways similar to nondeviant activities and can be understood as the product of similar forces and considerations.

Factors that are traditionally thought to influence delinquency operate in a somewhat different fashion when viewed within a decisionmaking framework. Family, school, and peer experiences channel decisions and structure preferences in patterned ways, but they do not rigidly force individuals into deviance. Instead, they affect the probabilities of leisure choices and alter the balance of legitimate and illegitimate activities in which all adolescents engage. Within a leisure decisionmaking framework, deviance is not an innate characteristic of activities. It is an attribute that can be variously applied depending on the situation. This application must be learned, often through direct experience. By extension, individuals are not inherently delinquent. Instead, actors choose from a mix of both deviant and nondeviant options whose delinquent character is seldom absolutely assured and whose outcomes can be predicted with varying degrees of certainty.

However, this variably deviant image of delinquency has some important implications for the way in which delinquency must be measured in an analysis that uses a leisure decisionmaking perspective. As noted earlier, delinquency is generally operationalized in terms of crime. Self-report measures have now been refined to the point that most delinquency researchers limit their work to analyses of activities that are legally prohibited. The most popular measures of delinquency are summary scales that cumulate these activities and differentiate between more or less delinquent individuals. We will employ a somewhat different measurement strategy in our analysis, in keeping with the image of delinquency implicit in a leisure formulation.

Throughout our discussion, we have emphasized the similarity in the processes by which adolescents make both potentially deviant and potentially nondeviant choices. In large part, the adequacy of our argument rests on the ability to demonstrate that similar patterns can be identified for a wide range of leisure activities, some potentially more deviant than others. For this reason, a strict "crime" definition of delinquency is not a useful reflection of the types of behavior we propose to study. We will not limit our attention to explicitly illegal behavior, but will examine patterns in activities ranging from status offenses, to serious crime, to modest forms of interpersonal conflict. Some of these qualify as crimes, others do not, but all are likely to occur within the context of adolescent leisure. Most delinquency researchers who employ this sort of broad operationalization of delinquency do so under the assumption that problem behavior is precriminal (see, for example, Shaw 1966, Short and Nye, 1958, and Stinchcombe, 1964, for just a few examples). This is not our justification for including noncriminal activities within our definition. Instead, there are leisure activities that are potentially deviant and likely to be responsive to many of the decisionmaking considerations outlined above.

We have measured these potentially deviant forms of leisure activity with familiar self-report survey questions, but we will not be cumulating them into an overall delinquency index as most self-report researchers do. Instead, items will be informally clustered and analyzed individually (for a detailed presentation of items to be used and the way in which they cluster see Chapter 3). While we could have developed scales consistent with a leisure definition of delinquency, scaling makes sense only after establishing the value of the underlying dimension which unites the items. In the case of delinquency, most people assume that this dimension is crime (see Hirschi, 1969, for a typical discussion of this underlying concept in scale construction). By posing a noncrime image of delinquency, we are challenging the utility of this assumption. To do so convincingly, we must show that leisure is a useful dimension in the study of delinquency. Were we to scale our measures from the outset, we would be asking the reader to assume what we would prefer to demonstrate. For this reason we will analyze delinquency items without scaling them, noting common patterns (and differences), and relating these patterns to the leisure decisionmaking model we propose.

Before turning to the analysis of these patterns we will present a brief description of our data in order to familiarize readers with our research. In the next chapter we will outline important features of our study of middle class delinquency (i.e., sampling, administration of questionnaires, etc.) and present our delinquency measures in greater detail.

NOTES

1. Among the authors who discuss the importance of infraction definitions of delinquency one might turn to Hirschi (1969) or Matza (1964).

2. The issue of "choice" has always been a difficult one for

delinquency theorists. Classical legal theorists emphasized the importance of individual calculation and free will in crime, but most criminologists rejected these ideas in favor of causal explanations modeled on natural science principles. In recent years there has been a resurgence of interest in utilitarian delinquency theories that allow individuals an element of choice. For comprehensive discussions of these see Matza (1964) or Taylor, Walton, and Young (1973).

3. Few delinquency theorists would argue that adolescents do not "choose" their delinquent activities, but this is seldom the focus of theoretical concern. It is difficult to find perspectives with explicit rather than implicit assumptions about individual choice or theories that attempt to specify the way in which delinquent choices are made. An obvious exception is the work of Matza (1964) and others who are interested in the potentially instrumental, political nature of adolescent deviance (see for example, S. Cohen, 1971, 1973; Ward, 1973; Taylor and Taylor, 1973; and other conflict theorists).

4. The microeconomic literature on deviance is growing rapidly. For an introduction to important issues see Becker (1974), Ehrlich (1974), and Sjoquist (1973). Much of this literature focuses on adult crime in general and issues of deterrence in particular (see for example, Ehrlich, 1975; 1977; Passel and Taylor, 1977), and the deterrent value of capital punishment has been an especially popular topic. Microeconomic perspectives on crime have sparked a great deal of debate both in terms of their implications for law enforcement policies (see for example Phillips, Votey, and Howell, 1976; Stigler, 1970; Mathieson and Passell, 1976) and in terms of the accuracy of the assumptions they require (for discussion of some of these issues, see Berk and Jurik, 1979). Readers interested in greater detail about utilitarian criminology should consult these references.

There are few microeconomic analyses of delinquency per se. Fleischer (1966) offers one of these and outlines an economic model of delinquency that shares many of the assumptions we will be making here. Like most economists, his analysis is based on aggregate level data (i.e., arrest rates); his work provides an intriguing example of how microeconomic principles can be applied to juvenile delinquency.

5. Those readers interested in a formal statement of most of these points should consult Ehrlich (1974). Perhaps the main difference between our presentation and Ehrlich's is that he does not consider the importance of gathering information about the consequences of one's actions.

6. By "marketable" we mean the skills that affect one's ability to earn a living. That is, they are arguments in one's earning function.

7. Leisure is an especially interesting issue in the middle class case since it is also differentially distributed according to affluence. Affluence frees adolescents from the need to work to supplement family income or to produce household commodities (presumably these can be purchased more readily by affluent families). This increases opportunities to invest leisure resources.

8. Time is clearly the major resource that teenagers have to invest, although nontrivial amounts of money may also be available. In our discussion we will concentrate on the former, but the same points are also applicable to monetary investments. Both time and money may be viewed as resources to be allocated, and indeed, Becker (1965), among other economists, typically combines both into an overall income constraint (see Becker, 1965, for detail on this issue).

9. The role of psychic rewards and costs is just now getting the attention it deserves in microeconomic theory. However, the introduction of psychic consequences into production processes raises hellish difficulties with formal microeconomic models, and this is one of the reasons that we have avoided formal model building here. Readers who wish to tackle some fairly demanding microeconomic theory should find the recent article by Block and Heineke (1975) helpful on this issue.

10. Although we will not discuss general theories of leisure in great detail, readers interested in sociological approaches to leisure should examine work by Dumagedier (1974), Parker (1975, 1971), Luschen (1973), Kaplan (1960), Bull (1963), or de Grazia (1962). Most of the leisure literature focuses on entertainment or consumption, and there are few direct links to models of deviance. Microeconomic perspectives on resource investment of the type outlined here offer one such link that we will discuss in some detail.

11. The literature on "play" covers a wide range of topics from detailed learning theories and theories of cognitive development to more general discussions of play as a vehicle for moral development. For a presentation of many of the most popular approaches to the latter of these topics see Reilly (1974).

12. Most of these points also apply to other significant actors in an adolescent's environment as well (e.g., parents, siblings, teachers, other authority figures). We will discuss these in greater detail below.

Chapter Three

The Study, Sample, and Data

INTRODUCTION: THE STUDY

Before examining our delinquency measures in detail it would be well to outline some of the important characteristics of the study on which this analysis is based. Our data come from adolescents living in an upper income suburb of Chicago. We have identified the area as middle class on the basis of the residents' occupational and educational characteristics. Most heads of household are employed in professional or business occupations that provide relatively high incomes. According to 1970 census figures, median family income in this community was $20,050, and 30.8 percent of all families had an income of over $25,000. Median years of schooling for adults over the age of twenty-five were 14.8, and 41.2 percent of all adults were college graduates. In addition, almost all of the residents of this community are white. Only 2.5 percent were listed as nonwhite in the 1970 census.[1]

Our analysis is drawn from a community wide survey of youth problems conducted in the spring of 1975. Questionnaires were administered to all public school children enrolled in the fifth through ninth and eleventh grades, a random half of the tenth graders, and a small purposive sample of twelfth graders.[2] The tenth graders included in this analysis are those enrolled in health courses that spring semester. Since enrollment in first or second semester health is essentially random, this sample should be representative of the grade as a whole. The twelfth grade sample is more of a problem. It is a convenience sample composed of students from sociology, psychology, and advanced chemistry courses and is an obviously unique subset of all high school seniors. These are among the most academically oriented students in the school, and their delinquency may be unique in both type and degree: one might predict that they would report less delinquency than other twelfth graders. Their responses will be included in this analysis, but findings about twelfth graders must be carefully interpreted in light of the potential biases introduced by these sampling procedures.[3]

Although we have been using the term sample in this discussion, this study represents a somewhat different kind of sample than is common in most survey research. Information was collected from the entire population of public school students for every grade except the tenth and twelfth. At the same time, we did not sample this particular population of suburban school children from some known universe of middle class suburbs. Instead, this community was chosen for study on the basis of informal criteria of typicality and convenience. Still, we feel that our findings can be generalized beyond this one suburb. This community is similar to nearby towns along a variety of dimensions including socioeconomic status, type of housing, employment and education patterns, and lifestyle. It is also similar in terms of the types of youth problems and delinquency that concern residents, and surveys of youth needs in surrounding towns have produced data quite similar to ours.[4] On this basis we would argue that our analysis can provide insight into the more general phenomenon of middle class delinquency. Obviously this generalization is based on theoretical assumptions of similarity, not on classical statistical inference.

Questionnaire Construction

Our analysis will draw on information from self-report questionnaires. The questionnaires consist of standard closed-ended survey items and short answer questions that follow the format used in other research on adolescents (e.g., Coleman, 1961, Stinchcombe, 1964, Kandel, 1974, Hirschi, 1969, etc.). The items provide information about several familiar topics. Independent variables cluster into four main groups: (1) attitudes, (2) family situation, (3) school experiences, and (4) peer relationships. Many of the items are similar to those used in other delinquency surveys, and all are familiar types of self-report questions. The dependent variables used to measure delinquency can also be grouped into clusters. We obtained measures of (1) vandalism, (2) drug use, (3) petty theft (shoplifting, etc.), (4) noncrime delinquency, (5) serious forms of delinquency, and (6) contact with law enforcement agencies.

The age range covered by this research poses some interesting issues in questionnaire construction. We expected fairly large differences in reading ability between students in elementary, junior high, and senior high school and for this reason constructed questionnaires for each age group. As much comparability as possible was maintained between instruments, and the questionnaires for junior and senior high respondents are the most alike. Occasionally the wording of an item was simplified for the younger group, but the major difference between the instruments is one of scope. Fewer items were included in the junior high questionnaire.

The fifth and sixth grade instrument differs in form as well as in content from the other two. Since few sociologists have administered self-report delinquency questionnaires to students this young, we found it difficult to anticipate how to pitch the survey items. We expected fifth and sixth graders to be unfamiliar with surveys but knew that they had had contact with standardized achievement tests used in the schools. This led us to model the instrument on achievement tests. Response categories were simplified to a yes-no pattern wherever possible, and few open-ended items were included. In addition, teachers took students through a short series of practice questions just as they do for standardized educational tests. While there was some danger that students would find this test format threatening, we hoped this could be minimized by careful explanations of the purpose of the survey and repeated assurances that this was not a test.

These efforts appear to have been largely successful. If teacher response is any indication, even the youngest children had little trouble answering the questionnaires. In fact, the younger students were the most careful of all respondents, qualifying their answers wherever possible and answering virtually every item. There is very little missing data from the elementary school set. However, there is some evidence to justify our original concern. Younger students may have had little difficulty with the mechanics of the task but they did not always share the conventional meaning of survey questions. For example, when asked "who do you live with," an occasional fifth or sixth grader would circle both "mother and father" and "other," specifying "my brother" or "my dog." Others would list "month, day, and year of birth" as "June, Tuesday, 1963." Interestingly enough, these responses are found only in the elementary students' data. None of the older respondents answered in this way, suggesting that junior and senior high students are more familiar with bureaucratic conventions. Still, the data provided by fifth and sixth graders seem sufficiently reliable to support analysis. In a highly educated, affluent community such as this, young students probably have strong enough language skills to answer a questionnaire clearly. As subsequent analysis will show, their responses follow systematic and readily interpretable patterns and cluster in meaningful ways. While this is not absolute proof of their reliability, it does indicate that meaningful analysis is possible.[5]

Questionnaire Administration

Classroom teachers administered questionnaire booklets to students during regularly scheduled class periods. Prior to distributing the booklets, teachers read instructions and answered students' questions according to guidelines provided by the researchers. Students had between forty and fifty minutes to complete the questionnaires, and most finished in less than the allotted time. Responses were completely confidential and measures were taken to visably ensure students' anonymity. A student volunteer from each classroom sealed the completed survey booklets in an envelope and delivered them to a central collection point monitored by the researchers. No school officials saw any of the completed instruments, and students were repeatedly assured of this.[6]

Response rates with this type of data collection procedure are high. Our response rate averages around 90 percent for all age groups based on total school enrollment. This rate reflects normal absences, refusals, and uninterpretable questionnaires. Usable questionnaires were obtained from 748 elementary school students, 852 seventh and eighth graders, and 1,250 high school students.

Response Rates and Non-Response Bias

Self-report delinquency research often encounters problems of bias introduced by differential cooperation. Seldom do researchers obtain data from 100 percent of their original sample, and this can influence the representativeness of findings. Our particular sampling and administration procedures tend to minimize this sort of bias, but there are still several issues worth noting. Normal absences are the major reason for our response rate of less than 100 percent, but since some students are more likely to be absent from school than others, this could create distortions. A smaller proportion of this nonresponse is the product of direct refusals to participate in the study. Parents could request that their child not participate, and some did. Students themselves could refuse to fill out a questionnaire, and booklets that were completed in an obviously frivolous manner were also discarded. Any of these procedures could have eliminated an important subgroup of respondents and threatened the representativeness of our survey.

Large blocks of missing data could in principle create several problems. Perhaps most important, subjects with extensive delinquent experiences may be underrepresented. Delinquency is correlated with truancy, and surveys of school populations that reflect normal rates of absenteeism may underrepresent students most frequently involved in delinquency. This same group may also be more likely to give frivolous responses to survey items or to fail to complete questionnaires, exacerbating problems of underrepresentation (see for example, Hirschi, 1969, for detailed discussion of these issues). However, nonresponse can also lead to the opposite form of bias. Parents usually requested that their child not participate in this study because they thought that participation would increase their child's curiosity about delinquency. Behind this reasoning is the assumption that their children have had few delinquent experiences up to this point. Were this the case, nonresponse would tend to underrepresent students with low levels of delinquency to report.[7]

In this study the actual impact of these potential biases appears to be limited. Our overall response rate is unusually high for self-report delinquency research, which in itself suggests that the chance of underrepresenting a major subgroup in this population is small. With response rates averaging around 90 percent, it is unlikely that large numbers of any special group have been excluded from the analysis. The potential bias introduced by discarding frivolous responses also appears to be slight. Only a few booklets were discarded because the respondent did not seem to take the task seriously. A handful of students failed to complete the questionnaire, and wherever possible we kept these, deleting them on a case-by-case basis during analysis. Nonresponse bias introduced by parental refusals also appears to be minimal. No more than two or three parents in any classroom asked that their children be excused and these numbers are not likely to produce major biases when Ns range from 748 to 1,250. To the best of our knowledge, there were no students who refused to fill out a questionnaire at the time of administration. Thus, direct refusals are likely to exert only a slight impact on the representativeness of these data.[8]

MEASURING DELINQUENCY:
QUESTIONNAIRE ITEMS

Our interest in the leisure context of delinquency led us to include a large number of delinquency measures in this survey. These have been grouped into clusters for the chapter-by-chapter analysis that follows. Before turning to these chapters, we would like to identify the range of measures we will be using and discuss the interrelationships that in part underlie our clustering procedures. Tables 3-1 through 3-3 present the distribution of basic responses to the delinquency measures and provide information about the types of delinquency favored by each of the three age groups. Tables 3-4 through 3-6 present the correlations that serve as guides for grouping these measures into chapter topics. (The actual wording of the items can be found in Appendix B.)[9]

Fifth and Sixth Graders: Basic Distributions of Delinquency

Delinquency is generally thought to be related to age in a curvilinear fashion, and it is not surprising that elementary students report the lowest levels of delinquency of any of the three age groups surveyed. They were asked two types of questions about delinquency, the first designed to assess their total history, the second their most frequent activities during the six months prior to the study. Reporting patterns for both sets of questions are similar. Most frequent are what might be categorized as minor forms of delinquency. About three quarters of these students have tried wine or beer, and almost 40 percent have done so more than once or twice in

Table 3-1. Fifth and Sixth Graders' Delinquency: Percentage of Students Reporting[a]

	Ever Tried			More than Once or Twice in the Last Six Months		
	Yes	*No*	*(N)*	*Yes*	*No*	*(N)*
Wine or Beer	74.1	25.9	(745)	37.3	62.7	(743)
Hard Liquor	23.3	76.7	(744)	9.0	91.0	(745)
Marijuana	3.9	96.1	(739)	2.6	97.4	(742)
Minor Shoplifting	26.1	73.9	(748)	9.7	·90.3	(749)
Major Shoplifting ($5 or more)	3.2	96.8	(748)	2.1	97.9	(750)
Damaged Property	8.7	91.3	(745)	3.3	96.7	(748)
Defaced Property	21.8	78.2	(747)	13.8	86.2	(749)
Bike Theft	1.5	98.5	(746)	.9	99.1	(746)
Fought with a Student	45.4	54.6	(749)	31.4	68.6	(748)
Truancy	5.2	94.8	(748)	2.1	97.9	(749)
Cheated on a Test	20.7	79.3	(744)	13.9	86.1	(747)
Run Away from Home	2.7	97.3	(728)			
Taken to Police Station More than Once or Twice	3.7	96.3	(732)			

[a]Exact wording of items can be found in Appendix B.

the last six months. Close to half have fought with another student; almost one-third have done so with some regularity during the current school year. Between 20 and 25 percent have tried hard liquor or been involved in minor shoplifting, defacing property, or cheating on a test at school. These are also among the more popular activities reported during the last six months.

Few have ever tried more serious delinquencies such as marijuana use, major shoplifting, or bike theft. Only a handful have ever ditched school or vandalized. Rates of recent activity are even lower for these items. Given the limited amount of serious delinquency reported here, it is not surprising that few fifth and sixth graders have had contact with the police. Less than 4 percent say that they have been taken to the police station more than once or twice.[10]

Seventh and Eighth Graders' Delinquency: Basic Distributions

Junior High students were asked to estimate involvement in potentially delinquent activities during the last six months (Table 3-2). Seventh and eighth graders are most likely to report drug or alcohol use, conflict with peers, school-related delinquency, minor theft, and vandalism during that period. Other forms of delinquency are much less common.

A good deal of junior high students' delinquency takes place in or around schools. Minor vandalism to school property is reported by 30-45 percent of these respondents. Over three-quarters claim to have cheated on a test at least once during the current year, and over half have done so more than once or twice. A fifth have ditched school. Conflict with other students is also fairly frequent. About half have stolen from another student or threatened to beat up someone, while about a quarter have actually gotten into a major fight.

Minor nonschool vandalism, minor shoplifting, and alcohol use are also reported with a good deal of frequency. Over half of these students have been out drinking during the last six months, and almost a fifth have done so more than five times. Seventeen percent have smoked marijuana at least once during the current school year.

Of the more serious forms of delinquency included in the survey, only major vandalism and major shoplifting are reported by more than 10 percent of these students. Still, it is interesting to note that about 15 percent claim some contact with the police and about 5 percent say that they have been taken down to the police station more than once or twice. Although these are small proportions of the total group the actual numbers (112 students) are nontrivial.

**Table 3-2.   Seventh and Eighth Graders' Delinquency:
Percentage of Students Reporting[a]**

	Never	Once	2-3	4-5	6+	N
			Number of Times in the Last Six Months			
Used Alcohol	45.2	7.5	17.0	9.2	18.2	(818)
Used Marijuana	83.4	2.7	3.3	3.3	7.2	(811)
Stole from a Student	53.4	18.9	13.1	4.3	10.2	(831)
Threatened a Student	52.5	19.2	11.2	4.3	11.6	(832)
Fought with a Student	73.1	16.2	6.2	1.9	2.6	(821)
Stole a Bike	95.6	2.7	0.6	0.2	0.8	(825)
Stole Auto Accessories	91.5	4.1	1.3	1.0	2.1	(827)
Stole a Car	97.5	1.1	0.2	0.1	1.1	(824)
Breaking and Entering	95.3	3.6	0.6	0.1	0.4	(816)
School Defacement	67.0	14.1	9.6	3.7	5.6	(821)
Minor School Damage	55.7	17.8	11.6	4.3	10.6	(830)
Major School Damage	93.0	3.9	1.0	0.6	1.6	(825)
Nonschool Defacement	73.8	11.9	9.2	2.2	2.8	(822)
Minor Non-school Damage	64.7	15.2	9.7	2.9	7.5	(828)
Major Non-school Damage	91.4	3.6	1.8	0.2	2.9	(824)
Minor Shoplifting	69.0	14.9	6.2	2.7	7.3	(825)
Major Shoplifting	87.6	4.3	3.1	1.2	3.8	(812)
Cheated on a Test	24.4	17.0	30.4	10.9	14.5	(807)
Truancy	78.8	11.8	3.8	3.2	3.1	(819)
			Number of Times in Entire Life			
Ever Brought to Police Station	85.1	9.8	2.7	1.4	1.5	(819)

[a]Exact wording of items can be found in Appendix B.

High School Students' Delinquency:
Basic Distributions

High school students were asked questions similar to those asked of seventh and eighth graders (Table 3-3). With a few exceptions, the rates of delinquent activity reported by high school students are equal to or lower than those of junior high respondents. Detailed age relationships for individual items will be discussed at later points in this analysis, but two general patterns can be seen in these marginal distributions. Contact with minor forms of delinquency tends to decline between junior and senior high while rates for the more

Table 3-3. High School Students' Delinquency: Percentage of
Students Reporting[a]

| | Number of Times in the Last Six Months | | | | | |
	Never	Once	2-3	4-5	6+	N
Used Alcohol	17.6	4.5	10.8	11.2	55.8	(1231)
Used Marijuana	47.1	3.2	7.3	3.2	38.2	(1234)
Stole from a Student	73.0	15.4	7.6	2.0	2.0	(1229)
Fought with a Student	85.0	9.0	4.3	0.9	0.8	(1223)
Stole School Property	72.4	14.3	9.7	2.5	1.1	(1234)
Minor Shoplifting	66.5	13.4	11.9	3.6	4.6	(1230)
Major Shoplifting	86.2	5.8	4.0	1.3	2.7	(1223)
Stole a Bicycle	95.4	2.9	0.8	0.3	0.5	(1240)
Stole Auto Accessories	94.6	2.7	1.0	0.7	1.0	(1231)
Stole a Car	98.7	0.8	0.2	0	0.3	(1229)
Breaking and Entering	95.1	2.8	1.5	0.3	0.3	(1219)
School Defacement	80.6	9.1	5.7	2.0	2.6	(1230)
Minor School Damage	75.6	11.4	8.4	1.9	2.6	(1234)
Major School Damage	95.6	2.5	0.9	0.3	0.7	(1228)
Damage to Private Property	71.6	12.8	8.4	3.3	4.0	(1240)
Damage to Public Property	92.2	4.2	2.0	0.8	0.7	(1230)
Cheated on a Test	16.9	9.2	26.5	17.2	30.3	(1232)
	Number of Times in Entire Life					
Ever Run Away from Home	88.4	8.5	2.5	1.0	1.3	(1225)
Ever Brought to Police Station	69.7	15.8	8.6	3.1	2.7	(1234)
Ever Appeared Before a Judge	90.8	6.7	2.2	0.4	0.3	(1236)

[a]Exact wording of items can be found in Appendix B.

serious types of delinquency tend to remain about the same for both
age groups.

Recreational drug and alcohol use are the most popular types of
delinquency reported by these high school students. Forty-five
percent have been out drinking more than six times during the
current school year, and only about a fifth have done no drinking at
all. Over half have smoked marijuana at least once during the same
time period. Close to 40 percent have done so more than six times.

School-related delinquency is also fairly common. Only 17 percent say they have not cheated during the current school year. Significant proportions have also stolen from another student, fought with a student, or stolen school property during that time. Twenty to twenty-five percent report minor forms of school vandalism.

Nonschool vandalism is less frequent than it is among junior high students, but still almost a third of these high school respondents say they have damaged nonschool property. One form of minor delinquency that does not seem to decrease among older age cohorts is minor shoplifting: approximately 35 percent have shoplifted something worth less than $5 in the last six months. Few of these older students report more serious forms of theft such as bike theft, auto theft, or stealing car accessories.

Interestingly enough, almost 30 percent of these high school students claim to have been taken to the police station at least once in their lives and 14 percent at least twice. This is about double the proportion found in the junior high data, but this does not necessarily mean that older students have more frequent contact with the police. Students were asked how many times they had "ever" been taken to the police station, which builds a history effect into the measure and automatically creates the potential for higher frequencies among older respondents. High school students were also asked how many times they had appeared before a judge. Almost 10 percent say they have done so. While this is again a small percentage, it represents a nontrivial number of students. Approximately 125 of these high school respondents claim to have appeared in court at some point in their lives.

Summary: Basic Distribution
of Delinquency

Since most popular delinquency theories lead one to expect relatively little delinquency among middle class adolescents, the levels reported here are quite striking. While fifth and sixth graders have had relatively few delinquency experiences, junior and senior high students report levels of delinquency that compare favorably with those found in other self-report surveys.[11] Meaningful proportions of these students have been involved in activities such as vandalism, shoplifting, drug use, or theft during the past year.

These students are most likely to report minor forms of delinquency. Relatively few say that they have been involved in activities such as car theft, breaking and entering, or other serious delinquencies in the past year. Still, nontrivial numbers of students report these activities, suggesting that they are worth further investigation. In spite of popular arguments that middle class adolescents seldom come into contact with the juvenile justice system, meaningful proportions of both junior and senior high respondents say that they have been taken to the police station. Close to 10 percent of the high school students also claim to have appeared before a judge.

Since these middle class adolescents report a wide range of delinquencies with a good deal of frequency, these items should be related to one another in systematic ways. Up to this point we have informally identified "major" and "minor" types of delinquency and outlined response patterns for variables that fit best in one or the other of these categories. Item intercorrelations offer additional detail about the relationships between these items and can be used to divide them into more definitive clusters.

Fifth and Sixth Graders' Delinquency:
Item Intercorrelations

Since elementary students report generally low levels of delinquency, there are few strong intercorrelations among delinquency items in the fifth and sixth grade data set (Table 3-4).[1][2] Zero order correlation coefficients between these dichotomized measures seldom exceed 0.30, and the degree of association among the most frequently reported items averages between 0.10 and 0.20. In spite of these small coefficients, the data do cluster in expected ways. For example, students who report recent use of wine or beer are also likely to report recent use of hard liquor ($r = 0.36$), and those who report using hard liquor also tend to report recent marijuana use. Minor and major shoplifting are correlated with police contact (rs of 0.23 or 0.31) in predictable ways.

This commonsense clustering is important evidence that these fifth and sixth graders' estimates are useful indicators of their actual behavior. Although many correlations are modest, it is important to recall that elementary students are just beginning to try out a variety of new and potentially delinquent activities. Their involvement is both limited and scattered. Systematic behavior patterns have not been established, making links between one form of delinquency and another rather tenuous. Until young students have enough chances to try, and then to repeat, delinquent activities, the relationships between different forms of delinquency are bound to be attenuated. In any event, the limited delinquent involvement at this age level means that conclusions about overall patterns must always be made with an eye to the potential problems introduced by highly skewed marginal response distributions.

The nature of these fifth and sixth grade measures poses some additional complications for our analysis. Half of these items refer to

Table 3-4.   Fifth and Sixth Grade Delinquency: Item Correlations (N = 584)

	1	2	3	4	5	6	7	8	9	10	11
1.	1.000										
2.	0.415	1.000									
3.	0.117	0.146	1.000								
4.	0.091	0.140	0.779	1.000							
5.	0.093	0.214	0.162	0.164	1.000						
6.	0.107	0.184	0.137	0.191	0.605	1.000					
7.	0.158	0.204	0.084	0.086	0.207	0.129	1.000				
8.	0.130	0.234	0.082	0.055	0.212	0.175	0.730	1.000			
9.	0.199	0.196	0.229	0.150	0.229	0.155	0.180	0.182	1.000		
10.	0.124	0.187	0.220	0.212	0.189	0.193	0.159	0.181	0.536	1.000	
11.	0.066	0.090	0.275	0.365	0.253	0.112	0.116	0.107	0.298	0.373	1.000
12.	0.014	0.122	0.241	0.319	0.144	0.149	0.102	0.097	0.219	0.408	0.752
13.	0.033	0.112	0.121	0.163	0.164	0.134	0.077	0.038	0.121	0.195	0.296
14.	0.050	0.075	0.073	0.100	0.099	0.179	0.040	0.068	0.105	0.147	0.283
15.	0.126	0.122	0.291	0.263	0.256	0.213	0.051	0.022	0.225	0.273	0.257
16.	0.091	0.100	0.222	0.232	0.164	0.246	0.039	0.026	0.215	0.343	0.365
17.	0.164	0.163	0.142	0.110	0.170	0.150	0.260	0.193	0.288	0.160	0.158
18.	0.167	0.217	0.143	0.107	0.172	0.168	0.210	0.197	0.255	0.201	0.176
19.	0.075	0.170	0.022	0.036	0.134	0.103	0.182	0.112	0.185	0.145	0.096
20.	0.044	0.175	0.015	0.022	0.129	0.092	0.162	0.159	0.157	0.123	0.064
21.	0.034	0.155	0.111	0.156	0.149	0.126	0.116	0.099	0.151	0.194	0.341
22.	0.076	0.148	0.212	0.234	0.173	0.191	0.038	0.067	0.193	0.234	0.289
23.	0.063	0.089	−0.043	−0.017	0.178	0.085	0.053	0.055	0.094	0.113	0.112
24.	0.076	0.058	0.123	0.097	0.070	0.018	0.120	0.088	0.109	0.041	−0.007
	1	2	3	4	5	6	7	8	9	10	11

1.000											
0.465	1.000										
0.230	0.629	1.000									
0.194	0.215	0.207	1.000								
0.319	0.343	0.441	0.605	1.000							
0.154	0.144	0.166	0.179	0.134	1.000						
0.213	0.233	0.215	0.206	0.220	0.711	1.000					
0.119	0.094	0.061	0.111	0.075	0.078	0.095	1.000				
0.104	0.074	0.054	0.063	0.084	0.080	0.090	0.736	1.000			
0.363	0.237	0.308	0.163	0.277	0.140	0.200	0.110	0.126	1.000		
0.309	0.275	0.170	0.201	0.234	0.136	0.132	0.053	0.095	0.164	1.000	
0.064	0.083	0.087	0.023	0.021	−0.028	−0.045	0.278	0.210	0.075	0.145	
0.001	0.028	−0.017	0.085	0.039	0.267	0.180	−0.004	−0.027	0.035	0.033	
12	13	14	15	16	17	18	19	20	21	22	

Table 3-4 continued

Variable[a]	Mean	Standard Deviation
1. Ever used wine or beer	0.742	0.438
2. Used wine or beer this year	0.374	0.484
3. Ever used marijuana	0.038	0.191
4. Used marijuana this year	0.023	0.151
5. Ever damaged property	0.083	0.276
6. Damaged property this year	0.031	0.176
7. Ever defaced property	0.210	0.408
8. Defaced property this year	0.130	0.337
9. Ever shoplifted—minor	0.261	0.439
10. Minor shoplifting this year	0.096	0.294
11. Ever shoplifted—major	0.030	0.172
12. Major shoplifting this year	0.020	0.141
13. Ever stole a bicycle	0.011	0.107
14. Stole a bicycle this year	0.007	0.085
15. Ever truant	0.054	0.225
16. Truant this year	0.023	0.150
17. Ever cheated	0.209	0.407
18. Cheated this year	0.136	0.343
19. Ever fought with a student	0.445	0.497
20. Fought with a student this year	0.310	0.462
21. Ever run away from home	0.026	0.160
22. Brought to police station	0.035	0.183
23. Sex	0.493	0.500
24. Grade	0.498	0.500

[a]Exact wording of variables can be found in Appendix B.

Variable Coding

Delinquency Variables
   0 = no
   1 = yes

Sex
   0 = female
   1 = male

Grade
   0 = 5th
   1 = 6th

delinquent experiences over the respondents' lifetimes, and this means that they are not strictly comparable to the information from older cohorts. In addition, it will be difficult to know how to interpret relationships between these lifetime measures and the independent variables, which are usually current attributes of the respondents. We do not know exactly when these activities took place, nor is there any assurance that the respondents' current attributes (e.g., family structure, attitudes) are the same as they were when the reported acts occurred. This time gap could be another explanation for the generally low correlations in the fifth and sixth grade data. At best we can argue that elementary students' lifetime experiences are likely to reflect fairly recent activities since they are too young to have lengthy histories of most forms of delinquency.

Still, the problem of temporal ordering must be kept in mind throughout our discussions of the patterns in the elementary school data.

Seventh and Eighth Grade Delinquency: Item Intercorrelations

Intercorrelations among the junior high delinquency measures are both stronger and more systematic than those observed for fifth and sixth graders. Delinquency measures were dichotomized (0 = none; 1 = once or more in the last six months) and correlated with one another; the intercorrelations are presented in Table 3-5.[13] Since it is somewhat unusual to dichotomize frequency estimates, our decision deserves some comment. We desired maximum comparability between data sets. By dichotomizing the junior and senior high responses, it is possible to compare results across all three age groups. Dichotomizing in this fashion also eliminates the outlier problem in those items that have highly skewed marginal distributions. For these reasons we will analyze dichotomized delinquency measures throughout the chapters that follow. (See notes 19 and 20 for further discussion of the advantages and disadvantages of this strategy.)

Once again there are predictable and readily interpretable relationships among different types of delinquency. For example, minor and major shoplifting are correlated at 0.54, theft of car parts and minor property damage at 0.37, minor shoplifting and minor property damage at 0.39, bike theft and major shoplifting at 0.38. Alcohol use has a zero order r of 0.38 with marijuana use, and the vandalism items are intercorrelated at levels that average around 0.35. The more serious forms of delinquency have higher levels of correlation with police contact than do less serious activities. These levels of association are similar to those found in general self-report delinquency research.

The most general clustering of these measures is into what might be loosly termed minor and major forms of delinquency. Activities such as minor vandalism, conflict with students, minor shoplifting, or minor theft are more strongly related to one another than they are with more serious forms of delinquency. Serious delinquencies are most closely related to other serious delinquencies. In fact, coefficients among these items are often quite impressive (e.g., an r of 0.53 between major school damage and major nonschool damage or of 0.48 between breaking and entering and bike theft). Again, however, these coefficients for serious forms of delinquency should be interpreted carefully in light of the relatively small number of students who report them.

Table 3-5. Seventh and Eighth Grade Delinquency: Item Intercorrelations (N = 830)

	1	2	3	4	5	6	7	8	9	10	11	12	13	14	15	16	17	18	19	20
1	1.000																			
2	0.382	1.000																		
3	0.220	0.190	1.000																	
4	0.311	0.220	0.314	1.000																
5	0.174	0.198	0.255	0.300	1.000															
6	0.303	0.207	0.469	0.375	0.302	1.000														
7	0.351	0.296	0.268	0.450	0.325	0.416	1.000													
8	0.202	0.196	0.229	0.275	0.533	0.403	0.440	1.000												
9	0.312	0.264	0.288	0.366	0.276	0.359	0.387	0.326	1.000											
10	0.233	0.274	0.227	0.277	0.433	0.384	0.388	0.464	0.545	1.000										
11	0.271	0.149	0.220	0.370	0.294	0.304	0.351	0.275	0.340	0.291	1.000									
12	0.117	0.175	0.192	0.232	0.487	0.245	0.278	0.469	0.284	0.377	0.210	1.000								
13	0.180	0.183	0.201	0.265	0.457	0.359	0.371	0.563	0.284	0.433	0.234	0.457	1.000							
14	0.115	0.147	0.158	0.185	0.430	0.295	0.283	0.471	0.244	0.399	0.190	0.481	0.432	1.000						
15	0.052	0.098	0.173	0.168	0.386	0.205	0.215	0.422	0.175	0.360	0.135	0.504	0.401	0.494	1.000					
16	0.303	0.376	0.219	0.282	0.214	0.250	0.305	0.243	0.276	0.179	0.211	0.182	0.226	0.196	0.159	1.000				
17	0.206	0.102	0.195	0.260	0.051	0.170	0.177	0.087	0.212	0.133	0.237	0.046	0.049	0.067	0.050	0.173	1.000			
18	0.161	0.102	0.115	0.205	0.312	0.199	0.270	0.271	0.218	0.240	0.278	0.205	0.286	0.196	0.200	0.149	0.091	1.000		
19	0.213	0.161	0.084	0.244	0.226	0.191	0.371	0.251	0.211	0.197	0.314	0.190	0.209	0.153	0.111	0.171	0.106	0.358	1.000	
20	0.244	0.321	0.172	0.238	0.311	0.212	0.312	0.388	0.294	0.293	0.205	0.310	0.347	0.248	0.243	0.253	0.085	0.173	0.217	1.000
21	0.164	0.125	-0.138	0.102	0.207	0.062	0.260	0.230	0.118	0.158	0.280	0.154	0.205	0.136	0.133	0.075	-0.043	0.250	0.435	0.254
22	0.104	0.100	0.029	-0.032	-0.017	-0.036	0.022	-0.011	-0.018	-0.036	-0.040	-0.053	-0.026	-0.056	-0.056	0.081	0.066	-0.099	-0.011	0.008

Submatrix blocks: A, B, C, D, E, F, G, H, I, J, K, L, M

MEAN INTERCORRELATIONS

Submatrix	$\bar{r}$
A	0.382
B	0.357
C	0.392
D	0.461
E	0.175
F	0.231
G	0.333
H	0.277
I	0.158
J	0.207
K	0.313
L	0.226
M	0.216

Variable[a]	*Mean*	*Standard Deviation*
1. Alcohol use	0.557	0.497
2. Marijuana use	0.198	0.398
3. School defacement	0.348	0.477
4. Minor school damage	0.451	0.498
5. Major school damage	0.088	0.283
6. Nonschool defacement	0.277	0.448
7. Minor nonschool damage	0.360	0.480
8. Major nonschool damage	0.105	0.307
9. Minor shoplifting	0.324	0.468
10. Major shoplifting	0.154	0.361
11. Stole from a student	0.472	0.499
12. Stole a bicycle	0.061	0.240
13. Stole auto accessories	0.098	0.297
14. Breaking and entering	0.075	0.263
15. Stole a car	0.045	0.207
16. Truancy	0.230	0.421
17. Cheated on a test	0.766	0.423
18. Fought with a student	0.286	0.451
19. Threatened a student	0.472	0.500
20. Brought to a police station	0.171	0.377
21. Sex	0.502	0.500
22. Grade	0.534	0.499

[a]Exact wording of variables can be found in Appendix B.

Variable Coding

Delinquency Variables
0 = not in the last six months
1 = one or more times in the last six months

Sex   Grade
0 = female   0 = 7th
1 = male   1 = 8th

The exceptions to this serious—less serious grouping are interesting ones. Both alcohol and marijuana use fail to fall cleanly in either camp. Alcohol use is among the most frequently reported of these items, and it correlates at modest levels with almost all of the other measures of delinquency. Marijuana use, perhaps because it is more rare, has levels of association with other items that average between 0.15 and 0.20, but these do not seem to vary in a systematic fashion. Both cheating and truancy operate in much the same way.

Within the broad categories of serious and minor delinquency are subgroups of variables that cluster in interpretable ways. These clusters include vandalism, drug and alcohol use, theft, serious delinquency, and noncrime delinquency. The matrix in Table 3-5 has been subdivided in order to make this clustering more readily apparent. The clusters were identified according to two sets of criteria—the degree of intercorrelation among measures and the degree to which measures fit into a substantively meaningful category. Purely empirical criteria for separating these measures were difficult to establish because so many of these items are correlated at roughly the same level. Levels of intercorrelation even among the most strongly associated items seldom exceed 0.4, and it is sometimes difficult to differentiate among those that range between 0.2 and 0.3 on empirical grounds alone. For this reason, we have used intercorrelations as a rough guide to grouping these variables into conceptually similar clusters. Correlational patterns that can be seen by inspecting the matrixes are consistent with those identified in a formal factor analysis.[14] We have separated these clusters in the matrixes in Tables 3-5 and 3-6 and computed their mean intercorrelations in order to facilitate cross-cluster comparisons. For example, the mean intercorrelation between the serious delinquency items (submatrix D: $\bar{r}$ = 0.46) is systematically higher than the mean intercorrelations between these serious items and measures of minor theft ($\bar{r}$ = 0.28), vandalism ($\bar{r}$ = 0.31), or noncrime delinquency ($\bar{r}$ = 0.18). At the same time there is a good deal of spillover between clusters, and it would be misleading to argue that they are totally discrete.

Although we have been emphasizing that the levels of intercorrelation among these measures are modest, it is important to note that they are no lower than those found in most self-report delinquency research. It is difficult to make direct comparisons with other studies because of differences in measurement strategies. However, the levels of association in these data are often higher than those that other researchers use to justify indexing strategies (see, for example, Hirschi, 1969). This is additional evidence that these data are likely to be useful in the analysis we propose.

High School Student's Delinquency:
Item Intercorrelations

Measures of high school students' delinquency also cluster in expected and readily interpretable ways. For example, police contact is most likely to be related to alcohol and marijuana use, bike theft, theft of auto accessories, breaking and entering, and major school vandalism. Minor vandalism items are systematically interrelated as are measures of nonschool vandalism. Students who report minor shoplifting are also likely to report major shoplifting, and those who drink are more likely to smoke marijuana than those who do not. Students who have stolen from another student are also more likely to report theft of school property, minor shoplifting, and vandalism.

As matrix 3-6 shows, these measures cluster in ways quite similar to those observed in the junior high data. Again, the measures of serious delinquency are the most closely interrelated (submatrix D: $\bar{r}$ = 0.37), and there is clustering among types of minor theft, vandalism, and drug use. Noncrime delinquency items show low levels of intercorrelation and relatively small associations with the other delinquency measures included in the analysis.

Intercorrelations and Accuracy
of Self-Reports

We have argued that both the marginal distributions and the patterns of intercorrelation among these delinquency measures can be taken as evidence that they are useful reflections of these students' delinquent activities. However, since the accuracy of self-report estimates of deviance is a topic of frequent debate, it would be well to examine this issue in greater detail. There are a number of ways to argue that self-reports are systematic and reasonably stable reflections of behavior, most having to do with response error or differential reporting among subgroups of the population surveyed.

Researchers are generally concerned with two types of bias that can affect the accuracy of self-reports—random measurement error and systematic response error. Formal discussions of reliability focus on the problem of measurement error, assuming that while unavoidable, measurement error is random and thus does not affect systematic patterns of response. Random error does increase the variance in any measure (making estimates of the variance larger than is actually the case), and this in turn means that correlations are likely to be attenuated.[15] Still, zero order patterns (especially in terms of mean values) should be useful even in the presence of random measurement error.[16]

Table 3-6. High School Delinquency: Item Intercorrelations (N = 1238)

	1	2	3	4	5	6	7	8	9	10	11	12	13	14	15	16	17	18	19	20
1.	1.000																			
2.	0.451	1.000																		
3.	0.108	0.127	1.000																	
4.	0.169	0.186	0.332	1.000																
5.	0.090	0.150	0.195	0.330	1.000															
6.	0.213	0.228	0.226	0.371	0.237	1.000														
7.	0.110	0.160	0.235	0.352	0.416	0.453	1.000													
8.	0.200	0.251	0.213	0.230	0.201	0.303	0.225	1.000												
9.	0.139	0.240	0.229	0.224	0.303	0.299	0.308	0.578	1.000											
10.	0.098	0.110	0.171	0.301	0.279	0.344	0.301	0.274	0.240	1.000										
11.	0.172	0.185	0.189	0.354	0.268	0.374	0.291	0.310	0.256	0.389	1.000									
12.	0.072	0.153	0.183	0.202	0.356	0.233	0.373	0.212	0.319	0.211	0.232	1.000								
13.	0.090	0.163	0.210	0.254	0.437	0.285	0.491	0.196	0.301	0.259	0.294	0.418	1.000							
14.	0.087	0.156	0.136	0.211	0.359	0.256	0.363	0.230	0.318	0.194	0.242	0.413	0.385	1.000						
15.	0.039	0.096	0.160	0.119	0.285	0.136	0.231	0.079	0.185	0.093	0.104	0.331	0.333	0.318	1.000					
16.	0.245	0.185	0.075	0.108	0.039	0.121	0.060	0.173	0.098	0.129	0.122	0.050	0.015	0.014	-0.036	1.000				
17.	0.098	0.167	0.129	0.199	0.237	0.168	0.202	0.141	0.201	0.251	0.184	0.214	0.237	0.140	0.159	0.040	1.000			
18.	0.091	0.167	0.124	0.079	0.061	0.088	0.057	0.125	0.132	0.073	0.097	0.113	0.076	0.105	0.126	0.022	0.155	1.000		
19.	0.170	0.278	0.086	0.179	0.225	0.186	0.235	0.140	0.147	0.172	0.194	0.221	0.206	0.193	0.069	0.055	0.173	0.131	1.000	
20.	0.091	0.161	0.050	0.100	0.131	0.047	0.097	0.080	0.094	0.002	0.091	0.129	0.079	0.181	0.065	-0.031	0.096	0.116	0.286	1.000
21.	-0.012	-0.057	-0.043	0.103	0.196	0.161	0.212	-0.026	-0.016	0.188	0.129	0.142	0.178	0.123	0.073	-0.117	0.163	0.015	0.262	0.175
22.	-0.134	-0.155	0.090	0.068	0.096	0.060	0.022	0.098	0.063	0.195	0.251	-0.012	0.037	-0.020	0.045	-0.010	0.058	0.015	-0.013	-0.133
23.	0.013	0.056	0.025	0.052	0.056	0.032	0.014	0.032	0.042	0.034	0.073	0.256	0.015	0.043	0.042	0.032	-0.019	0.035	0.042	-0.044
24.	0.101	0.120	-0.036	-0.056	-0.051	-0.023	0.007	-0.066	-0.042	-0.123	-0.069	-0.009	-0.023	0.003	-0.048	0.001	-0.021	-0.036	0.030	0.088
25.	0.039	-0.034	-0.101	-0.095	-0.049	-0.113	-0.056	-0.077	-0.092	-0.163	-0.070	-0.038	-0.032	-0.026	-0.047	-0.018	-0.046	-0.018	-0.006	0.110

Submatrix labels: A, B, C, D, E, F, G, H, I, J, K, L

MEAN INTERCORRELATIONS

Submatrix	$\bar{r}$
A	0.451
B	0.315
C	0.331
D	0.366
E	0.072
F	0.286
G	0.154
H	0.255
I	0.217
J	0.107
K	0.174
L	0.246

Variable[a]	Mean	Standard Deviation
1. Used alcohol	0.826	0.379
2. Used marijuana	0.532	0.499
3. School defacement	0.201	0.401
4. Minor school damage	0.248	0.432
5. Major school damage	0.053	0.225
6. Damage to private property	0.290	0.454
7. Damage to public property	0.086	0.280
8. Minor shoplifting	0.341	0.474
9. Major shoplifting	0.150	0.358
10. Stole from a student	0.277	0.448
11. Stole school property	0.280	0.450
12. Stole a bicycle	0.054	0.226
13. Stole auto accessories	0.061	0.239
14. Breaking and entering	0.065	0.247
15. Stole a car	0.021	0.146
16. Cheated on a test	0.832	0.374
17. Fought with a student	0.162	0.369
18. Ran away from home	0.127	0.332
19. Brought to police station	0.306	0.461
20. Appeared before a judge	0.095	0.293
21. Sex	0.573	0.494
22. Ninth grade	0.307	0.461
23. Tenth grade	0.217	0.412
24. Eleventh grade	0.376	0.485
25. Twelfth grade	0.090	0.286

[a]Exact wording of variables can be found in Appendix B.

Variable Coding

Delinquency Variables
  0 = not in the last six months
  1 = one or more times in the last six months

Grades
  0 = no
  1 = yes

Sex
  0 = female
  1 = male

The problem in self-report research is that there are always additional sources of systematic reporting bias that confound the issue of reliability. Factors such as respondent acquiescence or systematic under- or overreporting by subgroups of the population introduce problems that cannot be solved by assuming random distributions of error. Systematic response bias has been an especially important topic in self-report delinquency research since delinquency surveys ask for information about deviant and therefore socially undesirable behavior. Critics are quick to argue that people respond differently to such questions and that systematic over- or underreporting may obscure true behavior patterns. Ideally, one could establish the nature and degree of such bias by comparing self-reported delinquency to some other objective measure of behavior. Unfortunately, few self-report researchers have access to information that makes this sort of comparison possible. Methodologists have used a number of substitutes for actual behavioral data in assessing the accuracy of self-reports. For example, Clark and Tifft (1966) have compared self-reports to results obtained in lie detector tests, and Hirschi (1969) has compared self-reports to the incidence of officially recorded police contact. By demonstrating that self-report data are consistent with the patterns noted in other types of delinquency measures, authors hope to support the claim that self-report measures are useful reflections of actual behavior. Sudman and Bradburn (1974) have developed a more general method of assessing the degree of response bias in survey research by reviewing a variety of self-report studies and drawing conclusions about response error based on item characteristics (e.g., degree of threat, salience of item, interview situation, characteristics of respondents) or research strategies. In spite of their different approaches, each of these authors concludes that while there may be systematic biases in self-report delinquency data, the biases are small enough that they should not seriously affect the accuracy of general conclusions reached through careful analysis.[1][7]

Since we do not have objective measures of delinquency to compare with our self-reports, arguments about the accuracy of our data must be more informal than those above. We have already noted that there are few frivolous answers to these items and that the amount of missing data is small. This reduces the likelihood of bias due to differential nonreporting. These items are also quite similar to those used in the bulk of self-report research. Any errors that they elicit should not be substantially different from those found in other studies. Most methodologists conclude that self-report measures are sufficiently accurate to support careful analysis, and we see little reason to assume that our data are any different. Systematic intercorrelations among the delinquency measures (Tables 3-4 through 3-6) support this assumption. Were there little or no clustering of items along lines predicted either by theory or by prior research, one might wonder whether response biases were a major problem in this particular study. In fact, the associations observed here mirror those found in other studies and reach levels of correlation that in some instances are higher than those reported by other delinquency researchers. On this basis, these data seem to offer useful indications of patterns in these students' delinquency.

Researchers frequently worry that certain subgroups of a population will respond differently to self-report questions, thus introducing systematic reporting bias into survey results. Without objective information on behavior, it is difficult to know how much impact such bias may have on our analysis. However, correlations between delinquency items and age or sex offer some information about potential bias since both age and sex are dimensions along which such bias may occur. The correlations also provide insight into the age and sex distribution of the delinquency reported by these middle class adolescents.

AGE PATTERNS IN MIDDLE
CLASS DELINQUENCY

Slight differences between the questionnaires for each of the three age groups mean that age patterns must be discussed somewhat informally. Correlations between grade and each of the delinquency items are reported in the matrixes in Tables 3-4 through 3-6. Few of these coefficients exceed 0.10, and there are no obviously large age differences in any of the data sets. This does not mean that there are no meaningful age patterns in these data. Comparisons between rather than within data sets show that reported levels of minor delinquency do differ for the age groups surveyed. There are generally modest increases in delinquency among elementary and junior high age groups that then drop among high school cohorts. Unfortunately, it is difficult to know how much of this difference is due to distinct age patterns and how much to differences between questionnaires. The bulk of these differences appear to be substantive. Absolute levels of involvement in most forms of activity follow regular increments between eighth, ninth, and tenth grades in spite of the fact that estimates come from two different data sets. In addition, involvement in serious forms of delinquency varies little by the age of the respondent. Were there strong systematic reporting biases according to age, one would expect them to appear for all forms of delinquency included in the survey. The stability of proportions for the serious delinquency items suggests that age-linked response bias may be no greater than normal in these data

SEX PATTERNS IN MARGINAL REPORTING FREQUENCIES

Since girls' delinquency is generally presumed to be quite different from that of boys', some comments on the basic sex differences in these data are in order. While we will discuss sex patterns throughout this analysis, the zero order coefficients between sex and delinquency provide some initial information about the issue. The most striking thing about these associations is that they are generally so small. Among elementary students, the only noteworthy coefficients in the conventional direction are those between sex and conflict with other students ($r = 0.28$) and sex with police contact ($r = 0.15$). All of the others have zero order coefficients smaller than 0.10, and three have negative signs (more likely to be reported by girls than boys). Sex differences in the junior high data are larger, but with the exception of interpersonal conflict items, these differences are still modest. Junior high boys are marginally more likely to report most forms of delinquency, but only seven out of the twenty coefficients reach a level of 0.20 or higher. Most minor forms of delinquency have coefficients of 0.10 or less, and school defacement and cheating have negative signs, indicating that they are favored more by girls. While there is a tendency for junior high boys to report higher levels of delinquency than girls, it is not a strong one.

The sex differences in junior high delinquency are generally the largest of any in the three data sets. High school coefficients are smaller, largely because older boys report much lower basic frequencies than younger boys, while age differences in girls' involvement are less marked. There is only one high school item with a zero order coefficient with sex of 0.20 or greater—contact with the police. Boys are also more likely than girls to report interpersonal conflict, but the magnitude of these differences is modest (rs average around 0.17). Perhaps more interesting are the types of delinquency reported by a higher proportion of girls than boys. High school girls are *more* likely to report alcohol use, marijuana use, cheating, shoplifting (both minor and major), school defacement, and running away from home. The coefficients for these items are small (ranging between -0.03 to -0.08), but given strong sex stereotypes about the distribution of delinquency, they are worth noting. Since these negative correlations are balanced by equally small positive ones for most other measures, it seems best to conclude that there are few systematic substantive sex differences in the distribution of delinquency among high school respondents.

This is quite different from what the delinquency literature leads one to expect, but we would argue that the similarities are likely to reflect actual behavior patterns. The growing literature on sex differences indicates that the distribution of delinquency by sex is more complex than familiar theories anticipate and that sex differences may have been inaccurately characterized in much of the literature.[18] Were this the case, these patterns may be more typical than first appears. Regardless of the validity of conventional theories, there is little reason to believe that these patterns are the product of differential response bias. Overall patterns are inconsistent with most assumptions about how response bias should affect the sex distribution of delinquency. Girls are usually thought to be more sensitive to social pressure than boys and thus expected to provide socially acceptable responses to questions about deviance (see, for example, Sudman and Bradburn, 1974). This should lead them to systematic underreporting and, if true, would produce large sex differences in a stereotypic direction. However, girls' reports occasionally exceed levels reported by boys and most sex differences are moderate. Thus it would seem that differential response bias of this type is not solely responsible for these patterns. In short, sex and age patterns as well as item intercorrelations suggest that these data are sufficiently accurate to warrant use in an analysis of middle class delinquency. While their accuracy can never be proven, it does not seem that they reflect biases any different or any more severe than found in other self-report delinquency data.

TECHNIQUES OF ANALYSIS

Because of the differences between these three questionnaires, we cannot analyze them as a single aggregate. Instead, we will treat each data set individually, linking the findings in the course of our discussion. This requires some concise analysis techniques that provide comparable data for each age group. For this reason we have relied heavily on multiple regression in the chapters that follow. Most delinquency researchers in the past have presented their findings in the form of contingency tables. This strategy is still popular, despite the fact that other techniques, especially multiple regression, are well suited to most forms of self-report delinquency data (see, for example, Hirschi, 1969; Hirschi and Selvin, 1967). Multiple regression is particularly useful in this analysis, since this study covers a large number of independent and dependent variables that must be analyzed in a parsimonious way. In addition to the parsimony it offers, multiple regression is useful because it allows simultaneous controls for a wide range of independent variables. This is something that is difficult with more conventional contingency table techniques. Most important for our purpose, however, is that regression information can be compared across several data sets.

Our analysis will be based on several variants of basic multiple regression techniques. Junior and senior high respondents were asked for frequency estimates for each delinquency item. Their estimates have been dichotomized and regressed on nominal and interval level predictor variables. The dichotomous format of the fifth and sixth grade delinquency items are analyzed in the same fashion.[19]

Since our goal is to identify important patterns in middle class delinquency and to isolate major predictors, our discussion will center on several regression statistics. Zero order correlations provide some insight into the basic relationships in each data set. Our main focus, however, will be on the unstandardized slopes in regression analyses. The information they provide about direction and magnitude of relationships makes it possible both to discuss overall patterns in delinquency and to compare relationships found in one type of delinquent activity with those that appear in another. Since we will be using multiple regression with binary dependent variables, the unstandardized slopes also provide information that can be interpreted in a familiar probability metric. This helps ground the analysis and makes findings more immediately accessible.[20] In short, slopes provide detailed descriptions of the type most useful in the analysis we propose.

Each of the following chapters analyzes one of the variable clusters identified in Tables 3-4 through 3-6. The same basic format is followed in each chapter. First, the distributions of items within each cluster are outlined and sex and age patterns are examined in detail. Items are then dichotomized and correlated with measures of school experiences, attitudes, family situation, and peer relationships. Important correlates are reported, then the results of multiple regression analysis are discussed. This makes it possible to evaluate the predictive strength of these items under controlled conditions.

The regression equations in each chapter are constructed in a somewhat unusual fashion because of the unique characteristics of our sample and the requirements of comparability within each data set. Normally variables are included and/or interpreted in regression equations if their slopes are statistically significant. This familiar criterion is not especially useful in this analysis because of the relatively large number of cases included in each data set and the nature of the samples with which we are dealing. A slope's significance is affected by the number of cases used in the analysis. With Ns of 748, 852, and 1,250, many coefficients that are substantively trivial appear statistically significant. In addition, these data have not been sampled in the strict sense of the term. Instead they reflect responses of the virtual population of this community's public school students. The applicability of significance tests in such a case is an issue of frequent debate (see, for example, Winch and Campbell, 1969; Berk and Brewer, 1978), since significance tests ideally assess the impact of stochastic error on findings in numerous hypothetical replications.

As noted earlier, regression with dichotomous dependent variables gives information about predictors that can be interpreted in a substantively meaningful fashion. This can be used as an alternative criterion to significance tests when constructing regression equations. Since slopes can be used to compute the total probability impact of a predictor, it is possible to select or interpret useful predictors on the basis of their substantive impact as well as statistical significance (see note 20 for a discussion of this issue). In this analysis predictors were included in "final" regression equations if they altered the probability of the dependent variable by a total of at least ten percentage points. This is a clearly meaningful probability change, assuring that important predictors exert a substantive as well as statistically significant impact on the items under study.

Requirements of comparability between different data sets and between the various measures of delinquency included in each chapter cluster imposed additional constraints on the way in which regression equations were constructed. Substantively meaningful predictors of one dependent variable are not always identical to those for other dependent variables in the cluster. For this reason the final best regression equations include all predictors in a data set that produced meaningful probability changes in any of the dependent variables. This makes it possible to compare predictors of all the items in a single cluster in a concise fashion.[21]

This strategy differs from more conventional hypothesis testing with multiple regression in several ways. Researchers ideally specify a theoretical model of relationships among variables, then use multiple regression techniques to test whether significant patterns occur as predicted. However, this requires theoretical models that are quite explicit and parsimonious—something delinquency researchers usually lack. For this reason, our use of multiple regression will be primarily exploratory and descriptive following the procedures outlined above. The danger of including or deleting variables in the fashion we propose is that of capitalizing on type II errors when constructing regression equations. One might expect some terms to be dropped from the equations due to chance factors that make them appear unsignificant when they have a real role to play in the patterns under study. (Type I error can also be a problem. Chance factors may produce significant predictors that in reality are not.) There are several reasons for discounting potential chance effects in this analysis. First of all, statistical significance is not the only criterion used in constructing regression equations. As noted earlier, variables are excluded or included primarily on the basis of judgements about their substantive importance. More important, we will be analyzing data drawn from three separate student populations. Predictive patterns are quite similar for all age groups surveyed. The fact that the same variables appear important over and over for both junior and senior high students is reassuring evidence that these equations reflect substantive patterns rather than chance occurrances.

Each of the following chapters is devoted to a different aspect of middle class delinquency. Chapter 4 presents data on vandalism; Chapter 5 summarizes patterns in middle class drug use; Chapter 6 analyzes minor theft (including shoplifting); Chapter 7 examines serious forms of delinquency; and Chapter 8 discusses the issue of noncrime delinquency. In Chapter 9 we summarize overall patterns in middle class delinquency and evaluate the utility of a leisure model for understanding the patterns in these particular data. Contrasts between this model and more familiar approaches offer some interesting insights into middle class delinquency.

NOTES

1. Data drawn from General Social and Economic Characteristics: Illinois PC(1)—C15. We collected information on the occupation and education of individual respondents' parents as well. The distribution of these variables is consistent with our decision to identify these students as middle class: the vast majority have parents employed in traditionally white collar occupations and the educational levels of parents are quite high. Few fathers have less than a college education.

2. Parochial school students in grades five through eight were also included in the study but their responses will not be analyzed here. We were forced to delete several sets of survey questions in order to

gain access to the parochial school group and thus lack comparable information on several of the issues to be included in this analysis.

3. The important issue here is whether the patterns in twelfth graders' delinquency are similar to those of younger age groups. This sampling strategy is likely to focus on a group with fewer incidents to report, but it is difficult to know whether this lower incidence translates into different patterns of association among types of delinquency or between delinquency and major correlates. We have included twelfth graders in our analysis because so little is known about middle class delinquency that their responses can provide at least some insight into differential patterning.

4. Since we wish to preserve the anonymity of this community, we will not be citing these comparable studies directly.

5. A comment made by one sixth grade teacher confirms our belief that this was a task within these students' capabilities. After administering the questionnaire she asked us why we hadn't provided students with an IBM answer sheet like those used in standardized tests. Students could have marked their answers right on the sheets, and we could have saved time by having them machine read. Clearly she found the task familiar.

6. Students were told in advance that their answers would be protected in this fashion to encourage candor.

7. Again, lower levels of baseline reporting reflected in marginal distributions with atypical means may or may not affect patterns of association in the data. Processes underlying delinquent choices may be the same regardless of how often they are made. In such a case, underreporting is not a serious analytic problem.

8. Delinquency researchers are also concerned with the potential bias that results from the fact that dropouts are excluded from studies of school populations. Dropouts characteristically have more delinquent experiences than students still in school, and thus studies of school populations may underrepresent delinquent adolescents. In this study the problem posed by dropouts is minimal since in this upper SES suburb only a few students drop out of high school.

9. For purposes of introduction to the data, we will limit discussion of middle class drug use to the two most common forms—marijuana and alcohol. We will examine other drugs in Chapter 6, which is devoted to the issue of recreational drug use.

10. The fact that the items referring to activities done "more than once or twice" have consistently lower rates than those referring to "ever tried" adds some additional credibility to these data. This is what one would anticipate on substantive grounds, demonstrating that these items pattern roughly as one would expect for even the youngest respondents.

11. Additional comparisons with other research will be made in the chapters presenting the data analysis.

12. Often the dichotomized variables have such skewed marginals that intercorrelations between them are difficult to evaluate (i.e., there is no meaningful variance to study). For example, only three percent of these students have run away from home more than once or twice in their lives and only 2 percent have shoplifted merchandise worth $5 or more in the last year. The correlation coefficient between these two items is 0.36, but this absolute value must be treated cautiously given the limited variance in these measures.

13. Since all these items have been dichotomized, the matrix is a phi matrix.

14. Factor analysis is one traditional method of identifying clusters within a large number of variables. The way in which the measures load is assumed to reflect dimensions along which indexes can be safely constructed or analysis profitably organized. We used factor analytic procedures on these data but have not presented the results here, or used the solutions for index construction. In large measure this is because of the relatively modest and constant size of the zero order intercorrelations. If discrete factors are to emerge from a factor analysis, interrelationships among some items must be fairly strong, while others must be fairly weak. The associations between these items are generally of the same magnitude, and the factors that emerge are somewhat unstable. In addition, the dimensions that emerge from factor analyzing these measures differ little from those that can be identified through informal eyeball clustering of the original matrixes. In short, we felt that a factor analysis would have given an appearance of greater rigor than was actually warranted.

15. In multiple regression, even random measurement error in one's independent variables makes the regression coefficients biased and inconsistent, although the direction of bias may be positive or negative.

16. Like all survey researchers, we must assume that our data contain this form of random measurement error, which can never be completely eliminated.

17. Sudman and Bradurn (1974) also note that self-report measures that are dichotomized into yes or no categories are less likely to be systematically under- or overreported than those that require detailed frequency estimates. This is another reason that we prefer to dichotomize these variables.

18. For a review of the literature on sex differences in crime and delinquency see Klein (1973). Most familiar predictions are based on

research done on officially delinquent populations. Self-report research generally finds smaller sex differences than do studies of
official delinquents (see, for example, Nye, 1958; Jensen and Eve,
1976; Hindelang, 1971; Wise, 1967). Still, much more research is
necessary if sex differences in delinquency are to be understood. In
later chapters we will examine these differences in greater detail.

19. As noted earlier, there are several reasons for dichotomizing
these frequency estimates: (1) to make data sets as comparable as
possible, (2) to resolve the difficulty of ordinal versus interval
response sets in the older student's data, (3) to eliminate the problem
of outliers in highly skewed dependent variables, and (4) to minimize
response biases.

20. Multiple regression employing dichotomous dependent variables poses several important issues in this analysis. When binary
dependent variables are regressed on predictors, the associated slope
and intercept values can be interpreted in an accessible way (Kmenta,
1971:425-428). The information provided is similar to that in
cross-tabulation, although it comes in a more concise form. Dependent variables can take on a value of either 0 or 1. In such cases,
slopes of predictors represent the average change in the probability
of scoring a 1 on the dependent variable for each increment in the
scale on which the predictor is measured. In other words, the slope is
the average difference between the category proportions one would
see in a tabular analysis of the same variables. The intercept of the
regression equation is the probability of scoring 1 on the dependent
variable when all predictor variables in the equation take on a value
of 0.

There are several important issues involved in analyzing binary
dependent variables in a standard multiple regression format. While
binary regression predicts probabilities that theoretically range between 0 and 1, computational techniques can occasionally produce
predicted probabilities that exceed these values. Logit models have
been proposed as one solution to this problem, since they predict the
log of the odds ratios rather than probabilities *per se*. This is
particularly important when the binary dependent variable under
analysis has highly skewed marginals. These predictions are bounded
by (positive and negative) infinity, avoiding the problem of occasional predictions greater than 1 or less than 0 (Goodman, 1972;
Watson, 1974).

Dichotomous dependent variables also pose problems for estimation. A dichotomous dependent variable produces heteroskedastic
residuals. This results in estimators that do not have all the desirable
OLS properties. For example, significance tests for regression coeffi-

cients are biased (and inconsistent), although the parameter estimates themselves are unbiased. Estimators are also inefficient, although this is less of a practical problem when sample sizes are large. Logit approaches (among others) are designed in part to remedy these problems (Watson, 1974).

Despite the apparent advantages of logit formulations, we have chosen to use standard binary dependent variable regression here. This choice can be justified in several ways. Perhaps most important is the fact that these data are being treated not as a sample, but as an entire population. (For general justifications, see Berk and Brewer, 1979.) Difficulties associated with estimation (e.g., biased significance tests, inefficient estimators) occur only when one is estimating population parameters from sample data. The intercepts and slopes reported here are descriptive values (containing measurement error, of course) and not population estimates; thus, this issue is moot. In addition, once regression models are well specified there are few instances of realistic predictions outside the 0-1 range in this analysis. Finally, logit procedures produce special complications for our data. Many of our most important independent variables are continuous, which means that unless we wanted to treat them in a nominal form (risking serious artifacts and very small cell sizes), the Goodman algorithm is not applicable (see Goodman, 1972). The alternative of Nerlove-Press estimation techniques (see Nerlove and Press, 1973) would have been extremely expensive, and the resulting effect parameters would not have the simple interpretation possible with standard regression coefficients (i.e., they express the change in log odds). But perhaps most important, the use of logit techniques assumes that a logistic functional form exists between one's independent and dependent variables. This is a theoretical statement for which we see no particular justification here. Rather, we are relying on the more conventional assumption of linear relationships.

For those who want to interpret significance tests on our data, the most difficult problem with our use of a linear probability model is that of biased significance tests that are produced by heteroskedastistic residuals. We have run weighted least squares models for those dependent variables with the most highly skewed marginals (those most vulnerable to heteroskedasticity) and compared results to the OLS models (see Spilerman, 1976, for a similar procedure). There are few substantively meaningful differences between models that correct for heteroskedasticity and those that do not. For this reason we will report the more familiar OLS results. However, one might still feel uneasy about the use of the t distribution (or the F distribution) with data that clearly do not fit the multivariate normal distribution.

Some authors have recommended Chi square tests as a good way out (Grizzle, Starmer, and Koch, 1969) where applicable, but the Chi square tests and *t* tests are asymptotically identical. Since we have a very large sample, we can rely on this approximation. We do not want to dismiss these problems out of hand, but we do feel that the descriptive nature of our analysis makes OLS regression a useful, parsimonious approach. In order to identify important patterns here, we are simply partitioning variance and reporting the results in the language of regression coefficients.

21. Appendix C contains the marginal response distributions for the predictor variables used in these regression equations.

Chapter Four

Vandalism as a
Leisure Activity

INTRODUCTION

Vandalism is one of the few forms of delinquency that
authors identify as typically middle class. Although some
assume that rates of property damage are greater for lower
strata adolescents, middle class vandalism is difficult to ignore.
Recent years have seen a number of antivandalism programs instituted in middle class areas, and local newspapers often carry articles
about the increasing financial cost of vandalism in schools or to other
public property.

Popular images of vandalism stress its allegedly "irrational" or
"wanton" character, and many people find it difficult to explain
why children from good families should damage property. Vandals
are often thought to be bored and to seek excitement in the artificial
"kicks" of property damage. Parents are frequently criticized for
failing to instill proper respect for others' property; adolescents
themselves are often blamed for acting irresponsibly. Perhaps the
favorite explanation for vandalism is one that assumes that it is a
symptom of psychological maladjustment: property damage is
thought to express unresolved hostilities. Regardless of the explanation, popular remedies for vandalism are generally the same: coerce
children into responsibility for their actions and, at the same time,
provide them with wholesome activities that will divert them from
the artifical thrills of property destruction.

Social science theory and research on vandalism share many of
these popular assumptions. Vandalism has been explained in several

familiar ways including psychological maladjustment and general social pathology, and middle class vandalism is especially likely to be discussed in these terms (for a comprehensive review of perspectives on vandalism, see Ward, 1973). Images of individual maladjustment or general social pathology draw heavily on the apparently cathartic and aggressive nature of property damage. Vandalism is seen as the symbol and expression of destructive drives or general feelings of inferiority; both are evidence of underlying illnesses. These concerns are reflected in classic comments like these:

> Vandalism, like other types of pathological behavior, represents an outlet for aggression and feelings that have not been solved in a healthy or acceptable manner. It is usually an expression of deep unrest and a need to react with destruction of property or a creation of unhappiness [sic] in order to lessen the feelings of unrest. (Lippman, 1952:5-6)
>
> ... in the cases that are studied in a clinic one rarely fails to find evidences of deep emotional conflict with a feeling of inferiority and frustration and a need to punish others or get even for real or fanciful offenses against them. (Ibid., p. 5)

General images of psychic pathology are often specified in terms of sex role insecurity or masculinity anxiety. Property damage is thought to be active and aggressive, demonstrating the adultlike virility to which adolescent boys aspire (A.K. Cohen, 1955; Martin, 1961; Wade, 1967), and girls' sexual frustration during adolescence is blamed for outbreaks of apparently senseless property destruction in institutions (Mannheim, 1952). Other authors attempt to isolate the reasons for these individual maladjustment problems in socialization experiences within families or schools or in community patterns of social control over adolescents. Parents' inability to teach their children respect for property (whether because of confusion about values, divorce, maternal employment, or family breakup) frees children to vandalize. So does improper supervision or lax treatment on the part of teachers, clergy, or law enforcement agents.

In contrast to these familiar perspectives, we will place vandalism within the type of leisure framework outlined in Chapter 2. Vandalism seems especially well suited to this approach since most property damage takes place during leisure hours and is a fairly common experience for middle class adolescents. A leisure decision-making framework for vandalism has several advantages over more familiar approaches. Although people tend to discuss vandalism as if it were a unitary phenomenon, it is a label that can be applied to a wide range of activities under a variety of different circumstances. At times property damage may appear to be a relatively harmless prank (e.g., lighting firecrackers in mailboxes on Halloween), while at other times the same activity can be seen as wanton vandalism.[1] This gives vandalism the fluidly deviant character emphasized in our leisure model and suggests that it may be responsive to many leisure considerations.

Leisure time can be invested in vandalism just as it can in other potentially delinquent activities. Property damage can produce utility that is directly consumed (e.g., the "thrill" of knocking over mailboxes or the "fun" of shooting out street lights). Vandalism can also produce commodities for future consumption or investment (e.g., "trophies" to be admired by those involved) and can produce information and develop skills that add to an individual's nonmarket human capital (e.g., techniques for effective use of a BB gun, knowledge of the risk involved in breaking into school after hours, or the best way to coordinate group action during a series of Halloween pranks). While all of this should not be surprising, it does suggest that there can be a number of purposes underlying vandalism that make it more complicated than simple thrill seeking. Among the most interesting of these are the opportunities it affords for developing skills, gaining information about deviant versus nondeviant activities, and learning subtle rules of social interaction.

Vandalism can provide a chance to master leisure skills that are useful in a fairly wide range of situations. Some of these are rather technical. Authors have noted that vandalism can take on a "game" character where children challenge one another to demonstrate proficiency in such things as shooting BB guns or throwing rocks. The individual who can shoot out the most street lights or break the most windows in an abandoned building not only wins the game, but has a chance to refine shooting or throwing skills that may be useful later (perhaps by increasing the efficiency of subsequent vandalism). It is worth noting that the potentially deviant nature of these games may be of only secondary concern to the participants and that children can be surprised to find that their game is taken so seriously by adults. (For a more detailed discussion of this issue with respect to vandalism see S. Cohen, 1973.)

Much vandalism is also a group activity, and peers can be a necessary prerequisite for many forms of property damage. While a lone graffitist can make political statements, it is almost impossible to get several piglets, paint them with blue paint, and let them loose in school corridors during lunch without group effort. This suggests that vandalism can contribute to the development of interpersonal skills that are useful in subsequent property damage and that may also generalize to other leisure contexts. The group processes involved in decisions about vandalism and the apportionment of tasks between members may help refine individuals' roles and develop leadership and interaction skills. In short, one can learn the rules of peer interaction during vandalism and develop the ability to coordinate and manipulate peers effectively. This is likely to be a complex process involving an awareness of the sanctions and rewards that peers can offer (something that must be learned) and an understanding of the potential costs and benefits that vandalism can have for one's position within the peer group.

Peers are not the only ones who can provide costs and benefits for vandalism. It is also a risky activity because of the formal and informal sanctions that adults can impose. (Obviously, they can also offer rewards, as anyone familiar with Halloween tales will recall.) In order to choose vandalism effectively, one must learn what these risks are and learn to differentiate between harmless pranks and vandalism. Since these differences are seldom clear, this sort of learning is likely to require some direct experience with property damage.

Popular images of vandalism suggest that it can provide several types of direct utility for those involved. Quite apart from other considerations, property damage can be fun. It can take on many of the characteristics of a game, and can also provide excitement. Common images of vandalism as thrill seeking reflect this possibility. However, this is not the only satisfaction that vandalism can provide. It can also be a rather pointed way of expressing disaffection or of redressing grievances. For example, one can display an active interest in changing the balance of power within a school situation by breaking into a school and damaging the classroom of a hated teacher. Much neighborhood conflict between adults and children has this same tone. If children are used to taking a shortcut through someone's backyard and the owner puts up a fence, dismantling the fence may be one way of changing the situation. Although most such property damage is popularly characterized as wanton, malicious, or irrational, it need not be seen this way within a decisionmaking framework.[2] Instead, vandalism can be a reasoned, deliberately chosen activity designed to provide utility to the actor and selected in line with this goal. This is one of the main advantages of a decisionmaking framework over those usually applied to vandalism. Popular characterizations that emphasize arationality, expressiveness, and aggression make it appear to be little more than a frustrated response to ennui, largely beyond the actors' control or understanding. In contrast, a decisionmaking framework assumes that vandalism can meet a variety of needs and can take many forms consistent with these. Whether these goals are simple recreation and relaxation, investment in thrills, or attempts to redress grievances, property damage is not likely to be senseless and wanton. Instead, it can be chosen from among a number of leisure alternatives in light of the opportunities, costs, and benefits involved.

In short, there appears to be much more to the leisure context of vandalism than is implied in conventional discussions of boredom and aggression. In addition to direct consumption (e.g., fun, pleasure, thrills, or other psychic rewards), it can provide actors with skills and information that are useful in subsequent investments of their leisure time. They can learn how to more effectively manipulate peers, gain necessary technical skills, and learn how subtle distinctions are made between fun and vandalism. This involves understanding the viewpoints of different actors (e.g., peers, parents, other adults) and can be seen as part of the more general process of learning the moral prescriptions and proscriptions entailed in growing up. Decisions about when and how to vandalize should be made in light of considerations such as the costs and benefits supplied by different audiences (e.g., peers, parents, school officials) and the available options that structure leisure opportunities. These considerations should be reflected in the patterns followed by the property damage that middle class students report, and our analysis will concentrate on the most important of these patterns.

BASIC DISTRIBUTION OF VANDALISM

The marginal distribution of students' responses to questions about property damage are presented in Table 4-1. Our analysis is based on several items, and vandalism was operationalized in slightly different ways in each questionnaire. Fifth and sixth graders were asked two questions, one about damaging property and one about defacing property. Seventh and eighth graders were asked to estimate the degree of their property damage in school and nonschool settings, while high school students were asked questions that focused on different targets rather than degree of damage (for exact wording of items see Appendix B).

Vandalism is among the most commonly reported types of delinquency in all three questionnaires. Fourteen percent of the elementary respondents have defaced property more than once or twice in the last six months, although they report little other property damage. Nearly half the junior high students admit at least one instance of minor school damage in the six months prior to the survey. One-third claim to have been involved in at least one incident of school defacement. Nonschool vandalism is slightly less common, but substantial numbers of students still report such activities. Seven to nine percent also say that they have done major property damage in the last six months. Students in high school have lower rates of vandalism. Reports range from about one-fifth who have defaced school property to one-quarter who report minor school damage. Almost one-third have damaged private property during the same time period.

Table 4-1. Marginal Distribution of Vandalism[a]

Fifth and Sixth Graders		Ever Defaced Property	Defaced More than One or Two Times This Year	Ever Damaged Property	Damaged Property More than One or Two Times This Year
	yes	21.8%	13.8%	8.7%	3.3%
	no	78.2	86.2	91.3	96.7
		100	100	100	100
number reporting		(747)	(749)	(745)	(748)

Seventh and Eighth Graders		School Defacement	Minor School Damage	Major School Damage	Nonschool Defacement	Minor Nonschool Damage	Major Nonschool Damage
	Never	67.0%	55.7%	93.0%	73.8%	64.7%	91.4%
	Once	14.1	17.8	3.9	11.9	15.2	3.6
	2-3	9.6	11.6	1.0	9.2	9.7	1.8
	4-5	3.7	4.3	0.6	2.2	2.9	0.2
	6+	5.6	10.6	1.6	2.8	7.5	2.9
		100	100	100	100	100	100
number reporting		(821)	(830)	(825)	(822)	(828)	(824)

High School Students		School Defacement	Minor School Damage	Major School Damage	Damage to Private Property	Damage to Public Property
	Never	80.6%	75.6%	95.6%	71.6%	92.2%
	Once	9.1	11.4	2.5	12.8	4.2
	2-3	5.7	8.4	0.9	8.4	2.0
	4-5	2.0	1.9	0.3	3.3	0.8
	6+	2.6	2.6	0.7	4.0	0.7
		100	100	100	100	100
number reporting		(1230)	(1234)	(1228)	(1240)	(1230)

[a]Exact wording of items can be found in Appendix B.

Vandalism, Age, and Sex

Differences between questionnaire items make it necessary to assess the age patterns in these vandalism data somewhat informally. Minor forms of property damage are curvilinearly related to grade, with eighth and ninth graders reporting the highest frequencies of minor vandalism. In most cases, the incidence of minor vandalism drops noticibly among eleventh and twelfth graders. This is not the case with major forms of property damage, whose incidence does not vary a great deal between the age groups surveyed.

While these measures follow familiar age patterns, they are related to sex in somewhat unexpected ways. Most theorists interpret vandalism as an aggressive masculine activity and predict that boys should vandalize considerably more than girls. This is not the case here. Junior high girls are slightly more likely to report school defacement than are boys, and they are only marginally less likely to report minor school damage and nonschool defacement. Meaningful sex differences in the predicted direction do appear for the more serious forms of property damage and for minor nonschool damage, but they are not large. Coefficients between major vandalism and sex average around 0.25 in the junior high data and around 0.20 in the senior high (girls coded as 0; boys coded as 1).

Vandalism and Attitudes

Implicit in most discussions of property damage are assumptions about causal relationships between attitudes and vandalism. The most popular explanations of property damage focus on emotional forces such as rage, aggression, vindictiveness, or boredom that are assumed to motivate the behavior. But while vandalism is often characterized in this fashion, attitudes are seldom an important component of this analysis. Few attitudinal measures appear as major correlates of property damage, and only one or two are effective predictors. (For exact wording of attitude measures see Appendix B.) Despite assumptions about the masculine character of vandalism, feelings of sex role insecurity have little relationship to property damage. Neither do feelings of inferiority or general disaffection with life. Even boredom does not correlate with vandalism in a systematic way. The only attitude items that are meaningfully related to vandalism are those that measure students' anger at either parents or school officials. These anger items correlate with minor forms of vandalism at average levels of 0.18-0.25 in the junior and senior high data.

Vandalism and School Experiences

Since so much adolescent vandalism is directed at school property, one expects school experiences to provide some insight into patterns of property damage. We have a good deal of information about school-specific vandalism since both junior and senior high respondents were asked about damage to school property. It is surprising how few measures of school experience are correlated with these items. (See Appendix B for exact wording of items.)

Both school satisfaction and school performance are only modestly associated with vandalism. In the junior high data coefficients between performance and vandalism average around 0.11, while those with school satisfaction range between 0.15 and 0.20. Similar coefficients appear in the high school matrixes. More important, levels of association are no stronger for school-related vandalism than for nonschool property damage. The school variable with the strongest ties to vandalism is an attitude measure—anger at school officials. But while the correlations with anger are moderately higher than with other school items, anger still does not strongly differentiate between school and nonschool property damage. In the junior high data, anger at school officials is correlated at 0.21 with school defacement and 0.27 with nonschool defacement; at 0.28 for minor school damage and 0.32 for minor nonschool damage.

Vandalism and Family Variables

Permissive child-rearing practices or lack of parental supervision are often blamed for juvenile vandalism. On this basis, measures of family structure or parent-child interaction should be important components of our analysis. However, traditional structure variables such as broken homes or working mothers are not systematically related to the vandalism items. Other proxies for family background such as parents' occupation or education similarly fail to differentiate between students who report property damage and those who do not. Measures of family rule structure or rule enforcement techniques that reflect the impact of supervision or permissiveness are also unrelated to the levels of vandalism that these students report. Only parent-child conflict measures are useful correlates of middle class vandalism. (The exact wording of family variables can be found in Appendix B.)

Parent-child conflict is related to most vandalism items at the zero order level. Seventh and eighth graders who fight with their parents are more likely to report minor types of vandalism; so are elementary school respondents. Both junior and senior high students who disobey their parents report higher levels of vandalism than those who are obedient. Actual disobedience is generally a stronger correlate than fighting.[3] As noted earlier, feelings of anger directed at parents are also likely to be related to vandalism, and the coefficients between this anger and various forms of vandalism are about as high as those of the other two parent-child conflict measures.

Vandalism and Peer Relationships

The number of ones' friends who have vandalized is the strongest and most systematic correlate of property damage across all age groups. Zero order coefficients range from 0.29 to 0.39 for elementary students and 0.31 to 0.53 among seventh and eighth graders. High school respondents were asked more detailed questions about their friends' property damage. These parallel the activities included in the self-report items. Not surprisingly, the resulting correlations are somewhat higher than those that appear for younger age groups (ranging from 0.43 to 0.56). Respondents were also asked to estimate the number of their friends who had been involved in other forms of delinquency besides vandalism. Occasionally these assessments are also correlated with property damage, but at generally lower levels than the friends' items that refer specifically to vandalism. This suggests that a highly delinquent peer group does not appear to be a necessary component of vandalism. If it were, estimates of general peer delinquency should be more closely associated with self-reported vandalism. Subsequent regression analysis will show that under controlled conditions, only the most serious forms of property damage can be predicted by types of peer delinquency other than vandalism.

Other measures of peer contact were included in this study, but they seldom show a systematic relationship to vandalism. Students were asked about a number of peer-oriented leisure activities (i.e., group and club memberships, sports, etc.) and about the rules or restrictions that parents impose on choice of friends or the amount of time spent with friends. None of these correlate with property damage in a meaningful way, reinforcing the conclusion that vandalism does not require the support of highly delinquent peers.

Summary of Zero Order Associations

Peer relationships are the strongest correlates of vandalism in this analysis. Students whose friends have vandalized are likely to report more property damage than those without such friends. Those with friends who drink, use drugs, or who have been involved in various forms of theft also tend to report higher levels of vandalism, although the strength of these relationships is weaker than that for friends' vandalism *per se*. Both family and school variables are associated with vandalism at the zero order level, although these relationships are not as strong as those with peer items. Parent-child conflict may increase chances of property damage; so may anger directed at parents. General satisfaction with school and above average academic performance are negatively associated with vandalism and appear to reduce chances of reporting property damage. Anger at school officials seems to increase the likelihood of vandalism among all age groups.

REGRESSION ANALYSIS OF VANDALISM: INTRODUCTION

While several variables are associated with vandalism at the zero order level, their simultaneous impacts are more complex. Controlled relationships pattern in slightly different ways that are worth noting. Each of the vandalism items was dichotomized and regressed on predictors that altered the probability of at least one vandalism item (in that particular data set) in a substantively meaningful fashion. (For a more detailed discussion of this procedure see Chapter 3.) Predictors that altered probabilities of vandalism by 10 percent or more across their full range of impact were selected as best predictors to be included in regression equations. The only exception is sex, which appears in every equation in order to demonstrate the atypical sex distribution of many of these types of property damage. The equations are presented in Tables 4-2 through 4-4 along with zero order correlation coefficients between these predictors and the various vandalism measures.[4]

Fifth and Sixth Grade Vandalism

It is somewhat difficult to predict fifth and sixth graders' vandalism, since many of these measures have relatively limited variability. Still, several predictors are consistent enough to warrant mention. Among the best predictors of "ever" defacing property are disobedience to parents, fighting with parents, school performance, school satisfaction, and the number of one's friends who have vandalized. Respondents who claim that "almost all" of their friends have vandalized are almost forty-five percentage points more likely to have defaced property than those who have no such friends (ceteris paribus). Many of these same variables predict more recent property defacement, although the limited number of students responding to this item suggest cautious interpretation is necessary. There is an interesting anomaly in the equations predicting defacement. School performance is positively related to defacement under controlled conditions, indicating that students who are doing above average in their school work are more likely to report this item. There are a number of plausible explanations for this relationship, but given the small zero order correlation between these items and the somewhat limited variability in the dependent variable, it seems best not to overemphasize this one coefficient.

Relatively few items predict general property damage among fifth and sixth graders. With the exception of school dissatisfaction, the only items to show consistently meaningful coefficients with elementary students' property damage are measures of friends' delinquency (especially friends' vandalism). Still, the probability of damaging property can rise by as much as thirty-four percentage points if all of ones' friends have been involved in vandalism. These data also suggest that popular characterizations of vandalism as a uniquely masculine activity may be overdrawn. When sex is used to predict defacement, its coefficients are negative. Boys are only slightly more likely than girls to report other property damage once important predictors are controlled.

Junior High Vandalism

Seventh and eighth grade respondents were asked for estimates of school and nonschool vandalism in an effort to specify patterns in property damage in greater detail. We will discuss each of these types of vandalism in turn. As the equations in Table 4-3 indicate, the best predictors of school defacement include sex, fighting with parents, and friends' involvement in vandalism or alcohol use. Probabilities of minor school damage are affected by disobedience to parents, anger at school officials, and friends' vandalism, shoplifting, and alcohol use. Fewer items predict major school damage. Of these, the best are estimates of friends' vandalism and shoplifting.[5]

Sex is among the most interesting of all the predictors in the school vandalism equations. Once controls for friends' delinquency and parent-child conflict are exerted, girls are more than twenty percentage points more likely to report school defacement than boys and fifteen percentage points more likely to report minor school damage. These patterns are quite different from those that popular stereotypes lead one to expect. Boys are more likely to report major school damage, but even here the probability difference is about six percentage points. This difference is too small to support familiar assumptions that school vandalism is the exclusive province of boys.

The best predictors of junior high students' school vandalism are usually measures of friends' delinquency. The impact of family or attitude predictors is smaller and less systematic. For example, friends' vandalism can alter the probability of minor school damage by as much as forty percentage points under the controlled conditions presented here. Friends' shoplifting and friends' alcohol use also increase chances of minor school damage by substantively

Table 4-2.   Fifth and Sixth Grade Vandalism: Prediction Equations (N = 486)

	Ever Defaced				Defaced This Year				Ever Damaged				Damaged This Year			
	b	(SE)	t	r	b	(SE)	t	r	b	(SE)	t	r	b	(SE)	t	r
R^2	0.144				0.143				0.191				0.136			
Intercept	-0.026				-0.047				0.075				0.070			
Predictor Variables																
Sex	-0.017[a]	(0.36)[b]	0.480[c]	0.035[d]	-0.043	(.030)	1.400	-.006	0.068	(0.025)	2.674	0.193	0.006	(0.017)	0.344	.087
Disobedience to Parents	0.052	(0.028)	0.167	0.187	0.006	(0.024)	0.257	0.142	0.017	(0.020)	0.837	0.143	0.022	(0.013)	1.673	0.136
Fighting with Parents	0.044	(0.026)	0.161	0.167	0.065	(0.022)	2.860	0.205	-0.002	(0.018)	0.100	0.069	-0.019	(0.012)	1.581	0.005
Feelings of Anger	0.022	(0.021)	1.095	0.143	0.012	(0.018)	0.656	0.119	-0.014	(0.015)	0.917	0.048	-0.019	(0.010)	1.997	-0.017
School Performance	0.041	(0.024)	0.202	-0.001	0.028	(0.020)	1.371	-0.009	-0.010	(0.017)	0.557	-0.101	-0.003	(0.011)	0.247	-0.072
School Satisfaction	-0.048	(0.022)	2.121	-0.151	-0.019	(0.019)	1.048	-0.106	-0.030	(0.016)	1.868	-0.174	-0.022	(0.010)	2.168	-0.159
Friends' Vandalism	0.109	(0.026)	4.24	0.298	0.092	(0.022)	4.254	0.316	0.085	(0.018)	4.722	0.392	0.038	(0.012)	3.240	0.309
Friends' Shoplifting	-0.042	(0.030)	1.414	0.169	0.014	(0.025)	0.557	0.224	0.029	(0.021)	1.400	0.305	0.024	(0.014)	1.764	0.269
Friends' Alcohol Use	0.048	(0.017)	2.73	0.264	0.027	(0.015)	1.803	0.247	0.024	(0.012)	1.926	0.265	0.016	(0.008)	2.045	0.226

[a]Unstandardized slope (b).
[b]Standard error.
[c]t value.
[d]Zero order correlation coefficient.

VARIABLE CODING

Dependent Variables
Ever Defaced
Ever Damaged
Defaced More Than Once or Twice This Year
Damaged More Than Once or Twice This Year
0 = no
1 = yes

Predictor Variables
Sex
  0 = female
  1 = male
Disobedience to Parents
Fighting With Parents
  0 = not at all
  1 = a little
  2 = some
  3 = a lot
Feelings of Anger
  0 = never
  1 = hardly ever
  2 = sometimes
  3 = often
  4 = almost always
School Performance
  0 = far below average
  1 = below average
  2 = average
  3 = above average
  4 = far above average

School Satisfaction
  0 = not at all
  1 = a little
  2 = some
  3 = a lot
Friends' Delinquency: Estimates of Involvement
  Friends' Vandalism
  Friends' Shoplifting
  Friends' Alcohol Use
    0 = none
    1 = one or two
    2 = some
    3 = most
    4 = all

Table 4-3. Seventh and Eighth Grade Vandalism: Prediction Equations (N = 640)

	School Defacement		Minor School Damage		Major School Damage		Nonschool Defacement		Minor Non-school Damage		Major Non-school Damage	
R^2	0.190		0.224		0.220		0.227		0.320		0.237	
Intercept	0.121		0.301		-0.009		-0.030		0.002		-0.030	
Predictor Variables												
Sex	-0.211[a] (0.036)[b] 5.800[c]	-0.136[d]	-0.153 (0.037) 0.412	0.094	0.061 (0.021) 2.915	0.214	-0.021 (0.034) 0.616	0.072	0.095 (0.034) 2.762	0.239	0.086 (0.023) 3.688	0.241
Disobedience to Parents	0.020 (0.030) 0.663	0.213	0.053 (0.031) 1.712	0.256	0.024 (0.017) 1.389	0.177	0.042 (0.028) 1.490	0.259	0.019 (0.029) 0.686	0.225	0.026 (0.019) 1.342	0.209
Fighting with Parents	0.052 (0.026) 2.035	0.233	0.016 (0.026) 0.592	0.180	0.002 (0.015) 0.141	0.091	0.049 (0.024) 2.066	0.225	0.027 (0.024) 1.118	0.141	0.020 (0.016) 1.208	0.133
Anger at Parents	0.025 (0.023) 1.095	0.235	0.019 (0.023) 0.843	0.212	-0.012 (0.013) 0.954	0.067	0.009 (0.021) 0.424	0.214	-0.012 (0.021) 0.592	0.149	-0.012 (0.014) 0.835	0.106
Anger at School Officials	0.022 (0.018) 1.229	0.210	0.038 (0.018) 2.121	0.279	-0.066 (0.010) 0.635	0.145	0.040 (0.016) 2.464	0.272	0.051 (0.016) 3.095	0.319	0.012 (0.011) 1.030	0.212
School Performance	-0.015 (0.023) 0.656	-0.093	-0.002 (0.023) 0.095	-0.091	-0.024 (0.013) 1.808	-0.128	-0.022 (0.021) 1.039	-0.124	-0.030 (0.021) 1.375	-0.130	-0.034 (0.015) 2.335	-0.153
Friends' Vandalism	0.097 (0.020) 4.902	0.306	0.098 (0.020) 4.861	0.413	0.043 (0.011) 3.778	0.392	0.098 (0.018) 5.329	0.407	0.161 (0.018) 8.712	0.532	0.069 (0.013) 5.459	0.431
Friends' Major Shoplifting	0.024 (0.020) 1.158	0.263	0.051 (0.021) 2.433	0.361	0.065 (0.012) 5.550	0.410	0.065 (0.019) 3.442	0.370	0.004 (0.019) 0.200	0.362	0.046 (0.013) 3.521	0.375
Friends' Alcohol Use	0.027 (0.018) 1.562	0.248	0.035 (0.018) 1.967	0.338	0.003 (0.010) 0.316	0.271	-0.016 (0.016) 0.969	0.255	0.031 (0.016) 1.876	0.369	-0.008 (0.011) 0.705	0.260

aunstandardized slope (b).

bstandard error.

ct value.

dzero order correlations coefficient.

VARIABLE CODING

Dependent Variables

School Defacement
Minor School Damage
Major School Damage
Nonschool Defacement
Minor Nonschool Damage
Major Nonschool Damage
   0 = not in the last six months
   1 = one or more times in the last six months

Predictor Variables

Sex
   0 = female
   1 = male
Disobedience to Parents
Fighting with Parents
   0 = not at all
   1 = a little
   2 = some
   3 = a lot
Anger at Parents
Anger at School Officials
   0 = never
   1 = hardly ever
   2 = sometimes
   3 = often
   4 = almost always

School Performance
   0 = far below average
   1 = below average
   2 = average
   3 = above average
   4 = far above average
Friends' Delinquency: Estimates of Involvement
   Friends' Vandalism
   Friends' Major Shoplifting
   Friends' Alcohol Use
   0 = none
   1 = one or two
   2 = some
   3 = most
   4 = all

meaningful amounts (fourteen to twenty percentage points). The best predictors of major school property damage are friends' shop-lifting and anger at school officials, which can exert a potential change of twenty-six percentage points each.

The role of school variables in these school vandalism equations is quite interesting. Normally one would expect factors such as school satisfaction, performance, perceptions of pressure, or anger at school officials to predict school vandalism. However, their predictive ability here is rather unsystematic, and the most influential still exert only a modest impact on these probabilities. For example, poor school performance increases chances of major school damage to some degree, but the item's total influence is somewhat less than ten percentage points.

Seventh and eighth graders were also asked about nonschool vandalism. Many of the same factors that were important predictors of school vandalism are also important components of the nonschool equations. Nonschool defacement is best predicted by disobedience to parents, fighting with parents, anger at school officials, and the extent of friends' vandalism and major shoplifting. All of these alter probabilities by at least twelve percentage points. Minor nonschool damage can be predicted by fighting with parents, anger at school officials, poor school performance, and friends' vandalism or alcohol use. The probability of major nonschool property damage is altered by many of these same variables.

Under the controlled conditions presented in these equations, girls are a bit more likely to report nonschool defacement than boys. Boys have a higher probability of minor and major nonschool property damage, but controlled sex differences in these probabilities do not exceed ten percentage points. When these patterns are considered along with those for school vandalism, it seems that sex differences in junior high vandalism are smaller and often in opposite directions to those conventionally predicted. Girls are more likely to report modest school vandalism and nonschool defacement; boys are more likely to report nonschool vandalism. The patterns suggest that these sex differences may be more a function of differential oppor-tunity than sex role traits or sex differences in destructive urges. Nonschool property damage and major school damage generally take place out in neighborhoods after dark. Since parents are perhaps not as likely to allow their daughters out after dark as they are their sons, these sex distributions in vandalism should not be surprising. In situations where both sexes have similar opportunities (e.g., school), girls are at least as likely as boys to deface or damage property. Only in those instances where girls' opportunities may be more limited do girls report less vandalism than boys.

The best predictors of nonschool vandalism are estimates of friends' property damage and general delinquency, just as they were for school-related property damage. Interestingly, school predictors operate about equally well in equations for both school and nonschool vandalism. In fact, school performance is a slightly better predictor of nonschool vandalism than of school defacement or property damage. The impact of family variables is also generally modest for nonschool vandalism, operating in much the same way as for school-related property damage.

It seems that there are few systematic differences in the patterns of school and nonschool vandalism reported by these students. Instead of varying by target, these equations tend to vary according to the degree or seriousness of the property damage under consideration. Equations for minor versus major property damage differ in several ways. Patterns by sex are among the most obvious of these differences: boys are more likely than girls to report serious vandalism. Minor vandalism is predicted by a wider range of factors, including attitudes, school experiences, family situations, and friends' behavior. The only variables besides sex that operate as consistent and systematic predictors of major vandalism are those measuring friends' delinquent experiences. This implies that patterns in junior high vandalism may vary less by target (i.e., school versus nonschool property) than by the seriousness of the property damage under consideration (i.e., minor versus major damage).

High School Vandalism

High school respondents were asked questions about three possible targets for vandalism—school, private property, and nonschool public property. The most detailed information was obtained for school vandalism, since the questionnaire included three school items. Table 4-4 summarizes the best predictors for the high school vandalism items.

School-related property defacement can be predicted in ways similar to those noted for younger respondents. The best predictors include anger at parents, school performance, and the number of friends who have defaced school property. Disobedience to parents, anger at school officials, the extent of friends' minor school damage, and friends' major shoplifting alter the probability of minor school damage to a meaningful degree. However, only one predictor alters the chances of major school damage by more than ten percentage points—friends' major school damage. The probability of serious school property damage is not altered much by family variables or school experiences once peer variables are included in regression equations.

Table 4-4.   High School Vandalism: Prediction Equations (N = 821)

	School Defacement		Minor School Damage		Major School Damage		Damage to Private Property		Damage to Public Property	
R^2	0.332		0.301		0.212		0.312		0.237	
Intercept	0.041		-0.136		-0.021		-0.073		-0.072	
Predictor Variables										
Sex	-0.034[a] (0.025)[b] 1.375[c]	-0.067[d]	0.051 (0.027) 1.868	0.112	0.051 (0.016) 3.194	0.178	0.116 (0.029) 4.000	0.211	0.095 (0.019) 4.930	0.236
Disobedience to Parents	0.032 (0.020) 1.612	0.186	0.055 (0.022) 2.520	0.224	0.027 (0.012) 2.168	0.155	0.023 (0.022) 1.019	0.158	-0.005 (0.015) 0.335	0.084
Fighting with Parents	-0.033 (0.019) 1.758	0.086	0.001 (0.021) 0.000	0.121	-0.015 (0.012) 1.265	0.034	-0.020 (0.021) 0.940	0.093	-0.014 (0.014) 0.943	0.028
Anger at Parents	0.032 (0.017) 1.962	0.175	-0.007 (0.018) 0.361	0.136	0.000 (0.010) 0.000	0.063	0.042 (0.019) 2.211	0.166	0.015 (0.013) 1.175	0.076
Anger at School Officials	0.012 (0.013) 0.938	0.189	0.050 (0.014) 3.521	0.264	0.017 (0.008) 2.126	0.192	0.020 (0.015) 1.353	0.192	0.017 (0.010) 1.755	0.173
School Performance	-0.030 (0.015) 2.022	-0.075	0.001 (0.016) 0.077	-0.056	-0.017 (0.009) 1.800	-0.120	-0.026 (0.017) 1.517	-0.108	-0.003 (0.011) 0.257	-0.093
Friends' Vandalism (parallel type)	0.209 (0.012) 16.793	0.561	0.176 (0.014) 12.685	0.522	0.128 (0.012) 10.954	0.430	0.188 (0.014) 13.191	0.534	0.132 (0.013) 9.808	0.453
Friends' Major Shoplifting	0.010 (0.013) 0.735	0.234	0.027 (0.015) 1.761	0.309	-0.005 (0.008) 0.539	0.158	0.009 (0.017) 0.567	0.299	0.022 (0.011) 1.972	0.278
Friends' Alcohol Use	-0.004 (0.009) 0.490	-0.011	-0.003 (0.010) 0.361	0.014	0.002 (0.005) 0.265	0.031	0.029 (0.010) 0.292	0.030	-0.004 (0.007) 0.648	0.003

a unstandardized slope (b).
b standard error.
c t value.
d zero order correlation coefficient.

VARIABLE CODING
Dependent Variables
School Defacement
Minor School Damage
Major School Damage
Damage to Private Property
Damage to Public Property (nonschool)
 0 = not in the last six months
 1 = one or more times in the last six months

Predictor Variables
Sex
 0 = female
 1 = male
Disobedience to Parents
Fighting with Parents
 0 = not at all
 1 = a little
 2 = some
 3 = a lot
Anger at Parents
Anger at School Officials
 0 = never
 1 = hardly ever
 2 = sometimes
 3 = often
 4 = almost always
School Performance
 0 = far below average
 1 = below average
 2 = average
 3 = above average
 4 = far above average

Friends' Delinquency: Estimates of Involvement
Friends' School Defacement
Friends' Minor School Damage
Friends' Major School Damage
Friends' Damage to Private Property
Friends' Damage to Public Property (Nonschool)
Friends' Major Shoplifting
Friends' Alcohol Use
 0 = none
 1 = one or two
 2 = some
 3 = most
 4 = all

Damage to private property is best predicted by anger at parents, poor school performance, friends' vandalism, and friends' alcohol use. However, it should be noted that school performance and friends' alcohol use barely exert the percentage impact necessary for them to qualify as meaningful predictors in this analysis. Damage to public property follows many of these same patterns, although it is somewhat more difficult to predict because of the limited variability in reports. Boys are more likely to report damage to public property than girls, and friends who are also involved in public property damage can increase the probability of this form of vandalism by as much as fifty-three percentage points.

Sex differences in high school vandalism mirror those noted for seventh and eighth graders. Girls are more likely to report school defacement, and sex differences in the probability of reporting either form of school property damage do not exceed five percentage points. Larger differences appear for damage to private and public property, but these differences still average around ten percentage points. Again, this suggests an opportunity explanation for sex differences in vandalism rather than one based on assumptions about sex role traits or sex differences in psychic outlook. However, the uniformly best predictors of high school vandalism are estimates of friends' involvement in various forms of property damage. Seldom do estimates of friends' more general delinquency adequately predict high school students' vandalism; school and family predictors are occasionally important but do not operate in a systematic fashion across all types of vandalism.

SUMMARY AND CONCLUSION

The pattern of predictors identified here fits quite well with the leisure framework outlined in Chapter 2, while more familiar explanations find less support in these data. There is no strong evidence that vandalism is motivated by the individual pathologies frequently cited in the literature, whether they be feelings of inadequacy, boredom, or a generalized urge to destroy. In fact, the alleged masculine character of property damage is challenged by by these data; girls are often as likely to report vandalism as boys. Masculinity anxiety or sex role maladjustment do not seem to be useful accounts for these patterns, since measures of sex role insecurity do not differentiate between those students who have vandalized and those who have not. The sex differences that do appear seem more likely to be the product of differential opportunity than destructive propensities that are sex role linked.

Anger at authority figures has a systematic role to play in the patterns of minor vandalism. This suggests that popular characterizations that emphasize anger contain an element of truth. Still, vandalism need not be seen as evidence of an amorphous urge to destroy. The anger reported here is explicitly directed at parents and school officials. These are the adults most likely to impose rules and limitations on adolescents. Many of these rules are confining and likely to provoke disagreement. Anger may be one response to these limitations, but need not automatically provoke destructive behavior. Instead, both anger at authorities and property damage may be part of a complex response to the limitations of adolescence. Within a decisionmaking framework, this anger may serve to alter the balance of costs and benefits attached to vandalism. Not all adolescents are equally likely to find rules and limitations galling. Those who do may see vandalism as a more appealing option than those who do not.

Minor types of vandalism (those that are also most popular) show a generally curvilinear relationship to grade.[6] The highest incidence of minor property damage is reported by seventh through ninth graders, suggesting that experimentation with property damage is most common during the junior high years and that individuals in this age group may be the most actively involved in evaluating the costs and benefits involved in vandalism. This pattern is consistent with a leisure decisionmaking framework, since younger students should have the least information about the potentially delinquent character of property damage as well as the costs and benefits it entails. This relative lack of information should produce higher rates of involvement as junior high students experiment with vandalism in an effort to see what will happen. Once this experimentation period is over, the bulk of adolescents seem to decide that the costs of property damage outweigh the benefits and reduce their activity.

These costs and benefits can take many forms, including risk of detection, direct sanctions from parents or other authorities, and responses of peers. The strong role of peer variables in this analysis is consistent with a decisionmaking framework where peers can provide both positive and negative reinforcement for vandalism, may be part of the "apparatus" of property damage (some forms of vandalism cannot be done alone), and are one element of the situation that must be managed or manipulated. One of the things one can learn through vandalism is how peers will react and how to manage these reactions successfully. Thus, it is not surprising that the most systematic and the most powerful predictors in this analysis are those that measure peers' experiences. All other things being equal, students with a good many friends who have vandalized are the most likely to report property damage. The reverse is also true: those students with few peers who have vandalized are relatively unlikely to report vandalism. Both interpretations should be emphasized, since delinquency researchers have a tendency to assume that peers exert basically prodeviant influences on their friends.

The nature of the ties between peers' vandalism and respondents' own reports is a difficult problem. While there is always a temptation to conclude that the relationship is a causal one, this is a risky statement when based solely on statistical predictability. Since the incidence of vandalism varies by age, one might propose an epidemiological explanation for these patterns. It is possible that groups of teenagers undertake vandalism at about the same time as a function of other growth processes. This explanation is similar to what one might propose for a number of childhood maladies. For example, the incidence of acne rises markedly once children enter junior high. This does not mean that peer acne causes an individual's acne. Instead, adolescents get it at about the same time because of similar maturational processes. Ties between friends' and individuals' vandalism could be similarly spurious if vandalism is a response to life stage considerations rather than peer pressure per se. However there is at least modest evidence that peers play more than a spurious role in the genesis of vandalism. Regardless of the age group under question, variation in what close friends do affects the property damage that individuals report. The predictive power of this variation in peer involvement suggests that life cycle processes are not the only factors at work here. Peer influence also seems rather activity-specific, especially among older cohorts of students. This specificity must be interpreted carefully given the wording of items used in the different questionnaires, but does suggest that peer experiences exert a less generalized influence than most theories predict. The activity-specific nature of important predictors implies that peers offer explicit rewards, sanctions, and instructions for vandalism rather than some more amorphous influence tied to life cycle stage.

The positive links between friends' vandalism and individuals property damage also fits well within a leisure framework. If peers are a necessary prerequisite for some forms of vandalism, these activities should be a more viable option for individuals with many friends who have vandalized than for those with few such friends. If one is willing to make an additional assumption that friends who have vandalized are likely to positively reinforce vandalism, one would also expect the highest rates of property damage among respondents with many friends who have damaged property. Obviously this assumption is somewhat risky, since there is no assurance that friends who have vandalized will endorse the behavior, but there is likely to be some relationship between between experience and attitudes that could affect the balance of costs and benefits that peers offer. A leisure model that emphasizes the elements of this decisionmaking process (the costs and benefits) does not require a stronger causal interpretation than this in order for it to fit these patterns. Indeed, this is one of its advantages over more familiar perspectives that attribute vandalism almost entirely to peer pressure.

Peer variables are generally more important components of this analysis than family or school factors. This too is consistent with a leisure decisionmaking framework, since both family and school actors are less likely to be part of an adolescents' leisure situation than are peers. Family members do appear to have a modest effect on the probability of vandalism, but their impact is stronger for younger respondents than for older ones. As a decisionmaking framework predicts, zero order associations between vandalism and school experiences almost disappear under controlled conditions. Once peer variables are introduced into the analysis, school experiences lose most of their predictive power. This suggests that school is most important as a context for peer group contact that can affect the costs and benefits of vandalism that an individual anticipates from peers.

In sum, the overall patterns of property damage found in this middle class population fit a leisure model better than most other familiar alternatives. The best predictors of vandalism are those related to important reference groups that can structure opportunities, provide direct rewards or costs for the activity, and give individuals useful information about techniques and risks involved in property damage. Since these are the same actors who are likely to have important roles in other leisure decisions, there seems to be no need for an explanation of vandalism that differs from a more general model of leisure decisionmaking. Property damage can take many forms, and its deviant character can vary with the situation; peers and other reference groups seem able to affect decisionmaking in predictable ways and create a system of rewards and costs within which an individual must operate. There is little evidence that these middle class adolescents are forced into vandalism by the power of individual pathology, family breakdown, or peer pressure. Instead, these patterns are consistent with a more fluid image of how vandalism can be chosen in response to complex interrelationships between various opportunities, costs, and satisfactions. On this basis, a leisure decisionmaking framework is an attractive one for explaining patterns in middle class property damage. Its value in explaining patterns in other potentially delinquent leisure activities will be examined in the chapters that follow.

NOTES

1. Even the police have difficulty categorizing vandalism. An overview of vandalism reports in this community's police files uncovered several instances where vandalism had originally been identified as burglary and *vice versa*. There is a good deal of overlap between these two categories, which can produce uncertainty even in official reports (Richards, 1976).

2. This arational image of adolescent vandalism is quite strong in spite of the obvious links between vandalism and strategic property destruction of the type that occurs during political disputes, labor conflicts, or civil disorders. This may be because these forms of vandalism are generally done by adults and thus are more difficult to dismiss as wanton and meaningless. Not that this isn't attempted, since it makes it easier to ignore the political statements implicit in the property damage and to justify harsh measures for dealing with the protest vandalism may symbolize.

3. However, the causal direction here is very ambiguous and must be interpreted cautiously. Perhaps students who vandalize more are almost by definition disobeying their parents. The case for the causal impact of anger is also unclear. Throughout the narrative we will be quite hesitant to assume that there is a direct or clear causal link between vandalism and these variables.

4. While these predictors alter the probability of reports, in no sense does this predictive ability assure that they cause vandalism. We are using regression techniques here in order to partition the variance in vandalism (and other forms of delinquency) and describe important patterns. Causal statements must be made more carefully.

5. The equations in Table 4-3 explain meaningful amounts of the variance in the vandalism that these seventh and eighth graders report. R^2 values range from 0.19 (school defacement) to 0.32 (minor school damage) and are quite good for survey research on adolescent deviance (see for example, Hirschi, 1969, for reports of multiple R values for prediction equations, many of which are lower than the levels explained by these predictors).

6. Again, age patterns must be interpreted cautiously because it is difficult to separate cohort effects from age trends over time. These conclusions seem justified given the size of the differences between grade levels, but must be made with their cohort nature in mind.

Chapter Five

Leisure and Drug Use

INTRODUCTION

Lower class adolescents in inner city neighborhoods have been the traditional focus of public concern about drug use. The allegedly disorganized nature of urban poverty is often linked to various forms of individual pathology including the withdrawal that drug use is thought to symbolize. It is also seen as an individual coping strategy motivated by underlying psychic pathologies stemming from inadequate socialization into conventional roles. This is an especially popular interpretation among law enforcement officials, physicians, and conservative sectors of the public, who often favor reductionist accounts for difficult social problems.

Although drug use may once have been considered a uniquely lower class phenomenon, it is obviously popular among middle class youths as well. The growth of 1960s counterculture ideologies focused public attention on drug use among affluent adolescents. It also sparked an interest in drug research among academics. Most authors extended causal models of individual pathology to the middle class case, modifying theories of lower class drug use to fit patterns observed among middle class adolescents. Much of the literature assumes that drugs provide disturbed adolescents with a way of gratifying needs that they cannot meet in conventional ways, and terms such as "amotivational syndrome" are invoked to describe the psychic disturbances of middle class youths who use drugs as a way of "dropping out" (L. Johnston, 1973: 168). Models of individual pathology lead theorists to focus on disturbed psychological states, social isolation, histories of family problems, or other stresses that may lead to escapist coping strategies. Representative of this view is the statement that "The typical habitual user of marijuana may be described clinically as an immature, emotionally unstable individual, unable to meet the demands of reality or to endure deprivation, frustration, and discipline. He reacts to conflict with either explosive aggression or a need for immediate hedonistic gratification" (Ausubel, 1958: 100). This reasoning should be familiar, since it is similar to that often applied to vandalism. Drug use is assumed to be motivated by many of the same social or psychic maladaptations, but in the case of drug use, the target of destructive behavior is internal rather than external.

There are researchers who reject causal models of social disorganization (i.e., pathological families, poor socialization) in the study of middle class drug use. Since middle class drug users generally come from intact homes, the best schools, and pleasant neighborhoods, it is difficult to argue that social breakdown has produced the individual pathologies traditionally associated with the activity. "Youth culture" explanations are alternatives that focus on the unconventional value systems that affluence can support. According to these views, affluent adolescents use drugs as part of a lifestyle designed to combat the meaninglessness and estrangement of middle class life. They have learned conventional values but reject them, substituting a new morality (termed by some as the "Hang Loose Ethic") marked by irreverence toward tradition, tolerance for unconventional lifestyles, spontaneity, and the pursuit of diverse experiences (Suchman, 1968; Kenniston, 1968b; Weil and Zinberg, 1970; Turner, 1974; Coleman, 1965). In this view, middle class drug use is part of a unique, deliberate, and innovative lifestyle.

The problem with both individual pathology and youth culture models of middle class drug use is that they tend to make more of the activity than is warranted. Both imply that drug use is fairly serious deviance, whether motivated by illness or by explicit rejection of conventional values. Yet the most popular drugs used by adolescents—alcohol and marijuana—bear marked resemblance to those that are a commonplace form of recreation among adults. This implies that a more mundane image of drug use and its motivations has much to offer in an analysis of middle class drug use. A leisure framework is a particularly attractive alternative in light of similarities between popular forms of adolescent drug use and the social drinking of adults. Drug use can be fun or entertaining; it can also teach interpersonal skills that are a crucial part of effective social interaction. Both of these possibilities suggest that a closer look at the leisure context of drug use may provide insight into patterns in this form of adolescent deviance.

DRUG USE AS A LEISURE ACTIVITY

Since recreational drug use is such a popular phrase, a leisure framework is an intuitively appealing way of explaining adolescent drug use. However, our approach to leisure drug use differs from most popular perspectives. While most focus on the relationship between boredom and artificial excitement, there are other reasons for placing drug use within a leisure decisionmaking framework. Drug use is one activity whose deviant character is particularly fluid. This requires an explanation that does not assume that the activity is automatically and consistently deviant. This fluidly deviant character is perhaps easiest to see in the case of adolescent drinking. Alcohol use is acceptable for adults (within moderation) but illegal for children. Since alcohol use is so widespread, many parents attempt to introduce children to alcohol at home under "healthy conditions" (e.g., a glass of beer with dinner, champagne on special occasions). In such situations, adolescent drinking may be acceptable even though strictly illegal. However, the same activity in a different context is likely to be deviant (e.g., drinking beer with friends). The deviant character of other popular forms of drug use (e.g., marijuana, cigarettes) varies in similar ways. This fluidity is an important dimension of drug use that must be consistent with any explanations proposed.

Our leisure framework takes this fluidity into account by assuming that the deviant nature of drug use is one of the things that must be learned if one is to use drugs successfully. Drugs obviously supply satisfaction (utility) that can be consumed directly (i.e., "fun," "relaxation," "excitement"). However, a good deal of learning must occur before full satisfaction can be gained. The deviant character of drug use varies from situation to situation, and different audiences are likely to respond to drug use in different ways. One must learn to anticipate these responses, since they are important elements in the rewards and costs involved. This is obviously a complex process and may require active experimentation before responses can be predicted with a reasonable degree of assurance.

These same actors may also exert more subtle influences on choices via their impact on individual preferences. Tastes develop in response to others' activities: one may prefer bourbon over scotch because one's father drinks bourbon (one may prefer scotch for the same reason); one may prefer marijuana over beer because marijuana is the drug of choice among one's peers. Part of the influence of parental role models in drug use may be exerted through this sort of manipulation of tastes.

Skills and techniques must also be learned if one is to gain satisfaction from drugs. Often this is difficult to do without direct experience. Learning to hold one's liquor requires practice; one must learn to properly identify the effects produced by marijuana; one must learn to smoke cigarettes without coughing. These skills are learned in a social context that consists of both observation and direct instruction. Parents often attempt to teach "responsible" drinking habits by introducing their children to beer or wine, and peers coach one another in proper drug use techniques. Both parents and peers are likely to have an impact on drug use patterns for this reason as well as for the direct rewards or sanctions they provide.

Once skills have been developed to the point that satisfaction can be gained from drug use, these skills can be "reinvested." Reinvestment can take the form of additional consumption (i.e., drinking), but the group character of most drug use suggests that skilled drug use can also "purchase" other goods that provide utility to the individual. Much adolescent (and adult) sociability is lubricated by alcohol and other drugs, and once drug use skills have been acquired, they may be useful in wider social contexts. In other words, skills can be reinvested in general sociability and have an impact on peer relationships and peer group structure. Drugs can also heighten the satisfaction derived from other leisure activities. One may obtain more pleasure from listening to a record when high than when straight; it may be more fun to go dancing when drunk than when sober.

Overall, a leisure decisionmaking perspective appears to be an attractive way of analyzing patterns in adolescent drug use. In contrast to most popular explanations, it does not assume that drug use is abnormal or pathological or that it entails a rejection of dominant cultural values. Instead, drugs can provide an individual with a number of forms of satisfaction that can be directly consumed (relaxation, fun, excitement). Effective consumption requires the acquisition of nonmarket skills that can be reinvested both in drug use and in other activities (e.g., group sociability) that produce utility for the individual. These skills are learned in a complex social context where the deviant character of drug use is variably defined. All of this suggests that middle class drug use should follow the basic patterns outlined in Chapter 2 and that peer and family experiences should be especially important elements in these patterns.

Basic Distribution of Drug Use

Tables 5-1 and 5-2 present the marginal response distributions for the drug use questions included in this survey. The items vary slightly from questionnaire to questionnaire, and for this reason we have noted their exact wording in Appendix B. Fifth and sixth graders were asked questions about five different categories of drugs including alcohol (two items), marijuana, cigarettes, and "other" drugs. Questions were designed to assess both lifetime use and use during the current school year. Older students were asked about a wider range of drugs, and estimates of both experimentation ("ever tried") and frequency of recent use were gathered for each type of drug. These estimates have been grouped into convenient categories in Table 5-2.[1]

Alcohol is the most common drug used by respondents of all ages. Almost three-fourths of the elementary students have tried beer or wine, and approximately one-quarter have tried hard liquor. Eighty-three percent of the high school students report alcohol use in the six months. Cigarette smoking is also fairly common. About one-third of the elementary school respondents claim to have tried cigarettes, a proportion that rises to two-thirds among high school students. However, only about a third of these high school students claim to smoke cigarettes on a regular basis. Elementary students report little contact with marijuana (4 percent) or other drugs (1 percent). Use of marijuana appears in junior high (19 percent) and continues throughout high school. Almost three-fourths of these students claim to have tried marijuana by the time they are seniors. Contact with other types of drugs increases among high school respondents but is still relatively limited. Only about one-fifth of the older students claim to have tried drugs like psychedelics, uppers, and downers, and fewer than 10 percent report any experience with cocaine, heroin, or other narcotic drugs.

**Age and Sex Patterns in
Drug Use**

Although most forms of delinquency are expected to be related to grade in a curvilinear fashion, this does not appear to be true of drug use. The most popular drugs (i.e., alcohol and marijuana) are used with steadily increasing frequency among older cohorts of students, while use rates for less popular drugs (i.e., cocaine, heroin) do not vary much across cohorts once initial use levels have been established. Most elementary students have at least tried beer or wine (often under parental supervision); significant experimentation with

Table 5-1.   Marginal Distributions of Drug Experimentation[a]

Fifth and Sixth Graders: Percent of Students Reporting

	ever used wine or beer	ever used liquor	ever used cigarettes	ever used marijuana	ever used inhalants	ever used other drugs
no	25.9	76.7	72.8	96.1	92.8	98.7
yes	74.1	23.3	27.2	3.9	7.2	1.3
	100	100	100	100	100	100
	(745)	(744)	(743)	(739)	(741)	(742)

Seventh and Eighth Graders: Percent of Students Reporting

	ever used alcohol	ever used cigarettes	ever used marijuana	ever used psychedelics	ever used "pills"	ever used narcotics	ever used inhalants
no	40.7	42.7	80.4	97.4	94.5	98.1	96.9
yes	59.3	57.3	19.6	2.6	5.5	1.9	3.1
	100	100	100	100	100	100	100
	(805)	(803)	(801)	(794)	(795)	(793)	(794)

High School Students: Percent of Students Reporting

	ever used alcohol	ever used marijuana	ever used psychedelics	ever used "uppers"	ever used "downers"	ever used cocaine	ever used inhalants	ever used narcotics	ever used heroin
no	14.4	41.4	80.1	80.6	86.4	89.6	92.2	90.5	99.4
yes	85.6	58.6	19.9	19.4	13.6	10.4	7.8	9.5	0.6
	100	100	100	100	100	100	100	100	100
	(1,238)	(1,238)	(1,235)	(1,237)	(1,237)	(1,236)	(1,235)	(1,237)	(1,236)

[a]Exact wording of items can be found in Appendix B.

Table 5-2.   Marginal Distributions of Drug Use: Frequency in the Last Six Months[a]

Fifth and Sixth Grade: Percent of Students Reporting

	wine or beer	hard liquor	marijuana	inhalants	"other" drugs
no	62.7	91.0	97.4	96.6	99.2
yes	37.3	9.0	2.6	3.4	0.8
	100	100	100	100	100
	(743)	(745)	(742)	(739)	(743)

Seventh and Eighth Graders: Percent of Students Reporting

	alcohol	marijuana	"pills"	psychedelics	narcotics	inhalants	cigarettes[b]
never	43.9	80.3	93.6	96.0	98.3	97.6	never 69.5
1-4 times	27.3	6.8	2.7	1.8	1.4	2.2	once or more 30.5
5-9 times	10.8	3.0	1.1	0.2	0.1	0.0	
10+ times	17.9	10.0	2.6	2.0	0.2	0.1	
	100	100	100	100	100	100	100
	(818)	(811)	(825)	(829)	(830)	(828)	(837)

High School Students: Percent of Students Reporting

	alcohol	marijuana	"uppers"	"downers"	psychedelics	cocaine	heroin	other narcotics	inhalants	cigarettes[b]
never	17.5	46.9	83.7	89.6	83.0	91.3	99.3	91.9	95.5	never 66.2
1-4 times	19.6	12.2	8.1	6.0	10.6	6.1	0.3	5.6	3.2	once or more 33.8
5-9 times	13.5	5.2	3.0	2.3	3.5	1.2	0.2	0.8	0.6	
10+ times	49.4	35.8	5.2	2.1	2.9	1.4	0.2	1.7	0.7	
	100	100	100	100	100	100	100	100	100	100
	(1231)	(1234)	(1232)	(1234)	(1232)	(1234)	(1237)	(1233)	(1233)	(1233)

[a]Exact wording of items can be found in Appendix B.

[b]Measured according to packs per day and dichotomized for comparability.

marijuana does not appear to occur until junior high and early high school cohorts. However, use rates for these common drugs continue to increase throughout the high school group, suggesting that students are establishing regular use patterns after initial experimentation.

Despite popular assumptions that girls are less delinquent than boys, there are no large sex differences in the drug use reported by this group of middle class adolescents. Girls are slightly less likely to report alcohol or marijuana use in elementary and junior high school (correlations in the seventh and eighth grade data of 0.16 and 0.10) but slightly more likely in the high school grades (rs of —0.01, —0.07). High school girls are also more likely than boys to use cigarettes (r = —0.19), pep pills, and barbiturates. There are parallel differences in the junior high data. Although these correlations are not large, they suggest that drug use is one form of delinquency that is popular among both girls and boys. In fact, older girls may be even more likely than boys to use drugs.

Drug Use and Attitudes

Much of the drug literature focuses on emotions of powerlessness, boredom, anger, or alienation that are presumed to stimulate drug use. If drug use is a way of withdrawing from society or of acting out underlying problems, it should be closely associated with a variety of attitudes. Several attitude measures were included in our analysis, but most fail to show substantively meaningful correlations with drug use. Anger (at parents or school officials) is the only attitude item to show systematic patterns with drug use, and these associations are modest. In the elementary data, correlations with anger and various drug items average around 0.10; in junior high the coefficients range from 0.15 to 0.30, and in high school from 0.12 to 0.23. Overall there is some evidence that anger is associated with higher frequencies of reported drug use, but little evidence that individual pathology as measured by feelings of efficacy, world views, boredom, or sex role insecurity has a strong role to play in middle class drug use.

Drug Use and School Experiences

Most correlations between drug use and measures of school experiences are rather small. Dissatisfaction and poor performance are the most systematic of these school correlates, although their levels of association are not especially strong. Satisfaction and performance are associated with high school drug use at levels ranging from —0.14 to —0.32; performance has much more modest

correlations with drug use in junior high. Participation in extracurricular activities such as sports teams or school groups or clubs is not
meaningfully associated with these students' drug use; neither are
variables measuring occupational or educational goals of the type
stressed in strain theories of delinquency.

Drug Use and Family Variables

Adolescent drug use is frequently attributed to family disorganization or permissive child-rearing practices. However, variables such as
broken homes, working mothers, family rules or punishment
methods, and parental occupation or education are not important
variables here. There are modest correlations between family conflict
variables (i.e., fighting, disobedience) and many of the drug items. In
both the junior and senior high data these coefficients range from
0.21 to 0.34. There is also a small relationship between drug use and
the amount of spending money available to younger respondents, but
this is not true for older cohorts.

Respondents were asked about the drug use habits of various
family members in order to assess the accuracy of modeling theories
that predict that parents and siblings can set influential examples for
students' drug use. While there are positive correlations between
parents' drinking and respondents' drug use (particularly alcohol),
these are not strongly associated. Siblings appear to have more
of an impact than parents, increasing respondents' chances of drug
use in modest ways (zero order correlation coefficients between
siblings' alcohol use and respondents' use of drugs vary from 0.13 to
0.26).

Drug Use and Peer Relationships

Peer variables are the strongest zero order correlates with drug use
in all three questionnaires. Fifth and sixth graders whose friends use
alcohol are substantially more likely to report various forms of drug
use than those who have no friends involved in drinking. Correlations
between estimates of friends' drinking and individual drug use in
junior high range from 0.22 to 0.53, and there are similar levels of
association between drug use and estimates of friends' marijuana use,
cigarette smoking, and general drug use. High school data for the less
popular drugs (e.g., amphetamines, barbituates) show strong ties
between respondents' experiences and those of their friends. However, these correlations for alcohol and marijuana use are somewhat
smaller. It may be that these forms of drug use are so widespread
that there is not sufficient variation to produce large associations.

Summary of Zero Order
Correlations

The most systematic and impressive zero order correlates of middle class drug use are measures of friends' and siblings' drug use. Sex differences are generally smaller than delinquency stereotypes suggest, and there is little evidence of strong associations between drug use and individual maladjustment. Anger at parents or school officials increases chances of reporting most kinds of drugs, as do school dissatisfaction and poor school performance. However, the only family variable (aside from siblings' drug use) to show systematic correlations with drug use is parent-child conflict.

REGRESSION ANALYSIS OF
DRUG USE PATTERNS

Since these zero order correlations reflect uncontrolled patterns in these data, we have used them as the basis for a regression analysis similar to that presented in Chapter 4. We have chosen the most popular drugs for further analysis in order to isolate important patterns. The small number of students involved in serious drug use makes those items more difficult to study through multiple regression techniques, and since we are interested in the most common forms of delinquency among these middle class students, we will concentrate on the regular use of (as opposed to experimentation with) alcohol, marijuana, and common forms of amphetamines, barbituates, and psychedelics. As best as we can tell, the patterns of less popular drugs are similar to those in the more common subset we will be presenting.[2]

Fifth and Sixth Grade Drug Use

The relatively limited variability in fifth and sixth graders' drug use suggests that the coefficients in Table 5-3 must be interpreted cautiously. Still, some noteworthy patterns appear in these data. The best predictors of elementary students' drug use are measures of peers' drug experiences. Parallel friends' items can alter the probability of alcohol use by almost 50 percent, marijuana use by 60 percent, and cigarette use by approximately 58 percent (controlling for other variables in the equations). The probability impact of nonparallel friends' items tends to be smaller, but still meaningful. The drug experiences of siblings also contribute to chances of reporting drug use, although this relationship is not as strong as that of peers. Conflict with parents increases probabilities of drug use under these statistical controls, and school performance and satisfaction are sometimes useful predictors of drug use as well.[3]

Junior High Drug Use

Reports of drug use among junior high students follow many of the patterns noted for elementary school respondents. Peer variables are again the most important predictors of all types of drug use, altering probabilities by as much as 80 percent depending on the drug in question. Respondents whose brothers and sisters use alcohol are more likely to do so themselves, but this sibling measure is not a strong predictor of most other types of drug use. Disobedience to parents often increases the probability of common drug use in a meaningful fashion. For example, junior high students who disobey their parents "a lot" are almost 22 percent more likely to have used alcohol and almost 28 percent more likely to have used marijuana during the current school year. Both school performance and school satisfaction alter the probability of drug use under these statistical controls. Those who dislike school or who are doing poorly have a greater chance of reporting drug use than do those who are satisfied with school or whose grades are above average. Anger at school officials is a useful predictor of alcohol use, although it does little to alter use patterns for less common drugs such as marijuana, amphetamines, or barbiturates.

High School Drug Use

Six categories of high school drug use have been used in the regression analysis presented in Table 5-5. These are among the most popular drugs reported by older students and include alcohol, marijuana, cigarettes, psychedelics, amphetamines, and barbituates. The best predictors of any of these items are parallel measures of peers' drug use. The relative impact of peer items varies with the type of drug under study. It is strongest for the less popular drugs (e.g., psychedelics, amphetamines, barbiturates) and seems somewhat less important in the equations predicting alcohol or cigarette use. Siblings' drug experiences also contribute to the probability of some types of drug use that these high school students report. Respondents whose brothers or sisters have used alcohol or marijuana are likely to do so themselves. Disobedience to parents also has a systematic impact on these probabilities.

School variables show a mixed pattern of influence in these equations. Poor performance increases the probability of cigarette and psychedelic use but has little predictive power over other items. Students who dislike school run a substantively higher risk of cigarette, psychedelic, amphetamine, and barbiturate use under these statistical controls. However, anger at school officials is seldom a meaningful predictor of high school drug use.

Table 5-3. Fifth and Sixth Grade Drug Use: Prediction Equations (N = 473)

	Ever Used Alcohol		Current Alcohol Use		Ever Used Marijuana		Current Marijuana Use		Cigarette Use	
R^2	0.170		0.234		0.332		0.254		0.325	
Intercept	0.512		0.267		0.033		0.049		0.038	
Predictor Variables										
Sex	0.046[a] (0.037)[b] 1.258[c]	0.087[d]	0.057 (0.038) 1.472	0.100	−0.040 (0.016) 2.494	−0.091	−0.012 (0.014) 0.829	−0.025	0.017 (0.033) 0.525	0.025
Sibling Alcohol Use	0.060 (0.035) 1.736	0.221	0.099 (0.036) 2.753	0.279	0.047 (0.015) 3.222	0.331	0.044 (0.013) 3.361	0.325	0.072 (0.031) 2.329	0.306
Disobedience to Parents	0.063 (0.028) 2.205	0.201	0.056 (0.030) 1.876	0.204	0.033 (0.012) 2.619	0.284	0.023 (0.011) 2.054	0.260	0.070 (0.027) 2.616	0.280
School Performance	−0.039 (0.025) 1.559	−0.098	−0.055 (0.026) 2.136	−0.136	−0.017 (0.011) 1.629	−0.108	−0.020 (0.010) 2.088	−0.134	−0.048 (0.023) 2.135	−0.151
School Satisfaction	0.033 (0.023) 1.405	−0.010	−0.023 (0.025) 0.934	−0.127	−0.006 (0.010) 0.546	−0.134	−0.012 (0.009) 1.315	−0.170	0.023 (0.021) 1.090	−0.080
Friends' Parallel Drug Use	0.125 (0.017) 7.338	0.380	0.151 (0.018) 8.461	−0.438	0.145 (0.012) 11.633	0.560	0.100 (0.011) 8.923	0.480	e	
Fighting with Parents	e		e		e		e		0.043 (0.024) 1.778	0.265
Friends' Cigarette Use	e		e		e		e		0.146 (0.020) 7.252	0.511
Friends' Alcohol Use	e		e		e		e		0.058 (0.018) 3.172	0.431

[a] unstandardized slopes (b).
[b] standard error.
[c] t value.
[d] zero order correlation coefficient.
[e] terms excluded from model.

VARIABLE CODING

Dependent Variables

Ever used alcohol
Current alcohol use
Ever used marijuana
Current marijuana use
Cigarette use
0 = never
1 = one or more times in the last six months

Predictor Variables

Sex
0 = female
1 = male
Siblings' Alcohol Use
0 = none
1 = sometimes
2 = a lot
Disobedience to Parents
0 = not at all
1 = a little
2 = some
3 = a lot

School Performance
0 = far below average
1 = below average
2 = average
3 = above average
4 = far above average
School Satisfaction
0 = none
1 = a little
2 = some
3 = a lot

Friends' Delinquency: Estimates of Involvement
Friends' Alcohol Use
Friends' Marijuana Use
Friends' Cigarette Use
0 = none
1 = one or two
2 = some
3 = most
4 = all

Table 5-4.   Seventh and Eighth Grade Drug Use: Prediction Equations (N = 625)

	Alcohol Use		Marijuana Use		Use of "Pills"		Cigarette Use	
R^2	0.310		0.444		0.109		0.329	
Intercept	0.120		0.051		0.112		0.187	
Predictor Variables								
Sex	0.052[a] (0.035)[b] 1.500[c]	0.156[d]	0.016 (0.026) 0.596	0.102	−0.059 (0.019) 3.092	−0.058	−0.054 (0.041) 1.305	0.019
Disobedience to Parents	0.054 (0.025) 2.119	0.256	0.070 (0.019) 3.628	0.299	0.039 (0.014) 2.773	0.211	0.076 (0.030) 2.534	0.278
Anger at School Officials	0.030 (0.017) 1.829	0.289	0.001 (0.013) 0.045	0.257	0.004 (0.009) 0.397	0.150	0.002 (0.020) 0.084	0.240
School Performance	0.024 (0.023) 1.067	−0.047	−0.018 (0.017) 1.045	−0.160	−0.028 (0.012) 2.291	−0.147	−0.039 (0.027) 1.488	−0.157
School Satisfaction	−0.032 (0.022) 1.475	−0.244	−0.039 (0.017) 2.305	−0.303	−0.033 (0.012) 2.731	−0.191	−0.082 (0.026) 3.150	−0.288
Siblings' Alcohol Use	0.044 (0.024) 1.829	0.264	0.007 (0.018) 0.479	0.223	0.008 (0.013) 0.601	0.127	0.185 (0.028) 0.657	0.218
Friends' Parallel Drug Use	e		0.206 (0.015) 13.837	0.639	e		0.208 (0.025) 8.352	0.540
Friends' Alcohol Use	0.174 (0.016) 10.764	0.532	−0.074 (0.015) 0.479	0.465	0.025 (0.009) 2.849	0.221	0.033 (0.025) 1.311	0.443
Friends' "Other" Drug Use	0.004 (0.008) 0.514	0.132	−0.016 (0.006) 2.765	0.111	0.006 (0.004) 1.373	0.117	0.012 (0.009) 1.356	0.110

a unstandardized slope (b).
b standard error.
c t value.
d zero order correlation coefficient.
e term excluded from model.

VARIABLE CODING

Dependent Variables

Alcohol Use
Marijuana Use
Use of "Pills"
Cigarette Use
  0 = not in the last six months
  1 = one or more times in the last six months

Predictor Variables

Sex
  0 = female
  1 = male
Disobedience to Parents
  0 = not at all
  1 = a little
  2 = some
  3 = a lot
Anger at School Officials
  0 = never
  1 = hardly ever
  2 = sometimes
  3 = often
  4 = almost always
School Performance
  0 = far below average
  1 = below average
  2 = average
  3 = above average
  4 = far above average

School Satisfaction
  0 = not at all
  1 = a little
  2 = some
  3 = a lot
Siblings' Alcohol Use
  0 = none
  1 = sometimes
  2 = a lot
Friends' Delinquency: Estimates of Involvement
  Friends' Alcohol Use
  Friends' Marijuana Use
  Friends' Cigarette Use
  Friends' "Other" Drug Use
    0 = none
    1 = one or two
    2 = some
    3 = most
    4 = almost all

Table 5-5. High School Drug Use: Prediction Equations (N = 926)

	Alcohol Use	Marijuana Use	Use of "Uppers"	Use of "Downers"	Use of Psychedelics	Cigarette Use
R^2	0.239	0.532	0.455	0.401	0.407	0.356
Intercept	0.480	0.071	0.107	-0.001	0.076	0.196
Predictor Variables						
Sex	0.010[a] (0.023)[b] 0.448[c] -0.005[d]	-0.023 (0.023) 0.997 -0.066	-0.069 (0.019) 3.525 -0.152	-0.038 (0.017) 2.275 -0.079	0.010 (0.020) 0.503 0.016	-0.133 (0.017) 4.912 -0.189
Disobedience to Parents	0.058 (0.017) 3.510 0.245	0.074 (0.017) 4.413 0.345	0.020 (0.014) 1.398 0.221	0.022 (0.012) 1.825 0.218	0.049 (0.015) 3.295 0.272	0.029 (0.019) 1.515 0.239
School Performance	-0.001 (0.014) 0.089 -0.137	-0.024 (0.015) 1.606 0.253	-0.007 (0.012) 0.584 -0.195	-0.004 (0.017) 0.416 -0.176	-0.027 (0.013) 2.069 -0.253	-0.049 (0.017) 2.932 -0.251
School Satisfaction	-0.009 (0.015) 0.613 -0.176	0.008 (0.015) 0.555 0.277	-0.032 (0.012) 2.603 -0.253	-0.004 (0.011) 0.342 -0.226	-0.037 (0.013) 2.886 -0.321	-0.037 (0.017) 2.239 -0.260
Anger at School Officials	0.002 (0.012) 0.205 0.136	0.004 (0.012) 0.298 0.210	-0.012 (0.010) 1.161 0.139	0.003 (0.009) 0.373 0.226	0.012 (0.011) 1.141 0.220	0.005 (0.014) 0.336 0.213
Siblings' Alcohol Use	0.036 (0.014) 2.617 0.211	-0.008 (0.021) 0.386 0.257	0.011 (0.012) 0.947 0.158	0.016 (0.010) 1.568 0.151	0.012 (0.012) 0.960 0.161	-0.003 (0.016) 0.173 0.152
Siblings' Marijuana Use	e	0.057 (0.020) 2.890 0.362	e	e	e	e
Friends' Alcohol Use	0.092 (0.011) 8.129 0.461	0.028 (0.012) 2.438 0.563	0.025 (0.008) 3.367 0.354	0.007 (0.007) 1.016 0.286	0.017 (0.008) 2.101 0.335	0.031 (0.011) 2.866 0.371
Friends' Marijuana Use	0.025 (0.012) 2.102 0.394	0.184 (0.012) 14.896 0.710	e	e	e	e
Friends' Psychedelic Use	-0.020 (0.015) 1.300 0.191	0.010 (0.015) 0.648 0.398	0.022 (0.016) 3.525 0.521	0.062 (0.014) 4.424 0.534	0.226 (0.013) 17.610 0.606	0.082 (0.017) 4.912 0.375

Friends' Use of Parallel Drug	e		0.237 (0.016) 14.527	0.653	0.183 (0.015) 11.982	0.561	e	0.136 (0.013) 10.865	0.530

a unstandardized slope (b).
b standard error.
c t value.
d zero order correlation coefficient.
e term excluded from model.

VARIABLE CODING
Dependent Variables
Alcohol Use
Marijuana Use
Use of "Uppers"
Use of "Downers"
Use of Psychedelics
Cigarette Use
  0 = not in the last six months
  1 = one or more times in the last six months

Predictor Variables
Sex
  0 = female
  1 = male
Disobedience to Parents
  0 = not at all
  1 = a little
  2 = some
  3 = a lot
School Performance
  0 = far below average
  1 = below average
  2 = average
  3 = above average
  4 = far above average
School Satisfaction
  0 = not at all
  1 = a little
  2 = some
  3 = a lot

Siblings' Alcohol Use
Siblings' Marijuana Use
  0 = none
  1 = sometimes
  2 = a lot
Friends' Delinquency: Estimates of Involvement
  Friends' Alcohol Use
  Friends' Marijuana Use
  Friends' Use of "Uppers"
  Friends' Use of "Downers"
  Friends' Use of Psychedelics
  Friends' Cigarette Use
  0 = none
  1 = one or two
  2 = some
  3 = most
  4 = almost all

Summary of Patterns Across
Data Sets

Regression analysis points out several interesting characteristics of the drug use reported by these middle class students. Although the items differ somewhat from questionnaire to questionnaire, there are similarities in patterning that fit well with an image of drug use as a leisure activity. There are few meaningful sex differences in the drug use habits of these middle class students regardless of the age group under study. Sometimes it is girls who are more likely to report drug use, sometimes it is boys, but these differences seldom exceed five percentage points when statistical controls are exercised. The single exception is cigarette use among high school students. High school girls are 13 percent more likely to smoke than are boys under statistical controls.

Drug experiences differ with the age group under study. Older students use a wider variety of drugs and with a greater degree of frequency than younger students. It is difficult to separate cohort effects from age trends with data such as these, but it does seem that students are exposed to more types of drugs as they grow older and that with age, fairly stable use patterns are established for the most popular of these (i.e., alcohol, marijuana, and cigarettes).

A number of factors appear to contribute both to patterns in experimentation and patterns in regular drug use. Perhaps the most important of these are peer experiences. Peer variables are the most influential predictors of drug use at all ages and for all types of drugs. Family impact seems to vary more by age: sibling's drug experiences are more important components of our elementary and junior high analysis than of the high school, and the impact of parent-child conflict variables (fighting, disobedience) is greater among young students than older ones. School experiences have some predictive power in these regression analyses, but this too seems greater for elementary and junior high respondents than for high school students.

Although many theories of adolescent drug use stress the role of individual maladjustment or withdrawal, attitude measures reflecting these concerns fail to predict middle class drug use in a systematic way. Anger is the only attitude item that predicts drug use with any consistency, and it is among the weaker variables in these regression equations. Overall, there is little evidence that middle class drug use is accompanied by the psychological pathology frequently cited in the literature.

THE SOCIAL CONTEXT OF DRUG USE

Our leisure perspective leads us to assume that much adolescent drug use is social in character, since it can be an important element in sociability and since techniques and skills are learned from others. If this is true, the social nature of drug use should be reflected in the situations where adolescents choose to use drugs. We asked high school students to identify the most popular of these settings for us, and their responses are summarized in Table 5-6.

Most of the high school students who use drugs do so as part of social or recreational situations such as parties, movies, or dates. Some drink or use drugs when there is "nothing else to do" (about 20 percent), but relatively few appear to use them as aids in sleeping, studying, or sports. The distribution of these responses is interesting for several reasons. Not only do students appear to use drugs in the situations that our leisure framework predicts, but in situations quite similar to those in which adults use alcohol. This is additional evidence that middle class drug use is leisure and recreation oriented rather than the product of individual disturbance. Adolescents use alcohol and other drugs in ways that parallel drug use among adults and that may draw a good deal from adult models of recreational-social alcohol use.

Table 5-6.   The Context of Alcohol and Drug Use: High School Students

Situation	Percent of Alcohol Users Mentioning the Situation[a]	Percent of Marijuana Users Mentioning the Situation[b]
Parties or Dances	66	41
At a Small Gathering of Friends	56	40
Concerts, Movies	34	35
When Alone with Someone of the Opposite Sex	30	20
On Religious Occasions	22	na
On Dates	21	14
When There's Nothing to Do	19	21
Before Going to Sleep	4	5
Studying for Exams	2	3
Before Participation in Sports	2	3

[a]based on students who used alcohol (N = 1043 or 84 percent of all students).

[b]based on students who use marijuana (N = 595 or 48 percent of all students).

na = not applicable.

The social character of middle class drug use is also underscored by patterns in students' attitudes about various drugs. Table 5-7 presents high school students' responses to drug attitude measures and provides additional insight into these students' general orientations to alcohol and marijuana.[4] Although these students seem somewhat concerned about the physiological effects of these drugs, significant proportions feel that there are benefits to be derived from alcohol and marijuana. Most believe that alcohol and marijuana are worth trying, and over half agree that they can be relaxing or can make one feel good. The social utility of drugs is also emphasized by many respondents. Approximately 40 percent say that both alcohol and marijuana use can help one to be part of a group. In short, many of these high school students believe that alcohol and marijuana are worth trying and that drug use can provide several types of personal satisfaction.[5] Alcohol and marijuana can help one be part of a group (as is also true for adults), but this does not necessarily mean that drug use is the product of irresistible peer pressure. Correlations between this item and individual drug use are virtually zero (averaging about 0.01).

CONCLUSION

In light of these patterns, a leisure decisionmaking framework offers an attractive alternative to many familiar explanations of middle class drug use. We have already noted that there is little evidence that these students' drug use is accompanied by psychological maladjustment and that family pathology does not appear to be an important factor in this analysis. Instead, drug use is a popular activity among these students, is apparently social in character, and follows patterns that suggest that it is responsive to the types of considerations involved in leisure choices.

Table 5-7. **Attitudes About Alcohol and Marijuana: High School Students**

	Percent believing statement to be true for:	
	Alcohol[a]	Marijuana[b]
Worth Trying	75.5	61.9
Makes One Feel Good	56.8	61.4
Relaxing	50.8	53.8
Harmful	48.4	34.0
Addictive	46.3	19.5
Helps One to be Part of a Group	40.9	42.3
Use Leads to Guilt	13.2	18.0
Difficult to Get	5.6	6.6

[a]N's range from 1,192 to 1,219.

[b]N's range from 1,188 to 1,223.

Students' attitudes toward drugs indicate that leisure time can be invested in drug use in order to gain direct psychic satisfaction. A good portion of these respondents agree that alcohol and marijuana are relaxing or that they can make one feel good. These data also suggest that drug use can be a means to other forms of satisfaction such as group status. For example, many feel that alcohol or marijuana can help make one part of the group.

However, for drug use to facilitate sociability, proper techniques must be learned, and individuals must discover when different sorts of drug use are deemed appropriate. Both family members and peers can provide this sort of instruction, whether formally (e.g., direct coaching) or informally (e.g., through observation). Our data indicate that both groups have a role to play in adolescent drug use. Younger students seem more influenced by family factors than are older respondents (although comparisons must be made cautiously). Those whose siblings use drugs often have a greater chance of doing so themselves. Measures of the possible modeling impact of parents do little to alter these probabilities, but parent-child conflict (especially disobedience) systematically increases the likelihood of familiar types of drug use.

The overall influence of family variables seems weaker than that of peer measures, but this is not surprising within a leisure decision-making perspective that stresses the social character of adolescent drug use. Peers should be powerful predictors of drug decisions because of their role as coaches and as important actors in most drug use situations as well as because of the direct costs and benefits they offer. Parents may shape tastes indirectly (perhaps through modeling), but since they are less likely to be part of the social context of adolescent drug use, their major impact should be concentrated in the direct rewards or sanctions they provide. Of all the family variables in this analysis, those measuring parent-child conflict seem closest to reflecting possible rewards or sanctions.

The importance of peer predictors in this analysis does not necessarily mean that peer pressure as conventionally defined is responsible for adolescent drug use. Within a decisionmaking framework, friends can exert a number of types of influence. The social nature of the settings in which drugs are used tends to build in automatic associations between an individual's drug use and that of his or her peers. As noted earlier, these students often use drugs in group contexts where drinking or smoking marijuana is an adjunct to other activities (e.g., parties, dates, etc.). In such situations, drug use may be a basically incidental accompaniment to group interaction. Peers contribute to the informal shaping of individual tastes; they can also tutor one another in techniques of drug use and help identify inappropriate and appropriate use. Through peers one learns something of when drug use is acceptable and when it is not, and one refines one's understanding of its variably deviant character. Obviously, peers also reward drug use in direct ways (what one might conceptualize as peer pressure), but it is important to remember that not all adolescents endorse drug use and that peers can sanction as well as reward it. In other words, decisions about drug use may be influenced by the potential rewards peers offer, but this is by no means the only, or even the most influential, way in which peers work in the process.

The school variables in this analysis seldom exert as systematic an influence as peer or family items. Once again, schools seem to be important for the opportunity they afford for establishing peer groups rather than for possible pro- or antideviant influences of academic performance or school satisfaction *per se*. These variables do have some modest impact, but nothing like strain or subcultural theories of delinquency lead one to expect.

One of the main advantages of a leisure framework is that it does not assume that adolescent drug use is pathological or abnormal. These data support our earlier assumption that individuals who use drugs are not likely to be radically different from those who do not. In fact, use patterns for the most popular drugs (i.e., alcohol, marijuana) appear quite similar to those found among adults. This underscores the everyday nature of most middle class drug use and suggests that these students may be using alcohol and marijuana in many of the same ways and for many of the same reasons as adults. General age patterns are consistent with this interpretation. More serious drugs are least common among younger students and are not reported often enough even among high school students to suggest that a significant number have established regular patterns of use. Instead, serious drug use follows patterns with age that are consistent with experimentation. Once students try these drugs, find them relatively less satisfying than others, or learn that the benefits do not outweigh the costs, most seem to discontinue regular use. This does not seem to be true of alcohol, marijuana, or cigarettes. Use levels for these drugs increase steadily across age groups, and high school respondents seem to have established fairly stable patterns that most adults would find familiar. Older students who use both alcohol and marijuana do so in situations that parallel those of adult alcohol use. In short, there is little reason to think that the bulk of middle class students' drug use is prompted by unusual motivations or accompanied by unfamiliar desires.

So far we have seen that a leisure decisionmaking framework is consistent with patterns in middle class vandalism and drug use. There are other forms of delinquency that may also fit within this perspective. Minor theft is one of these, and in the following chapter we will extend a decisionmaking framework to the shoplifting and minor theft that these middle class students report.

NOTES

1. The categories in Table 5-2 represent fairly clear breaks in the marginal distributions of these items. In addition, the questions asked of fifth and sixth graders differentiate between the use of beer or wine and the use of hard liquor. Conversations with students and parents indicated that children are likely to try wine and beer with adult permission at family meals or religious ceremonies. Use of hard liquor is less likely to be encouraged in this legitimate fashion.

2. Regression analyses have been done on the less common forms of drug use, and while we do not report results here, the basic patterns are the same as those noted for amphetamines and barbiturates.

3. Slightly different models were constructed for fifth and sixth graders' cigarette use and other types of drug use, as Table 5-3 indicates.

4. Seventh and eighth graders were asked similar attitude questions. Basic patterns are similar, and for this reason, we have presented only the high school data here.

5. When asked to similarly evaluate the less popular drugs such as psychedelics, amphetamines, and barbiturates, more than three-quarters of the high school respondents believed these drugs to be dangerous and not worth trying. Hard drugs like these tend to be evaluated in a much more negative light than do popular drugs such as alcohol and marijuana.

✳ *Chapter Six*

Minor Theft and Leisure

INTRODUCTION

Shoplifting and other forms of minor theft have become topics of controversy in middle class communities. People recognize that children from good families and affluent neighborhoods are often involved in these activities yet find it difficult to explain why. It is hard to argue that affluent adolescents steal out of economic necessity, and this has led many people to favor theories ranging from psychoanalytically phrased accounts of individual pathology (e.g., kleptomania) to less clinical notions of boredom and thrill seeking.

Minor theft is also a favorite topic in delinquency research. Since it is among the most popular forms of adolescent deviance, self-report studies have taken it to be an important component of delinquency. Several theft scales can be found in the literature, and one of them has become a classic in delinquency research (Dentler and Monroe, 1961). Researchers often replicate theft studies using scales as originally developed, and measures of minor theft serve as important items in delinquency indexes. Questions about minor or major shoplifting are especially likely to be included in delinquency surveys.

This tendency to see minor theft as an integral part of general delinquency has meant that most researchers rely on familiar delinquency theories when explaining the behavior. With the exception of psychologically oriented theories of compulsive stealing, few explanations have been constructed of minor theft *per se*. Implicit in popular accounts of minor theft are standard assumptions about the nature of the tie between leisure and adolescent deviance: the risk involved in shoplifting or minor theft provides the excitement sought by bored adolescents. This reasoning is virtually identical to that noted for standard approaches to vandalism or drug use and encounters many of the same limitations as those outlined earlier. Models of thrill seeking or kicks are especially likely to be invoked to explain activities that appear senseless or irrational to the observer. Since most adolescents, particularly those from middle class backgrounds, do not really need to steal, their risk taking seems easiest to understand as a search for thrills or kicks. While this interpretation may have an element of truth, it produces an image of minor theft that emphasizes the potential arationality of the actor and limits its meaning to that of expressing frustration or boredom.

The irrational or compulsive image frequently attached to minor theft seems to stem from explanations that actors themselves give for their behavior. Individuals caught for shoplifting often have difficulty explaining their motives (I don't know why I did it; I just couldn't help myself), and the fact that they often have enough money in their pockets to pay for the merchandise makes their behavior seem especially mysterious. However, there are a number of alternative interpretations that do not require assumptions of irrationality. A statement that "I don't know why I did it" may be quite true, not because the actors do not know why they wanted the merchandise, but because in retrospect they cannot understand how they could have miscalculated the risk so radically. Having enough money to pay for stolen merchandise is no mystery if one assumes that resources are scarce. Spending money on merchandise that can be stolen is not an optimal allocation of scarce resources, all other things being equal. Finally, *post hoc* claims about compulsion or confusion may also provide the individual with a comforting way of reducing the dissonance created by a self-image as thief. Appeals to psychological urges remove the actor's responsibility and place it on forces beyond individual control.[1]

A leisure framework for minor theft offers an attractive alternative to images of arationality, boredom, or compulsion for several reasons. First of all it assumes that minor theft is just one of a variety of leisure options. Leisure is not automatically boring; thus it produces no inherent pressures toward thrill seeking or risk taking that are expressed through theft. Minor theft may be an exciting outlet for adolescents who are bored (i.e., it may be fun), but there are other factors besides boredom and recreation operating within a leisure context.

Initial experimentation with shoplifting can teach individuals a variety of skills that are useful in subsequent leisure investments. While middle class adolescents obviously do not need to steal to survive, they live in a consumption-oriented world. The affluence of American teenagers is considerable, and a number of delinquency theorists have suggested that a consumption ethic is the backbone of adolescent culture (see for example, Bernard, 1967; Coleman, 1961; Scott and Vaz, 1967). To participate effectively one must have the goods that are evidence of this consumption (i.e., records, clothing, entertainment). However, adolescents are generally dependent on adults for the money needed for this form of consumption. Parents' own resources are limited, and they can refuse to provide (or be unable to provide) the necessary money. In such a case adolescents may search for alternative sources of supply (e.g., "theft"). The general dependence on adults for money or resources may also give affluent adolescents other justifications for theft. Shoplifting may indicate that adolescents can acquire goods without taking money from their parents. In other words, it may show an ability to "purchase" goods without being dependent on parents and give one a chance to learn to take care of material needs on ones' own (one of the important characteristics of "maturity"). When seen in this light, shoplifting appears quite rational and can be a way of producing commodities that can be consumed or reinvested at a later point.

A number of skills are required for successful shoplifting and minor theft, many of which are likely to be learned from peers. These range from technique (e.g., coats with large inside pockets) to a knowledge of the formal and informal sanctions one can expect if detected. Peers are likely to pass on many of these things and thus to be an important component in the decisionmaking process around leisure-based theft. Peers also provide informal sanctions (both positive and negative) for theft, and the character and extent of these sanctions must be learned either by watching and listening or by active participation. Thus it should not be surprising that adolescents frequently shoplift in pairs or that small groups of adolescents are often involved in theft. Given this group character, peer management can be another skill learned in the process of leisure theft. However, it is important to emphasize that peers do not necessarily provide positive reinforcement for these activities. Not all adolescents admire shoplifters or endorse petty thievery. This means that there is variability in the extent to which peers support leisure-based theft and that they may be instrumental in deterring as well as promoting the activity.

Shoplifting can also be a useful way of testing the parameters of adult-imposed rules. It is obvious that while stealing is almost universally condemned, there are a number of situations in which it is likely to be considered normal operating procedure. For example, cheating on income taxes can be justified in a number of ways; picking up "lost" articles (e.g., a jacket left lying on a chair) or taking hotel towels isn't "really" stealing; gatecrashing at baseball games isn't much more than a prank. These exceptions to general prohibitions against theft are numerous and often subtle. To understand these subtleties, adolescents must learn to separate words from deeds. Much of this information can be reliably evaluated by actually trying various types of minor theft.

Obviously, most adolescents are aware of the potentially deviant character of theft, and the activity can also be chosen precisely because of this potential. Stealing on a dare is a good example of this, often underscored by explanations adolescents themselves provide for their shoplifting. Here theft assumes the nature of a game made more interesting because of the risk posed by its deviant nature. Theft as a game also gives experience in managing risk, danger, and excitement. Still, this does not necessarily make shoplifting or minor theft any more expressive or compulsive than other forms of competitive leisure activity. In fact, there is often little to distinguish competitive horsing around in a shopping center from the sorts of shoplifting that can take place at the same time and for many of the same reasons. They both supply similar types of utility that can be directly consumed (e.g., psychic outcomes such as fun or excitement) and may be chosen in light of many of the same considerations.

Overall, a leisure framework seems an attractive alternative to many of the most familiar explanations of minor theft. It gives the activity a meaning which is difficult to find in theories of compulsion or simple thrill seeking and allows for a fluid conception of adolescent theft which neither requires nor precludes its deviant potential. Theft can provide a way of learning subtle rules and also can be a skill which is invested to produce utility difficult for adolescents to gain in other ways.

BASIC DISTRIBUTION OF MINOR THEFT

Several measures of minor theft were included in each of our questionnaires. The questions concentrate on shoplifting, although older students were also asked about theft of school property or theft from peers. The distribution of responses to these items are presented in Table 6-1. (For the exact wording of these questions see Appendix B.) Shoplifting was the only minor theft topic asked of

Table 6-1. Marginal Distribution of Minor Theft[a]
(percent)

| | | *Minor Shoplifting (less than $5)* | | *Major Shoplifting ($5 or more)* | |
		Ever	*More than One or Two Times This Year*	*Ever*	*More than One or Two Times This Year*
Fifth and Sixth Graders	yes	26.1%	9.7%	yes 3.2%	2.1%
	no	73.9	90.3	no 96.8	97.9
	number reporting	100 (750)	100 (749)	100 (748)	100 (750)

		Minor Shoplifting (less than $5)	*Major Shoplifting ($5 or more)*	*Stole from a Student*
Seventh and Eighth Graders	Never	69.0%	87.6%	53.4%
	Once	14.9	4.3	18.9
	2-3	6.2	3.1	13.1
	4-5	2.7	1.2	4.3
	6+	7.3	3.8	10.2
	Number reporting	100 (825)	100 (812)	100 (831)

		Minor Shoplifting (less than $5)	*Major Shoplifting ($5 or more)*	*Stole from a Student*	*Stole School Property*
High School Students	Never	66.5%	86.2%	73.0%	72.4%
	Once	13.4	5.8	15.4	14.3
	2-3	11.9	4.0	7.6	9.7
	4-5	3.6	1.3	2.0	2.5
	6+	4.6	2.7	2.0	1.1
	Number reporting	100 (1230)	100 (1223)	100 (1229)	100 (1234)

[a]For exact wording of items see Appendix B.

elementary students. About a quarter have "ever" shoplifted something worth less than $5; fewer than 10 percent have done so more than once or twice in the last year. Only a handful report any experience with major shoplifting, particularly within the previous six months. While some of these percentages are small, shoplifting is still among the most common types of delinquency reported by fifth and sixth graders. For this reason, it is worth detailed examination.

Shoplifting is more popular among junior high respondents. About 30 percent have stolen something of minor value in the last six months, while close to 12 percent claim to have stolen something worth $5 or more. Seventh and eighth graders were also asked whether they had stolen anything from a fellow student. Almost half said that they had; approximately one-fourth had done so more than twice. High school students report approximately the same amount of shoplifting as seventh and eighth graders, but fewer older students steal from their peers. Only about a quarter claim to have done so in the last six months. High school respondents were also asked whether they had stolen school property. Over a quarter say they have taken something from school, although few have done so more than once.

Sex and Age Patterns in Minor Theft

These basic distributions indicate that minor theft, particularly shoplifting, is a common activity among these middle class students. The theft items were dichotomized and correlated with grade and sex in order to examine sex and age patterns in greater detail, and the results are quite intriguing. Theft from a fellow student is the only item to show the familiar curvilinear relationship with grade. The incidence of both minor and major shoplifting is virtually identical for junior and senior high respondents and suggests that this is one form of delinquency less open to maturational reform than most.

Shoplifting is often thought to be popular among girls as well as boys. Studies of shoplifting often concentrate on women (e.g., Cameroun, 1964), and studies of sex differences in delinquency generally find small differentials in self-reported shoplifting (e.g., Wise, 1967). This also seems true of these data. Most zero order correlations with sex are small in all three data sets, and several of the high school coefficients are negative (more girls report shoplifting than boys). Boys are slightly more likely to report major shoplifting, but the pattern is not a strong one ($r = 0.19$ in the junior high data). In short, shoplifting seems almost as popular among girls as it is among boys.

Sex differences are larger and more typical for other forms of minor theft. Boys are more likely to steal from fellow students ($r = 0.30$ in junior high; $r = 0.19$ in high school) and are more likely to report theft of school property ($r = 0.22$).

Minor Theft and Attitudes

Anger at parents or school officials are the only attitude variables in this survey that correlate meaningfully with minor theft. This is surprising since so many popular theories explain theft in terms of motives such as thrill seeking or the pathology of compulsive stealing. Anger at school officials or parents increases the chances that these students will report shoplifting. Coefficients average around 0.20 in both junior and senior high, and the generalized anger expressed by fifth and sixth graders is also positively correlated with shoplifting. The relationships are much the same for other forms of minor theft, suggesting that this is a pattern worth further study under (statistically) controlled conditions.[2]

The fact that feelings of boredom are not correlated with shoplifting or school theft suggests that a search for kicks may not be as important in these students' decisions to shoplift as stereotypes expect. The absence of correlations with feelings that are often associated with maladjustment (e.g., feelings of inferiority, efficacy, autonomy, persecution) also challenges the utility of explanations based on models of psychological illness.

Minor Theft and School Experiences

Several school variables appear as modest zero order correlates of minor theft. Among the strongest of these are measures of school performance and school satisfaction. High levels of both tend to decrease the frequency with which respondents report these theft items. Coefficients average around —0.10 to —0.20 across both junior and senior high respondents and across both school items. This relationship also does not vary much between general shoplifting and the kinds of minor theft that take place in a school context. Anger at school officials is the school variable with the largest zero order association with these minor theft items. Still the coefficients are not large, suggesting that school experiences do not have a strong impact on the probability of reporting minor theft.

Minor Theft and Family Situation

Many of the most familiar family variables cited in the delinquency literature fail to correlate with the minor forms of theft reported here. As was the case for vandalism and drug use, family structure variables do not differentiate between those students who report minor theft and those who do not. Children from broken homes are no more likely to have been involved in minor theft; neither are respondents whose mothers are employed outside the home. Measures of family rule structure or rule enforcement patterns are similarly unrelated to these items. Interestingly, students whose parents give them spending money (whether a token amount or a substantial allowance) are not substantially less likely to shoplift than other respondents. This implies that the psychic rewards of theft may be more important to these middle class students than the monetary value of the goods obtained.

The family measures that are meaningfully correlated with theft and shoplifting are those related to parent-child conflict. High school students who say they disobey their parents are more likely to report minor theft (rs averaging around 0.17); junior high students who report fighting with their parents as well as disobedience also report larger amounts of shoplifting and theft from fellow students. The same is true for fifth and sixth graders.

Minor Theft and Peers

Once again, peer variables are the strongest correlates with these delinquency items. The best of these reflect peer involvement in minor theft; peer experience with other types of delinquency seems to have less impact, especially for older students. This suggests that peer influence may be more activity-specific among older students than younger, a possibility that can be examined in greater detail under statistical controls. Other peer items included in this study failed to correlate meaningfully with shoplifting or minor theft. For example, formally organized peer groups such as sports teams or student organizations have little relationship to minor thefts.

REGRESSION ANALYSIS: MAJOR PREDICTORS OF SHOPLIFTING

The prediction equations for these minor theft items have been divided into two categories to make discussion easier—shoplifting and other forms of theft. The regression equations for shoplifting are presented in Tables 6-2 through 6-4. The best predictors of elementary students' shoplifting are sex, parent-child conflict, school performance, and measures of friends' delinquency.[3] Many of the same predictors alter the probability of recent shoplifting as well. Disobedience to parents and friends' shoplifting are especially likely to increase the chances of reporting shoplifting in the last six months.[4]

Anger at parents, disobedience, school satisfaction and performance, and friends' shoplifting or vandalism are the best predictors of minor shoplifting among junior high respondents. Seventh and eighth graders who are "almost always" angry at parents are almost 22 percent more likely to report minor shoplifting than those who are "never" angry (controlling for other variables in the equation). The total direct impact of disobedience exceeds 10 percent, and the impact of friends' shoplifting approaches 40 percent. Once controls are exercised, junior high girls are slightly more likely to report minor shoplifting than are boys.

Major shoplifting follows many of the same patterns. Friends' experiences are the best predictors of major shoplifting, and those respondents who report that "almost all" of their friends have shoplifted increase their own chances by more than sixty percentage points over those who estimate that "none" of their friends have ever done so. Boys are slightly more likely to report major shoplifting than are girls, but actual percentage differences are small (6 percent). Disobedience to parents and poor school performance tend to increase the probability of major shoplifting, although the impact of these variables is modest. The overall variance that these equations explain (24 to 34 percent) is quite good for survey research on delinquency.

High school students' shoplifting can also be predicted in familiar ways. Disobedience to parents can alter the probability of minor shoplifting by more than 10 percent. So can pressure to get good grades, as well as school performance. Again friends' shoplifting is the most powerful predictor in these equations and can change the likelihood of minor shoplifting by as much as 56 percent. There are, however, fewer meaningful predictors of major shoplifting. Anger at parents exerts a modest impact, as does anger at school officials. Otherwise no school or family factors have a major role to play in these high school equations. Almost all of the power is exerted by friends who have shoplifted.

There are several interesting coefficients in these high school equations that are too small to exert a substantive impact on probabilities of shoplifting but that are nonetheless worth some comment. Sex has a small negative coefficient for both major and minor shoplifting, indicating that girls and boys are about equally likely to have shoplifted in the last six months. Friends' general delinquencies seem to have relatively little impact on the shoplifting experiences reported by these high school students. Once the degree of friends' contact with shoplifting is entered into the equations, none of the other friends' delinquency measures alter probabilities in a substantively meaningful way.

REGRESSION ANALYSIS: MAJOR PREDICTORS OF MINOR THEFT

Questions about minor theft were asked only of junior and senior high respondents. There are only a few differences between the best predictors of these items and those of shoplifting. Sex is the most obvious of these. Girls are about as likely to report shoplifting as boys, but boys are more likely to report other forms of minor theft. This difference is largest among junior high students, approaching 20 percent in one case (theft from another student).

This probability of minor theft is also affected by anger at parents and school officials, degree of school satisfaction, and a variety of

Table 6-2.   Fifth and Sixth Grade Shoplifting and Minor Theft: Prediction Equations (N = 439)

	Minor Shoplifting		Minor Shoplifting More than One or Two Times This Year		Major Shoplifting		Major Shoplifting More than One or Two Times This Year	
R^2	0.258		0.218		0.309		0.289	
Intercept	0.065		-0.142		0.014		0.026	
Predictor Variables								
Sex	0.080[a] (0.037)[b] 2.144[c]	0.119[d]	0.048 (0.027) 1.760	0.101	0.027 (0.016) 1.702	0.100	0.008 (0.013) 0.616	0.046
Disobedience to Parents	0.063 (0.031) 2.037	0.264	0.105 (0.023) 4.647	0.354	-0.004 (0.013) 0.282	0.200	0.015 (0.011) 1.341	0.226
Fighting with Parents	0.050 (0.027) 1.843	0.234	0.041 (0.020) 2.073	0.244	0.035 (0.011) 3.098	0.244	0.009 (0.010) 0.948	0.163
Feelings of Anger	-0.008 (0.022) 1.140	0.112	0.006 (0.016) 0.346	0.139	0.006 (0.009) 0.670	0.123	-0.012 (0.008) 1.549	0.014
Amount of Spending Money	-0.008 (0.021) 0.374	0.066	0.188 (0.015) 1.224	0.131	0.015 (0.009) 1.702	0.170	0.033 (0.007) 4.460	0.279
School Performance	-0.032 (0.025) 1.276	-0.143	-0.006 (0.018) 0.316	-0.102	-0.031 (0.010) 2.983	-0.192	-0.025 (0.009) 2.828	-0.165
Friends' Major Shoplifting	0.044 (0.035) 1.264	0.328	0.047 (0.026) 1.843	0.308	0.088 (0.015) 5.991	0.477	0.048 (0.012) 3.893	0.426
Friends' Cigarette Use	0.120 (0.026) 4.505	0.452	0.038 (0.019) 1.974	0.333	-0.006 (0.011) 0.509	0.331	0.015 (0.009) 1.612	0.365
Friends' Marijuana Use	-0.012 (0.038) 0.300	0.341	-0.005 (0.028) 0.000	0.280	0.061 (0.016) 3.885	0.427	0.047 (0.013) 3.507	0.420
Friends' Alcohol Use	0.031 (0.022) 1.410	0.366	0.015 (0.016) 0.421	0.291	0.002 (0.009) 0.173	0.305	-0.005 (0.008) 0.591	0.285

| Friends' Vandalism | 0.024 (0.028) 0.848 | 0.328 | 0.007 (0.021) 0.355 | 0.268 | -0.016 (0.012) 1.341 | 0.310 | -0.011 (0.010) 1.095 | 0.300 |

[a] unstandardized slope (b).

[b] standard error.

[c] t value.

[d] zero order correlation coefficient.

VARIABLE CODING

Dependent Variables

Minor Shoplifting
Major Shoplifting
Minor Shoplifting More than Once or Twice This Year
Major Shoplifting More than Once or Twice This Year

   0 = no
   1 = yes

Predictor Variables

Sex
   0 = female
   1 = male
Disobedience to Parents
Fighting with Parents
   0 = not at all
   1 = a little
   2 = some
   3 = a lot
Feelings of Anger
   0 = never
   1 = hardly ever
   2 = sometimes
   3 = often
   4 = almost always

Amount of Spending Money (per week)
   0 = under $1.00
   1 = $1.00-$2.99
   2 = $3.00-$4.99
   3 = $5.00-$9.99
   4 = $10.00-$14.99
   5 = $15.00 or more
School Performance
   0 = far below average
   1 = below average
   2 = average
   3 = above average
   4 = far above average

Friends' Delinquency: Estimates of Involvement
   Friends' Major Shoplifting
   Friends' Cigarette Use
   Friends' Marijuana Use
   Friends' Alcohol Use
   Friends' Vandalism
      0 = none
      1 = one or two
      2 = some
      3 = most
      4 = all

Table 6-3. Seventh and Eighth Grade Shoplifting and Minor Theft: Prediction Equations (N = 595)

	Minor Shoplifting		Major Shoplifting		Theft From a Student	
R^2	0.239		0.339		0.230	
Intercept	0.163		−0.013		0.158	
Predictor Variables						
Sex	−0.016[a]	0.098[d]	0.062	0.190	0.197	0.305
	(0.038)[b]		(0.029)		(0.041)	
	0.435[c]		2.190		4.857	
Disobedience to Parents	0.034	0.261	0.048	0.262	0.023	0.211
	(0.030)		(0.022)		(0.031)	
	1.183		2.236		0.754	
Anger at Parents	0.054	0.250	0.005	0.166	0.039	0.179
	(0.021)		(0.016)		(0.022)	
	2.588		0.346		1.760	
Anger at School Officials	0.008	0.243	0.010	0.230	0.042	0.267
	(0.018)		(0.013)		(0.019)	
	0.469		0.748		2.190	
Pressure for Good Grades	0.004	0.159	−0.004	0.170	0.022	0.197
	(0.018)		(0.014)		(0.019)	
	0.244		0.282		1.131	
School Satisfaction	−0.046	−0.235	0.003	−0.199	−0.047	−0.246
	(0.023)		(0.017)		(0.025)	
	2.002		0.200		1.923	
School Performance	−0.035	−0.167	−0.043	−0.186	−0.012	−0.111
	(0.023)		(0.017)		(0.025)	
	1.486		2.463		0.479	
Friends' Major Shoplifting	0.096	0.409	0.151	0.544	0.024	0.285
	(0.021)		(0.016)		(0.023)	
	4.505		9.481		1.067	
Friends' Marijuana Use	−0.013	0.261	−0.012	0.275	−0.027	0.175
	(0.020)		(0.015)		(0.022)	
	0.655		0.774		1.224	
Friends' Alcohol Use	0.000	0.293	−0.017	0.300	0.000	0.247
	(0.021)		(0.016)		(0.023)	
	0.000		1.090		0.000	
Friends' Vandalism	0.077	0.398	0.043	0.444	0.095	0.388
	(0.020)		(0.015)		(0.021)	
	3.860		2.898		4.502	

[a]unstandardized slope (b).
[b]standard error.
[c]t value.
[d]zero order correlation coefficient.

VARIABLE CODING
Dependent Variables
   Minor Shoplifting
   Major Shoplifting
   Theft from a Student
      0 = not in the last six months
      1 = one or more times in the last six months

Table 6-3 continued

Predictor Variables

Sex	School Performance
0 = female	0 = far below average
1 = male	1 = below average
Disobedience to Parents	2 = average
0 = not at all	3 = above average
1 = a little	4 = far above average
2 = some	Friends' Delinquency: Estimates of Involvement
3 = a lot	Friends' Major Shoplifting
Anger at Parents	Friends' Marijuana Use
Anger at School Officials	Friends' Alcohol Use
0 = never	Friends' Vandalism
1 = hardly ever	0 = none
2 = sometimes	1 = one or two
3 = often	2 = some
4 = almost always	3 = most
Pressure for Good Grades	4 = all
School Satisfaction	
0 = not at all	
1 = a little	
2 = some	
3 = a lot	

friends' delinquencies including shoplifting, marijuana use, and vandalism.[5] Seventh and eighth graders who are "almost always" angry at their parents or at school officials increase their chances of this form of theft by sixteen percentage points, and those who report that "almost all" of their friends have vandalized are 38 percent more likely to have stolen something from another student than respondents with no friends who vandalize.

High school students' chances of stealing from peers are most strongly affected by sex, anger at school officials or parents, pressure from their parents to get good grades, and the number of their friends who have stolen from another student. The single strongest predictor is once again the friends' item: high school students who claim that "almost all" of their friends have stolen from peers are 76 percent more likely to report such activity themselves than those who have no friends who have done so. Interestingly enough, other types of friends' delinquency do not emerge as useful predictors under these controlled conditions. Neither friends' shoplifting, vandalism, or drug use affect the probability of stealing from another student.

High school students were also asked to estimate the number of times they had stolen school property in the last six months. Both disobedience to parents and anger at parents are useful predictors of school theft, but school experiences such as satisfaction, performance, or pressure for good grades are not. Again, the strongest

Table 6-4.   High School Shoplifting and Minor Theft: Prediction Equations (N = 826)

Predictor Variables	Minor Shoplifting	Major Shoplifting	Theft from a Student	Theft of School Property
R^2	0.164	0.164	0.306	0.302
Intercept	0.131	0.019	−0.102	−0.089
Sex	−0.036[a] (0.033)[b] 1.067[c] 0.043[d]	−0.003 (0.026) 0.141 −0.016	0.077 (0.029) 2.664 0.193	0.073 (0.030) 2.428 0.220
Disobedience to Parents	0.025 (0.025) 1.004 0.180	0.002 (0.019) 0.1 0.150	−0.005 (0.021) 0.264 0.137	0.040 (0.022) 1.843 0.178
Anger at Parents	0.062 (0.019) 3.193 0.204	0.030 (0.015) 1.972 0.151	0.036 (0.016) 2.190 0.186	0.018 (0.017) 1.090 0.108
Anger at School Officials	0.017 (0.017) 0.100 0.162	0.035 (0.013) 2.626 0.203	0.036 (0.014) 2.489 0.240	0.010 (0.015) 0.685 0.125
Pressure to Get Good Grades	−0.027 (0.017) 1.549 0.041	−0.015 (0.013) 1.140 0.040	0.044 (0.014) 3.033 0.179	0.017 (0.015) 1.122 0.090
School Satisfaction	−0.024 (0.019) 1.264 −0.146	0.021 (0.015) 1.378 −0.157	−0.005 (0.016) 0.316 −0.109	0.006 (0.017) 0.346 −0.080
School Performance	−0.034 (0.020) 1.702 −0.117	−0.020 (0.015) 1.264 −0.124	−0.022 (0.017) 1.264 −0.118	−0.017 (0.017) 0.989 −0.068
Friends' Parallel Delinquency Item	0.140 (0.021) 6.610 0.356	0.129 (0.015) 8.774 0.371	0.190 (0.016) 12.247 0.510	0.219 (0.106) 13.892 0.590
Friends' Major Shoplifting	0.012 (0.022) 0.519 0.269	e	0.013 (0.016) 0.768 0.254	0.003 (0.017) 0.173 0.216
Friends' Alcohol Use	−0.007 (0.013) 0.519 0.030	−0.002 (0.010) 0.200 0.038	−0.004 (0.011) 0.374 −0.015	0.005 (0.010) 0.387 −0.024

	b / (se) / t	r	b / (se) / t	r	b / (se) / t	r	b / (se) / t	r
Friends' Marijuana Use	0.009 (0.012) 0.787	0.055	0.003 (0.009) 0.316	0.043	−0.010 (0.010) 0.974	−0.027	−0.006 (0.010) 0.600	−.024
Friends' Vandalism (Minor Nonschool Damage)	−0.003 (0.017) 0.173	0.201	−0.008 (0.013) 0.616	0.187	0.015 (0.014) 1.086	0.288	0.012 (0.014) 0.830	0.277

[a] unstandardized slope (b).

[b] standard error.

[c] t value.

[d] zero order correlation coefficient.

[e] omitted to avoid duplication with parallel friends' predictor.

VARIABLE CODING

Dependent Variables
Minor Shoplifting
Major Shoplifting
Theft from a Student
Theft of School Property
 0 = not in the last six months
 1 = one or more times in the last six months

Predictor Variables
Sex
 0 = female
 1 = male
Disobedience to Parents
 0 = not at all
 1 = a little
 2 = some
 3 = a lot
Anger at Parents
Anger at School Officials
 0 = never
 1 = hardly ever
 2 = sometimes
 3 = often
 4 = almost always

Pressure to get Good Grades
School Satisfaction
 0 = not at all
 1 = a little
 2 = some
 3 = a lot
School Performance
 0 = far below average
 1 = below average
 2 = average
 3 = above average
 4 = far above average

Friends' Delinquency: Estimates of Involvement
 Friends' Minor Shoplifting
 Friends' Major Shoplifting
 Friends' Theft from a Student
 Friends' Theft of School Property
 Friends' Alcohol Use
 Friends' Minor Nonschool Damage
  0 = none
  1 = one or two
  2 = some
  3 = most
  4 = all

single predictor of school theft is the degree of friends' involvement in similar activities. Other friends' general delinquency items exert a negligible impact in this regression equation. The minimal effect of school experiences here is somewhat puzzling, since one might expect such activity to be linked to performance or general school satisfaction. It would be easy to characterize the theft of minor items from in and around school as a response to negative experiences. However, even at the zero order level, these items are not highly correlated. Not even anger at school officials significantly alters chances of reporting theft of school property.

SUMMARY AND CONCLUSIONS

Shoplifting follows basic patterns that are quite similar to those noted for other types of middle class delinquency. The generally small sex differences suggest that shoplifting is popular among both boys and girls. Attitudes other than anger do not differentiate between those with a high or low probability of reporting shoplifting. This challenges the adequacy of individual maladjustment theories. Peer variables are generally the most powerful predictors in these equations, although their impact relative to family and school items seems to vary between age groups. Parent-child conflict exerts an apparently stronger influence on fifth and sixth graders' shoplifting than on the shoplifting reported by older students, and the same appears true for school variables such as satisfaction and performance.

There is also a modest age difference in the patterns followed by important peer predictors. There is little evidence that shoplifting requires the support of strongly delinquent peers, although peer influence seems somewhat more diffuse among younger respondents. In the case of elementary students, there are several friends' predictors that are almost as powerful as friends' shoplifting itself (i.e., friends' cigarette use, drinking, and vandalism). There are only two meaningful peer predictors in the junior high data (friends' shoplifting and vandalism), while friends' shoplifting is generally the only important peer variable in the high school equations. It is difficult to know how many of these differences are due to differences in the items used in the three data sets, but the peer context for shoplifting does seem more activity-specific among older students than among younger.

With the exception of an occasional sex difference, patterns in minor theft are similar to those for shoplifting. Once again, the most useful predictors are estimates of peers' delinquency. The predictive power of peer variables is more activity-specific for older students than for younger, and family and school experiences seem to have a stronger impact on younger respondents. Again, it is difficult to know the extent to which these differences reflect differences between the data sets rather than actual patterns, but they seem sufficiently systematic to suggest that there are age differences in the relative weight of family, school, and peer factors on decisions about minor theft.

The overall patterns in Tables 6-2 through 6-4 point to several important characteristics of middle class theft. They seldom fit well with the most popular explanations offered for the activity. For theories of compulsive stealing to be useful here, measures of attitudes and psychic outlook should be a prominent part of this analysis. Although several such items were included in the study, they fail to predict either minor theft or shoplifting. Anger at parents or school officials can increase the probability of minor theft, but the absence of other attitude predictors makes it difficult to argue that this anger is evidence of the maladjustment stressed by popular psychogenic theories. Boredom and general disaffection should operate as predictors if theft can be understood primarily as a search for thrills or kicks. Yet neither of these items is a systematic component of these equations.

A leisure explanation is an interesting alternative for these patterns. For example, shoplifting shows few sex differences under controlled conditions and is best predicted by item-specific peer measures. This is one activity readily available to both boys and girls, and both sexes may have ample leisure opportunities for shoplifting. Given similar chances, both boys and girls may choose shoplifting.

The importance of peer variables in this analysis is again consistent with a leisure model that assumes that peers are an important reference point for opportunities for leisure deviance and as a source of costs and benefits for minor theft. The causal links between peer variables and self-reports are complex, and this suggests caution in concluding that peers pressure their friends into deviance. Peers provide both costs and benefits for theft, and it would be a mistake to assume that all peers endorse minor theft or shoplifting. Those respondents who have few friends involved in shoplifting are less likely to be involved themselves. This may be because they lack opportunities to shoplift (which are often structured by peer relationships); it may also reflect a deterrent impact. Without friends who shoplift, individuals may encounter fewer rewards for theft or learn fewer skills that make theft a viable option. The relatively activity-specific nature of best peer predictors (especially for older students) suggests that peers can structure opportunities for shop-lifting as well as provide direct costs and benefits. To the extent that peers are an important structural element in theft one would expect the extent of peer involvement to be a powerful predictor. Measures of friends' general deviance should be less useful since they are less likely to reflect the situational importance of peers in activities like minor theft that often have a peer group as an important prerequisite for the behavior.

As a leisure framework predicts, peer variables are better predic-tors of theft than are school or family measures. Leisure theft is likely to take place in situations where peers may be an important element in decisionmaking, but where parents or school authorities have no direct role to play. The fact that school and family variables are better predictors in the elementary and junior high data than in the high school data is also consistent with a leisure perspective. School actors and family members should be a relatively more important source of costs and benefits for deviance among younger children whose peer contacts are somewhat more restricted. As children age, peers should assume greater importance in leisure decisions.

The fact that the incidence of shoplifting does not show a strong curvilinear relationship with age suggests that many respondents find it so rewarding that they tend to routinize their initial experimenta-tion. In other words, shoplifting may provide a good deal of utility, perhaps by making it possible to obtain goods that may be otherwise unavailable. Adolescents' financial resources are limited, and this may encourage the expenditure of (leisure) time rather than money in the acquisition of goods. Once the skills and orientations necessary for successful theft are learned, it is an apparently popular form of leisure investment. At the same time, this does not mean that adolescents are driven to shoplift. The majority have not stolen anything during the prior six months, and the rather small amount of money involved in most shoplifting or theft has strong parallels to normal adult theft such as cheating on taxes or lifting hotel towels.

Overall, a leisure framework that focuses on individual decision-making offers a useful way of understanding the minor theft reported by these affluent adolescents. There are a number of similarities in the patterns of minor theft and those noted for the vandalism and drug use items analyzed in earlier chapters. This suggests that a leisure model may be applicable to a number of different forms of minor deviance or delinquency. Its applicability to less common and less typical delinquent activities is an issue we will investigate in the next chapter.

NOTES

1. For a detailed discussion of this issue, see Cameroun (1964).

2. As always, the causal relationships between attitudes and behavior are difficult to specify. Positive correlations between anger and minor theft should not be taken as proof that anger causes theft, since it is obvious that the causal direction could conceivably go the opposite way as well.

3. The equations for the elementary students should be interpreted cautiously because of the relatively small number of fifth and sixth graders who claim experience with major shoplifting and minor shoplifting more than once or twice. They are included here in order to make comparisons across the full age range.

4. Again, the causal direction between these items is ambiguous, and it should be stressed that the predictive strength of these items is no absolute assurance of a direct causal impact on minor theft or shoplifting.

5. There are some intercept values in these tables that are below zero (for example, less than —0.10) that could create some difficulties in use of a linear probability model. The data are coded in such a way that the intercept reflects the probability of minor theft when scoring 0 in all predictors simultaneously. Fortunately, the negative probabilities reported here do not pose a serious difficulty for interpretations since there are not likely to be any individuals who actually score 0 on all of the predictors included in these equations. In other words, empirical configurations of these predictors are likely to produce probabilities that are larger than zero.

✳ *Chapter Seven*

The Leisure Context of
Serious Delinquency

INTRODUCTION

Delinquency researchers seldom expect middle class adolescents to be involved in serious forms of delinquency. In
part this is a reflection of class stereotypes about deviant
behavior. Activities such as gang fighting, assault, violence, and
serious theft are important components of popular images of delinquency but are generally thought to characterize the behavior of
lower class gang youths. Since the causes of this delinquency are
sought in the daily experiences of lower class life (e.g., family
structure, strains), there is usually little reason to think that middle
class adolescents would be involved in these activities.

However, this *West Side Story* picture of lower class delinquency
is difficult to establish empirically. Popular images may stress the
often violent and predatory nature of delinquency, but self-report
research finds that the bulk of even lower class delinquency is
incidental and small scale. Few adolescents of any class seem heavily
involved in serious delinquency, and it is rare to find self-report data
that identify more than a handful of respondents with extensive
experience in serious delinquency. The exact proportions of adolescents involved in such activities are often difficult to establish
because of researchers' tendency to combine measures into summary
scales (and then to divide serious from nonserious delinquents along
some rather arbitrary cutting point), but the incidence of serious
delinquent activities seems small in most noninstitutionalized adolescent populations.

147

Serious forms of delinquency are generally divided into two categories—property crimes (e.g., auto theft, grand larceny, breaking and entering) and serious interpersonal conflict (often violent; e.g., assault, gang fighting). Questions about property delinquency are easier to ask than those about interpersonal violence and can be interpreted in a more straightforward manner. Items such as, Have you ever threatened to beat up someone if they didn't do what you told them, or Have you ever been in a serious fight, are familiar measures of interpersonal violence or assault in self-report research. However, it is difficult to know whether such items measure predatory assault or mundane forms of playground conflict. We will analyze items of this type in our chapter on noncrime delinquency, since the response patterns for these items are more consistent with expectations about modest interpersonal conflict than the personal violence usually thought to characterize serious delinquency. In this chapter we will focus on bike theft, theft of auto accessories, auto theft, and breaking and entering.

Since the literature generally assumes that middle class delinquency is confined to minor forms of deviance, it provides little guidance about what patterns to expect in this analysis. Beyond broadly phrased comments about psychological maladjustment or a search for kicks that might motivate delinquency, there are few clues about which factors should be related to serious delinquency. Our discussion will center on the issue of whether a leisure model can be profitably extended to the serious types of delinquency analyzed in this chapter.

BASIC DISTRIBUTION OF
SERIOUS DELINQUENCY

Fifth and sixth graders were asked only one question that falls within our category of serious delinquency. We expected few elementary students to have experience with serious delinquency and so chose to concentrate on minor delinquency in this age group. To check this assumption, we asked one question about bike theft, a type of serious delinquency that they may have encountered more often than most others. As the distribution of their responses shows, few fifth and sixth graders have ever stolen a bicycle, and less than 1 percent have done so in the last six months (Table 7-1). These proportions are so small that further analysis is difficult. For this reason, the rest of the chapter will be devoted solely to the responses of junior and senior high students. (For exact wording of these items see Appendix B.)

Table 7-1. Marginal Distribution of Serious Delinquency[a]
(percent)

			Bike Theft	
		Ever	*More than One or Two Times This Year*	
Fifth and Sixth	yes	1.5%	0.9%	
Graders	no	98.5	99.1	
		100	100	
	number reporting	(746)	(746)	

		Bike Theft	*Theft of Auto Accessories*	*Breaking Entering*	*Auto Theft*
Seventh and Eighth Graders	Never	95.6%	91.5%	95.3%	97.5%
	Once	2.7	4.1	3.6	1.1
	2-3	0.6	1.3	0.6	0.2
	4-5	0.2	1.0	0.1	0.1
	6+	0.8	2.1	0.4	1.1
	Number	100	100	100	100
	Reporting	(825)	(827)	(816)	(824)

		Bike Theft	*Theft of Auto Accessories*	*Breaking and Entering*	*Auto Theft*
High School Students	Never	95.4%	94.6%	95.1%	98.7%
	Once	2.9	2.7	2.8	0.8
	2-3	0.8	1.0	1.5	0.2
	4-5	0.3	0.7	0.3	0
	6+	0.5	1.0	0.3	0.3
	Number	100	100	100	100
	Reporting	(1240)	(1231)	(1219)	(1229)

[a]Exact wording of items can be found in Appendix B.

Serious delinquency is somewhat more common among junior high students, although only a handful report more than one or two incidents in the last six months. Fewer than 10 percent say that they have stolen auto accessories, and under 5 percent report bike theft, auto theft, or breaking and entering. While this is a small proportion of the total group, the actual numbers are nontrivial. The 8 percent who report theft of auto accessories represents approximately sixty-six students; about twenty respondents claim to have stolen a car in the last six months. In a community of the size studied here, this is probably a meaningful number of individuals.

The proportions of high school students involved in these more serious delinquencies is similar to that of seventh and eighth graders. Fewer than 5 percent report any single activity, but again this probably represents a nontrivial number of students in a community of this size. About sixty-five high school students say that they have stolen auto accessories in the last six months, while sixty report at least one incident of breaking and entering, and about sixteen say that they have stolen a car. When these numbers are combined with those in the junior high data, almost one hundred and twenty of this community's students claim to have stolen auto accessories, and about thirty-five report car theft.[1] Although the extreme skewness of these distributions poses some problems for further analysis, absolute numbers of this size suggest that a more detailed investigation of patterns in these items is worthwhile.[2]

Age and Sex Patterns in Serious Delinquency

Each of the items in Table 7-1 was dichotomized into "never" and "once or more" and correlated with school, family, and peer variables. Despite highly skewed marginal distributions, several interesting patterns appear with sufficient regularity to suggest that they reflect reliable characteristics in serious delinquency.

One of these is the relationship between serious delinquency and sex. Popular images lead one to expect activities such as auto theft, bike theft, or breaking and entering to be an almost exclusively male activity. Although these middle class boys are more likely to report serious delinquencies than girls, sex differences in these items are small.[3] The correlation coefficients between these items and sex range from 0.14 to 0.22 in junior high and average about 0.12 in the high school data. One usually expects larger coefficients on the basis of popular stereotypes, but it appears that for these middle class students such expectations are misplaced. These correlations reflect absolute differences that average around 5 percent. For example, 7 percent of the junior high boys report breaking and entering compared to 2 percent of the girls, and 7 percent of the high school boys say they have stolen a bike compared to 1 percent of the girls. Sex differences are largest for theft of auto accessories, which is reported by 14 percent of the junior high boys and 9 percent of the high school boys but by less than 3 percent of the girls in either age group.

A comparison of the basic distributions of response between junior and senior high students shows that the incidence of serious delinquency does not vary substantially between these two age groups. Correlation coefficients with grade are also negligible. Unlike minor forms of delinquency outlined earlier, these items do not appear to be cuvilinearly related to grade level. Few respondents of any age are likely to report serious delinquency. However, it is well to remember that the incidence of these activities is so low that large age differences are unlikely.

Serious Delinquency and Attitudes

Serious delinquency often appears both threatening and inexplicable to the general public, and this makes explanations based on theories of individual pathology especially appealing. Given familiar maladjustment assumptions, one might expect these items to be associated with measures of respondents' attitudes and feelings. However, measures of serious delinquency are not meaningfully related to the attitude and adjustment items included in this survey. Even measures of anger at parents or school officials fail to correlate with serious delinquency at levels similar to those observed for other types of minor delinquency. Seldom do anger coefficients exceed 0.15, and in the high school data, the average correlation between anger at school officials and the serious delinquency items averages about 0.15. With associations of this magnitude, it is difficult to argue that strongly phrased theories of individual pathology are useful accounts of these patterns.

Serious Delinquency and
Family Experiences

The absence of meaningful associations between these items and familiar measures of family structure or organization should no longer be a surprise to the reader. These factors are frequently invoked to explain serious delinquency, usually under the assumption that they lead to the individual pathology thought to motivate committed delinquents. This does not appear to be true in this case. Measures of broken homes, working mothers, or permissive rule enforcement do little to separate students who report serious delinquency from those who do not. At the same time, the measures of family conflict that do correlate with minor forms of delinquency are less strongly associated with serious delinquency than with the minor forms outlined in earlier chapters. Fighting with parents shows no systematic relationship to these items at either grade level, and disobedience works in the familiar fashion only among junior high respondents. Neither measure of parent-child conflict is substantively correlated with high school students' serious delinquency. Whatever the forces operating to affect probabilities of serious delinquency, these family experiences do not seem as important as stereotypes lead one to expect.[4]

Serious Delinquency and
School Experiences

Of the school variables included in this analysis, only performance and satisfaction emerge as systematic correlates of serious delinquency. Systematic may be a bit strong a term, since these coefficients tend to be lower than those observed for the minor types of delinquency analyzed in previous chapters. This is especially true of the high school data, where even school performance does not systematically distinguish between students who report serious delinquency and those who do not.

Serious Delinquency and Peers

After so many null relationships, it is reassuring to discover that serious delinquency is correlated with friends' delinquency in familiar ways. Were it not for the direction and magnitude of these associations, one might suspect that absence of relationships to attitudes, family, or school variables was due solely to the limited variability in the dependent variables. The fact that they correlate with friends' measures is at least modest evidence that the data pattern in interpretable, meaningful ways.

Junior high students with friends who vandalize, shoplift, or drink are more likely to report serious delinquency. Correlation coefficients among these items are relatively high, especially in the case of friends' vandalism and friends' major shoplifting. (They average at about 0.30, which is typical of this form of delinquency research.) The parallel friends' items in the high school data tend to be even more strongly associated with these serious delinquency measures. Bike theft and friends' bike theft correlate at 0.36; breaking and entering with friends' breaking and entering at 0.42; friends' theft of auto accessories with auto accessories at 0.56; and auto theft with friends' auto theft at 0.32. Coupled with the levels of intercorrelation among the serious delinquency items themselves, which are again typical of self-report research, these coefficients suggest that these data are tied to friends' delinquency in familiar ways.

REGRESSION ANALYSIS: SERIOUS DELINQUENCY

The simultaneous impact of the correlates described above differs somewhat from the zero order relationships. In order to outline these patterns, the measures of serious delinquency were dichotomized and regressed on those variables that are substantively meaningful predictors of at least one form of serious delinquency (Tables 7-2 and 7-3).[5]

Bike Theft

Bike theft is among the most frequently reported forms of serious delinquency. Seventh and eighth graders' bike theft is best predicted by school performance and the number of their friends who have shoplifted (the one friends' theft predictor available for this age group). Boys are more likely to report bike theft than girls, although actual probability differences are small (around five percentage points). Under statistical controls, there are no family items that exert a meaningful impact in these equations.

There are only two important predictors of bike theft among high school students—school performance, whose total probability impact is barely greater than 10 percent, and the extent of friends' bike theft. There are no other measures of friends' delinquency that predict the activity with assurance once friends' bike theft is controlled.

These equations explain relatively small amounts of total variance in bike theft. R^2 values for both junior and senior high respondents average 0.15. R^2s of this magnitude are to be expected, since relatively few respondents claim to have stolen a bike in the last six months. This is likely to attenuate any correlations in the data, reducing the amount of variance that can be explained in a regression analysis.

Theft of Auto Accessories

Almost 10 percent of the junior high students say that they have stolen auto accessories during the last six months; so do almost 5 percent of the high school students. Among the best predictors of junior high responses are disobedience to parents, poor academic performance, and friends' vandalism. This is again the most useful predictor in this equation. Friends' vandalism can alter the probability of theft of auto accessories by as much as twenty-four percentage points; none of the other general friends' deviance items included here exert a meaningful impact on this probability.

The pattern of predictors for high school students is simpler than this. When comparable variables are included in the regression equation, the only item to show a meaningful influence on the likelihood of theft of auto parts is the number of friends who have been involved in the same activity. This item-specific peer variable seems to have an important impact on the amount of variance explained in these regression equations since the R^2 value is substantially higher in the high school analysis than in the junior high, which lacks an item-specific predictor.

Breaking and Entering

Breaking and entering is difficult to predict in either the junior or senior high data. School performance has a small impact on its

Table 7-2.   Seventh and Eighth Grade Serious Delinquency: Prediction Equations (N = 646)

	Bike Theft	Breaking and Entering	Theft of Auto Accessories	Auto Theft
R^2	0.134	0.117	0.192	0.081
Intercept	0.064	0.028	-0.051	-0.010
Predictor Variables				
Sex	0.051[a] (0.018)[b] 0.185[d] 2.771[c]	0.042 (0.020) 0.143 2.073	0.076 (0.023) 0.220 3.286	0.048 (0.016) 0.157 3.082
Disobedience to Parents	0.010 (0.013) 0.151 0.741	0.025 (0.015) 0.153 1.673	0.039 (0.017) 0.222 2.345	0.016 (0.011) 0.122 1.414
Anger at School Officials	0.008 (0.009) 0.172 0.927	-0.001 (0.010) 0.112 0.141	0.022 (0.011) 0.242 2.049	0.004 (0.007) 0.101 0.489
School Performance	-0.035 (0.012) -0.176 3.016	-0.030 (0.013) -0.135 2.302	-0.031 (0.015) -0.148 2.097	-0.020 (0.010) -0.111 2.024
School Satisfaction	-0.017 (0.011) -0.205 1.506	0.004 (0.013) -0.114 0.331	-0.003 (0.014) -0.188 0.173	0.009 (0.010) -0.077 1.014
Friends' Major Shoplifting	0.033 (0.010) 0.283 3.255	0.045 (0.011) 0.285 3.949	0.019 (0.013) 0.295 1.506	0.028 (0.009) 0.224 3.357
Friends' Vandalism	0.016 (0.010) 0.270 1.673	0.030 (0.011) 0.274 2.756	0.060 (0.012) 0.383 4.806	0.011 (0.008) 0.205 1.378
Friends' Alcohol Use	0.000 (0.009) 0.205 0.000	-0.015 (0.010) 0.144 1.516	0.002 (0.011) 0.247 0.173	-0.009 (0.007) 0.111 1.264

[a] unstandardized slope (b).
[b] standard error.
[c] t value.
[d] zero order correlation coefficient.

VARIABLE CODING

Dependent Variables
Bike Theft
Breaking and Entering
Theft of Auto Accessories
Auto Theft
  0 = not in the last six months
  1 = one or more times in the last six months

Predictor Variables
Sex
  0 = female
  1 = male
Disobedience to Parents
  0 = not at all
  1 = a little
  2 = some
  3 = a lot
Angry at School Officials
  0 = never
  1 = hardly ever
  2 = sometimes
  3 = often
  4 = almost always

School Performance
  0 = far below average
  1 = below average
  2 = average
  3 = above average
  4 = far above average
School Satisfaction
  0 = not at all
  1 = a little
  2 = some
  3 = a lot
Friends' Delinquency: Estimates of Involvement
Friends' Major Shoplifting
Friends' Vandalism
Friends' Alcohol Use
  0 = none
  1 = one or two
  2 = some
  3 = most
  4 = all

Table 7-3.   High School Serious Delinquency: Prediction Equations (N = 988)

Predictor Variables	Bike Theft		Breaking and Entering		Theft of Auto Accessories		Auto Theft	
R^2	0.156		0.191		0.333		0.127	
Intercept	0.022		−0.011		−0.071		−0.029	
Sex	0.032[a] (0.014)[b] 2.302[c]	0.151[d]	0.025 (0.015) 1.673	0.127	0.056 (0.013) 4.159	0.191	0.015 (0.008) 1.843	0.059
Disobedience to Parents	0.005 (0.010) 0.519	0.109	0.000 (0.011) 0.000	0.108	0.005 (0.010) 0.479	0.124	0.012 (0.006) 2.044	0.095
Anger at School Officials	0.023 (0.007) 0.458	0.121	0.013 (0.008) 1.643	0.131	0.015 (0.007) 2.121	0.180	0.016 (0.004) 3.754	0.155
School Performance	−0.027 (0.008) 3.361	−0.177	0.008 (0.009) 0.927	−0.101	−0.002 (0.008) 0.458	−0.118	−0.001 (0.005) 0.264	−0.072
Friends' Delinquency Parallel Item	0.087 (0.011) 8.246	0.363	0.151 (0.013) 11.545	0.423	0.165 (0.010) 16.754	0.560	0.109 (0.011) 10.242	0.321
Friends' Major Shoplifting	0.000 (0.008) 0.000	0.199	−0.007 (0.009) 0.781	0.202	−0.005 (0.008) 0.360	0.266	−0.005 (0.005) 0.921	0.077
Friends' Vandalism (Damage to Private Property)	0.013 (0.007) 1.949	0.220	0.015 (0.007) 1.974	0.228	0.010 (0.007) 1.612	0.300	−0.008 (0.004) 1.870	0.041
Friends' Alcohol Use	0.004 (0.005) 0.964	0.080	0.001 (0.005) 0.316	0.058	−0.001 (0.005) 0.223	0.057	−0.002 (0.003) 0.959	0.016

[a] unstandardized slope (b).
[b] standard error.
[c] t value.
[d] zero order correlation coefficient.

VARIABLE CODING
Dependent Variables
Bike Theft
Breaking and Entering
Theft of Auto Accessories
Auto Theft
0 = not in the last six months
1 = one or more times in the last six months

Predictor Variables
Sex
0 = female
1 = male
Disobedience to Parents
0 = not at all
1 = a little
2 = some
3 = a lot
Anger at School Officials
0 = never
1 = hardly ever
2 = sometimes
3 = often
4 = almost always

School Performance
0 = far below average
1 = below average
2 = average
3 = above average
4 = far above average
Friends' Delinquency: Estimates of Involvement
Friends' Bike Theft
Friends' Breaking and Entering
Friends' Theft of Auto Accessories
Friends' Auto Theft
Friends' Major Shoplifting
Friends' Damage to Private Property
Friends' Alcohol Use
0 = none
1 = one or two
2 = some
3 = most
4 = all

probability among seventh and eighth graders, but peer's delinquency exerts the strongest impact on the chances of breaking and entering. Both friends' shoplifting and vandalism alter the probability of breaking and entering by more than ten percentage points for younger students. However, the only predictor in the high school equation to have a substantively meaningful impact is the parallel measure of friends' delinquency. Respondents who claim that "almost all" of their friends have some experience in breaking and entering are 60 percent more likely to have done so themselves than those respondents who have no such friends. The R^2 values for these equations reflect the general difficulty in predicting breaking and entering. Only 12 percent of the variance in the junior high reports is explained by these predictors; 19 percent for high school students. Again, this is not surprising given the limited variability in these dependent variables.

Auto Theft

So few of these students report auto theft that it is difficult to derive much information from a regression analysis. There are no really strong predictors in the seventh and eighth grade equation. Friends' major shoplifting is the best, altering the probability of auto theft by somewhat more than 10 percent. Much the same is true for the high school equation, only this time it is the extent of friends' experiences with auto theft that exerts the only meaningful predictive impact. Family or school predictors do little to alter probabilities of auto theft. Given the limited variability in this item, it seems best not to place too much emphasis on any of these single predictors.

SUMMARY AND CONCLUSION

Although serious delinquency is relatively rare among these middle class students, there are some interesting patterns that are similar to those observed for the minor forms of delinquency. Sex differences in serious delinquency are smaller than popular stereotypes lead one to expect. This suggests that serious delinquency is not likely to be motivated by masculinity anxiety, nor is it likely to be the expression of manly virility that the literature frequently assumes. In addition, serious delinquency does not seem to be closely linked to individual pathology. The ties between serious delinquency and attitude or adjustment measures are no stronger than those that were found for adjustment and minor delinquency.

Family and school predictors exert a greater impact on the serious delinquency reported by seventh and eighth graders than on that reported by high school students. This is again similar to patterns observed in earlier chapters. Peer predictors also operate in ways that readers should find quite familiar. For older students, the only systematic peer predictors are those measures that parallel the type of delinquency under study. Younger students show somewhat more generalized peer influence, but peers' overall impact seems no stronger than found in the analyses of minor delinquencies. There is little evidence that serious delinquency occurs within a peer context that is radically different from that noted in other forms of leisure deviance. This is important, since serious delinquency is often taken as evidence of a strong commitment to a general delinquent lifestyle that is peer generated and defined. Were this the case, peer pressure should be strongest for more serious types of delinquency. However, there is little evidence of this sort of relationship in these equations. The fact that the best peer predictors of serious delinquency are activity-specific is further evidence that even serious delinquencies do not require the presence of an influential peer group strongly committed to general delinquency.

There are some differences between serious and minor forms of delinquency that need to be noted. The most obvious is one of frequency. Serious delinquency is relatively less frequent than the minor activities analyzed in previous chapters. Popular images of serious deviance stress its allegedly atypical character. This often leads to assumptions that serious delinquency is an activity limited to atypical or abnormal adolescents. These abnormalities include psychological maladjustment (compulsion, innate aggressiveness) or unusual peer or family situations. Since such abnormalities are relatively rare in any adolescent population, the incidence of serious delinquency linked to these abnormalities should also be low. The difficulty with this explanation for the low incidence of serious delinquency is that it assumes that it is quite different from minor delinquency and that it requires a unique explanatory model (i.e., individual abnormality). A leisure framework does not require a special model of individual behavior to explain why serious delinquency is relatively rare. If one assumes that serious delinquency is more risky than minor delinquency, it should be more costly (all other things being equal). This means it should be chosen less often than other potentially delinquent activities. Yet individuals may still choose serious delinquency in much the same way that other leisure choices are made. The patterns in this analysis suggest that the processes underlying these choices resemble those for minor delinquency. What may differ are the relative costs and benefits attached to each or differences in tastes that make serious delinquency relatively less attractive leisure option.

The fairly stable age patterns are consistent with what one would expect for higher risk choices. There are minor forms of delinquency that show fairly stable rates across age cohorts (i.e., shoplifting) but at a consistently higher level than is found for more serious delinquency. Earlier we argued that this stability suggested that adolescents could be reinvesting skills in leisure activities that were likely to provide goods unavailable in other ways. The stable but lower incidence of serious delinquency suggests experimentation rather than consistent investment in serious delinquency. Since the costs attached to serious delinquency are relatively high, one may learn that things like stealing autos just aren't worth it (i.e., do not provide sufficient utility). This would reduce the likelihood of reinvestment and limit the frequency with which such activities occur.

Still, it does not seem that the skills learned in serious delinquency need to be formally different than those learned through investing in minor forms of potentially deviant activity. During serious delinquency one can learn mastery of risky situations (including peers as co-actors or necessary prerequisites) as well as useful social skills. This is consistent with the power of peer predictors in these equations. One could also learn the boundaries of permissible behavior, although the potentially deviant character of serious delinquency would seem to be less ambiguous than that of minor activities. If less ambiguous, there is less reason to test the borders of rules through direct experience. This too could reduce the frequency with which serious delinquency is chosen without relying on a unique model of the individual in order to explain why serious forms of delinquency are relatively rare.

In sum, we would argue that the similarities in patterning between minor and major forms of delinquency suggest that a leisure decisionmaking framework can be profitably applied to both. The basic patterns in these prediction equations follow those noted in earlier chapters, and this is additional evidence that the data on serious delinquency are accurate reflections of behavior in spite of their relatively limited variability. The major difference between serious and minor forms of delinquency is not in how they pattern but in their baseline frequency. A decisionmaking framework that stresses relative costs and benefits can account for frequency differences quite well. Those (serious) delinquencies with higher costs should be chosen less often than others, but the choice process seems to follow the basic principles common to the bulk of leisure decisions.

NOTES

1. These absolute numbers would likely be higher were it not for the sampling done in the tenth and twelfth grades. Of course this does not mean that there were this many actual incidents of serious delinquency in the community, since these activities are generally group based. The same incident could be reported by more than one individual.

2. Although relatively few of these students report serious forms of delinquent activity, these data seem consistent with the incidence of such activities found in other self-report studies. Direct comparisons to other research are difficult since our measures reflect estimates within the last six months rather than more conventional time frames of one year or the respondent's lifetime. Still, the data seem consistent with what one would expect based on information provided by Wise (1967), Short and Nye (1958), and Stinchcombe (1964), among others, and there is little reason to think that these middle class students report markedly lower rates of serious delinquency than most other adolescents.

3. Obviously, the generally low incidence of involvement in serious delinquency makes large percentage differences between the sexes unlikely.

4. Other studies seem to indicate that family factors do affect serious delinquency, but this may be due to the different ways in which delinquency is operationalized or different class composition of samples. Since most of these analyses are based on indexes composed of both minor and serious forms of delinquency, a division of respondents into more and less delinquent does not necessarily mean that those who are more delinquent are significantly more involved in the type of serious activities outlined here. They may be more delinquent by virtue of more persistent or frequent involvement in minor forms of delinquency. This is likely, given the fact that most summary delinquency indexes (the most familiar kind—weighted indexes are less common) are based on a greater number of minor components than major. When total experiences are measured in this way, family factors that predict minor infractions may also differentiate between more and less serious delinquents.

5. The skewness of most of these distributions poses a problem for standard regression analysis. We outlined these difficulties in Chapter 3, but they are worth noting again. In order to see whether the skewness affects the basic outlines of our conclusions we analyzed high school students' responses with a weighted least squares regression procedure that adjusts for the problem of heteroskedasticity.

Comparison of these findings with OLS regression turned up no substantively meaningful differences, so we have chosen to present OLS regression results here. This makes it more convenient to compare patterns in this chapter with those found in other chapters.

6. There are several other ways of accounting for lower frequency, but most are less appealing than these based on a leisure framework. For example, one might argue that serious delinquency is less frequent because opportunities for serious delinquency are more limited than those for other activities. In part this may be true, but if one considers the types of serious activities examined here, it is difficult to argue that opportunities *per se* are radically different. There are autos everywhere from which one can steal hubcaps, just as there are numerous targets for vandalism; breaking and entering is a loose term for a variety of activities that might more accurately be characterized as trespassing. This is especially true given the wording of the items we have used here.

❋ Chapter Eight

Leisure and Noncrime Delinquency

INTRODUCTION

So far, all of the potentially delinquent activities we have analyzed could be classified as crimes. Individuals of any age could be legally prosecuted for these actions, and while their seriousness varies widely (e.g., defacement of property *versus* auto theft), they are united by the fact that they are against the law. There are other activities that many researchers include in studies of delinquency that are either (1) problem behaviors not strictly illegal or (2) status offenses—activities that are illegal only for children. We have included several of these in this study and in this chapter will examine patterns in fighting with other students, threatening peers, cheating on tests, truancy, and running away from home.

As noted earlier, these are usually defined as delinquency under the assumption that they are the precursors of crime. This image of predelinquency or precrime is the justification for their place in most delinquency analyses. Our reason for including them in this study is related to our interest in a leisure rather than a crime model of delinquency. Activities such as ditching school or conflict among peers may be as much a part of this complex of leisure behavior as the more potentially delinquent activities outlined in previous chapters. In order to examine this possibility, we will analyze patterns in these noncriminal activities and note whether they can be predicted in the same fashion as other measures of delinquency or whether other models are required to explain the patterns they follow.

Since most delinquency studies use questions about peer conflict (fighting, threatening one another) as measures of serious interpersonal violence, some explanation for their inclusion in our noncrime category is in order. As noted in Chapter 7, it is always difficult to interpret responses to questions such as these since one never knows whether they reflect assault within a rather narrow definition of the term or more informal conflict among peers. The patterns observed here suggest that these measures are not likely to reflect serious forms of interpersonal violence. Instead of assigning them to the conventional category of serious delinquency, it seems better to include them in an analysis of delinquencies that would not even qualify as crime. The reasons for this decision should become clear in the course of the analysis.

BASIC DISTRIBUTION OF
NONCRIME DELINQUENCY

Table 8-1 presents the marginal response distributions for the items included in our noncrime category. (For exact wording of these items see Appendix B.) Several of these are among the most frequently reported of all questions examined thus far. Even fifth and sixth graders have a good deal of experience with noncrime delinquency. Forty-five percent say they have "ever" fought with another student, and twenty-one percent report ever cheating on a test at school. Truancy or running away from home is much less common: under 5 percent of the elementary respondents admit to these activities.

Almost a quarter of the junior high respondents report that they have been in a serious fight with another student during the last school year. Almost half claim to have threatened another student during that same time period. Truancy is also more common than it is among younger students: over 20 percent claim to have ditched school at least once in the prior six months. A large proportion of these junior high students have cheated on a test during that same time period.

Fewer high school students appear to be involved in the kind of peer conflict that breaks out into fistfights (15 percent), but cheating is widespread. Only 17 percent say that they have not cheated during the current school year. Unfortunately, the innovative organization of class time in this particular school made it impossible to ask high school students about truancy. However, about 12 percent claim to have run away from home at some point in their lives.

Table 8-1. Marginal Distribution of Noncrime Delinquency[a]
(percent)

		Fighting with Another Student		*Cheating on a Test*		*Truancy*		*Run Away from Home*
		Ever	*More than One or Two Times This Year*	*Ever*	*More than One or Two Times This Year*	*Ever*	*More than One or Two Times This Year*	*Ever*
Fifth	yes	45.4%	31.4%	20.7%	13.9%	5.2%	2.1%	2.7%
and	no	6	68.6	79.3	86.1	94.8	97.9	97.3
Sixth	number	100	100	100	100	100	100	100
Graders	reporting	(749)	(748)	(744)	(747)	(748)	(749)	(728)

		Fighting with Another Student	*Threatening a Student*	*Cheating on a Test*	*Truancy*
Seventh and Eighth	never	73.1%	52.5%	24.4%	78.8%
Graders	once	16.2	19.2	17.0	11.8
	2-3 times	6.2	11.2	30.4	3.8
	4-5 times	1.9	4.3	10.9	3.2
	6+ times	2.6	11.6	14.5	3.1
	number reporting	100	100	100	100
		(821)	(832)	(807)	(819)

		Fighting with Another Student	*Cheating on a Test*	*Times Ever Run Away from Home*
High School	never	85.0%	16.9%	88.4%
Students	once	9.0	9.2	8.5
	2-3 times	4.3	26.5	2.5
	4-5 times	0.9	17.2	1.0
	6+ times	0.8	30.3	1.3
	number reporting	100	100	100
		(1223)	(1232)	(1225)

[a]Exact wording of items can be found in Appendix B.

Sex and Age Patterns in
Noncrime Delinquency

Peer conflict variables (fighting and threatening) have the highest correlations with sex of any type of delinquency in this analysis. Coefficients range from 0.30 (elementary students' fighting) to 0.42 (junior high students' threatening), making boys substantially more likely to report peer conflict than girls. (These coefficients reflect sex differences in percentages ranging from 20-45 percent.) Sex differences are smaller in the high school data, but boys are still more likely to report these forms of peer conflict.

The opposite is true of sex differences in school deviance (cheating and truancy). Girls are generally more likely to report these activities than boys. Although these sex differences are small, they are worth noting because they run in a direction opposite to conventional expectations. Atypical patterns also appear in the correlation between sex and running away from home. Despite strong stereotypes that running away from home is a favorite female form of delinquency, boys are slightly more likely to report this item.

Minor forms of delinquency are usually expected to be related to age in a curvilinear fashion. This appears to be true of the types of peer conflict examined here, but the incidence of school-related delinquency increases with the age of these respondents. High school students cheat more frequently than seventh and eighth graders; junior high students are more likely to be truant than elementary respondents. Age patterns in running away from home are difficult to isolate because of the history effect built into the measure.

Noncrime Delinquency and Attitudes

Interpersonal conflict is one form of delinquency that is often expected to be associated with feelings of aggression and anger. These data are generally consistent with these expectations. Fifth and sixth graders who are "angry" are more likely to report fighting ($r = 0.20$), junior high respondents who are angry at school officials report higher incidence of both threatening another student and fighting (rs of 0.25, 0.19), and high school students who are angry report higher levels of fighting ($r = 0.16$). However, other measures of attitudes or individual adjustment (including anger at parents) are not meaningfully correlated with interpersonal conflict.[1]

Cheating and truancy are also positively associated with feelings of anger. These correlations are strongest in the junior high data. High school students who have run away from home at some point in their lives are more likely to report anger at parents than those who have not ($r = 0.20$). While other measures of attitudes or world views correlate with these items in familiar directions, they seldom do so at levels that suggest that they will be important predictors of noncrime delinquency under controlled conditions.

Noncrime Delinquency and
Family Factors

Traditional family structure variables (broken homes, working mothers, etc.) do not differentiate between students who report noncrime delinquency and those who do not. However, measures of parent-child conflict are often positively correlated with cheating, truancy, and fighting with other students. These associations are small in the elementary school data but reach substantively meaningful levels among junior and senior high respondents. Disobedience is the most systematic parent-child conflict correlate, although actual levels of association are modest. For example, disobedience is positively correlated with running away from home ($r = 0.14$ in elementary school; $r = 0.18$ in high school) and so is fighting with parents ($r = 0.26$ in high school). The familiar direction of these associations suggests that family conflict may have a modest role to play in noncrime delinquency, although the causal direction here is obviously difficult to establish with certainty.

Noncrime Delinquency and School Experiences

Since cheating and truancy are often assumed to indicate dissatisfaction with school, one might expect them to be systematically related to measures of school experiences. Items such as school performance or satisfaction are associated in expected directions, but seldom at anticipated levels. For example, fifth and sixth graders who have cheated or ditched school are somewhat more likely to report below average academic performance (rs averaging around -0.15) and to be dissatisfied with school (rs between -0.17 and -0.05). However, performance is only slightly related to these items in the junior high data (rs of -0.06 and -0.13), and zero order associations with satisfaction are only marginally higher (rs of -0.13 and -0.23). Neither performance or satisfaction is meaningfully related to the cheating that high school students report, and only anger at school officials reaches the systematic levels of association with school delinquency that one expects.

School experiences exert a similarly modest impact on interpersonal conflict. Junior high respondents who are dissatisfied with school are somewhat more likely to report fistfighting or threatening other students; anger at school officials operates in much the same way. However, neither of these items is a particularly useful correlate of the fighting that high school students report.

Noncrime Delinquency and Peers

The strongest correlates to appear in this analysis are those that measure friends' delinquency. For example, elementary respondents whose friends have vandalized report higher levels of cheating ($r = 0.26$) and truancy ($r = 0.24$) and are more likely to have run away from home ($r = 0.20$). Correlations with the number of friends who have tried marijuana are somewhat higher. Although modest, these levels of association do suggest that friends' experiences may help specify patterns in noncrime delinquency among fifth and sixth graders.

Friends' delinquency items are somewhat more strongly correlated with the noncrime delinquency reported by junior high respondents. Friends' vandalism is the most systematic of these. Estimates of friends' delinquency are also positively related to the incidence of noncrime delinquency among high school students. For example, estimates of friends' fighting are correlated with respondents' self-reports at 0.46. The absence of parallel items for cheating or running away makes it more difficult to identify strong peer correlates for these forms of noncrime delinquency.

In order to trace the simultaneous impact of these zero order correlates, measures of noncrime delinquency were dichotomized and regressed on important predictors according to the procedures followed in earlier chapters. To make discussion easier, we will divide the noncrime delinquency items into (1) measures of school-related noncrime delinquency, (2) measures of interpersonal conflict, and (3) a measure of family-related noncrime delinquency (i.e., running away from home) and deal with each in turn. Equations for each of these variable sets are presented in Tables 8-2 through 8-4.

NONCRIME DELINQUENCY IN A
SCHOOL CONTEXT

Cheating on a test is one of the most commonly reported types of delinquency included in this study. Even fifth and sixth graders report enough cheating to make a regression analysis of their estimates truly viable. Among the best predictors of fifth and sixth graders' reports are disobedience to parents, actual school performance, school satisfaction, and the extent of their friends' contact with shoplifting, alcohol use, and vandalism. Disobedience alters the probability of having ever cheated on a test by over 30 percent; the extent of friends' shoplifting can also change probabilities by almost thirty percentage points. School satisfaction exerts a substantive impact on cheating, and girls are slightly more likely to cheat than boys. (However, the sex difference under statistical controls does not exceed 10 percent.) Many of these same variables are also meaningful predictors of recent cheating (more than once or twice in the last year).

Anger at parents or school officials and peers' deviance (vandalism and alcohol use) are the best predictors of cheating among junior high respondents. No school or family variables other than anger

Table 8-2. Fifth and Sixth Grade Noncrime Delinquency: Prediction Equations (N = 479)

	Fought with Student		Fought with Student More than One or Two Times This Year		Ever Cheat on Test		Cheat More than One or Two Times This Year	
R^2	0.148		0.117		0.162		0.201	
Intercept	0.219		0.055		0.227		0.332	
Predictor Variables								
Sex	0.267[a] (0.043)[b] 6.131[c]	0.304[d]	0.196 (0.041) 4.753	0.244	-0.055 (0.035) 1.549	-0.059	-0.085 (0.029) 2.949	-0.059
Disobedience to Parents	0.000 (0.033) 0.000	0.088	0.028 (0.031) 0.894	0.121	0.079 (0.027) 2.932	0.244	0.090 (0.022) 4.086	0.268
Feelings of Anger	0.087 (0.025) 3.449	0.196	0.080 (0.024) 3.331	0.187	0.008 (0.021) 0.400	0.121	-0.045 (0.017) 2.666	0.004
School Performance	-0.033 (0.029) 1.131	-0.097	-0.040 (0.028) 1.449	-0.106	-0.042 (0.024) 1.777	-0.144	-0.039 (0.019) 1.905	-0.166
School Satisfaction	-0.016 (0.027) 0.600	-0.113	0.018 (0.026) 0.707	-0.056	-0.042 (0.022) 1.897	-0.165	-0.072 (0.018) 3.974	-0.235
Friends' Vandalism	0.042 (0.031) 1.371	0.202	0.051 (0.029) 1.740	0.198	0.026 (0.025) 1.034	0.256	0.028 (0.021) 1.378	0.258
Friends' Shoplifting	0.016 (0.037) 0.435	0.155	0.029 (0.035) 0.824	0.161	0.070 (0.030) 2.355	0.285	0.056 (0.024) 2.315	0.281
Friends' Alcohol Use	0.025 (0.021) 1.140	0.168	0.000 (0.020) 0.000	0.124	0.060 (0.017) 3.494	0.293	0.042 (0.014) 2.004	0.260

[a] unstandardized slope (b).
[b] standard error.
[c] t value.
[d] zero order correlation coefficient.

Predictor Variables	Truancy		Truancy More than One or Two Times This Year		Run Away from Home	
R^2	0.109		0.107		0.073	
Intercept	0.057		0.067		0.052	
Sex	-0.028 (0.020) 1.378	-0.012	-0.020 (0.015) 1.378	-0.015	0.009 (0.012) 0.721	0.075
Disobedience to Parents	0.027 (0.015) 1.816	0.174	0.034 (0.011) 3.162	0.202	0.018 (0.009) 1.897	0.138
Feelings of Anger	-0.006 (0.011) 0.479	0.048	-0.021 (0.008) 2.469	-0.033	-0.009 (0.007) 1.319	-0.003
School Performance	-0.029 (0.013) 2.121	-0.133	-0.012 (0.010) 1.224	-0.114	-0.007 (0.008) 0.888	-0.102
School Satisfaction	0.007 (0.012) 0.574	-0.050	-0.010 (0.010) 1.140	-0.105	-0.015 (0.008) 1.951	-0.141
Friends' Vandalism	0.024 (0.014) 1.700	0.238	0.019 (0.010) 1.854	0.223	0.017 (0.009) 1.964	0.203
Friends' Shoplifting	0.045 (0.017) 2.705	0.266	0.029 (0.012) 2.345	0.239	0.019 (0.010) 1.838	0.195
Friends' Alcohol Use	0.017 (0.010) 18.220	0.209	0.005 (0.007) 0.728	0.153	-0.004 (0.006) 0.640	0.087

Table 8-2 continued

VARIABLE CODING

Dependent Variables

Ever Fought with a Student
Ever Cheated on a Test
Ever Truant
Ever Run Away from Home
Fought with a Student More than Once or Twice This Year
Cheated on a Test More than Once or Twice This Year
Truant More than Once or Twice This Year

   0 = no
   1 = yes

Predictor Variables

Sex

   0 = female
   1 = male

Disobedience to Parents

   0 = not at all
   1 = a little
   2 = some
   3 = a lot

Feelings of Anger

   0 = never
   1 = hardly ever
   2 = sometimes
   3 = often
   4 = almost always

School Performance

   0 = far below average
   1 = below average
   2 = average
   3 = above average
   4 = far above average

School Satisfaction

   0 = not at all
   1 = a little
   2 = some
   3 = a lot

Friends' Delinquency: Estimates of Involvement

   Friends' Vandalism
   Friends' Shoplifting
   Friends' Alcohol Use

   0 = none
   1 = one or two
   2 = some
   3 = most
   4 = all

Table 8-3. Seventh and Eighth Grade Noncrime Delinquency: Prediction Equations (N = 641)

	Threatened a Student		Serious Fight with Student		Cheated on a Test		Truancy	
R^2	0.257		0.115		0.109		0.230	
Intercept	0.199		0.048		0.518		-0.075	
Predictor Variables								
Sex	0.370[a] (0.036)[b] 10.099[c]	0.423[d]	0.155 (0.036) 4.242	0.224	-0.089 (0.033) 2.664	-0.057	-0.013 (0.031) 0.424	0.088
Disobedience to Parents	0.012 (0.029) 0.412	0.144	0.036 (0.029) 1.236	0.154	-0.003 (0.026) 0.141	0.152	0.020 (0.025) 0.787	0.232
Anger at Parents	0.015 (0.021) 0.721	0.089	0.012 (0.021) 0.565	0.102	0.058 (0.019) 3.082	0.234	0.031 (0.018) 1.752	0.232
Anger at School Officials	0.060 (0.018) 3.391	0.247	0.033 (0.018) 1.897	0.189	0.036 (0.016) 2.213	0.220	0.037 (0.015) 2.428	0.299
School Performance	-0.053 (0.023) 2.323	-0.137	-0.021 (0.023) 0.927	-0.088	0.000 (0.021) 0.000	-0.058	-0.027 (0.020) 1.341	-0.131
Friends' Vandalism	0.058 (0.020) 2.949	0.328	0.055 (0.020) 2.787	0.271	0.034 (0.018) 1.897	0.198	0.060 (0.017) 3.507	0.383
Friends' Major Shoplifting	0.026 (0.020) 1.264	0.239	0.025 (0.020) 1.236	0.211	0.002 (0.019) 0.141	0.169	0.029 (0.018) 1.612	0.340
Friends' Alcohol Use	-0.019 (0.018) 1.224	0.197	-0.011 (0.018) 0.785	0.167	0.043 (0.016) 2.666	0.232	0.070 (0.015) 4.582	0.398

[a] unstandardized slope (b).

[b] standard error.

[c] t value.

[d] zero order correlation coefficient.

VARIABLE CODING

Dependent Variables

Threatened a Student
Fought with a Student
Cheated on a Test
Truant
    0 = not in the last six months
    1 = one or more times in the last six months

Predictor Variables

Sex
    0 = female
    1 = male
Disobedience to Parents
    0 = not at all
    1 = a little
    2 = some
    3 = a lot
Anger at Parents
Anger at School Officials
    0 = never
    1 = hardly ever
    2 = sometimes
    3 = often
    4 = almost always

School Performance
    0 = far below average
    1 = below average
    2 = average
    3 = above average
    4 = far above average
Friends' Delinquency: Estimates of Involvement
Friends' Vandalism
Friends' Major Shoplifting
Friends' Alcohol Use
    0 = none
    1 = one or two
    2 = some
    3 = most
    4 = all

Table 8-4.   High School Noncrime Delinquency: Prediction Equations (N = 973)

	Fought With a Student		Cheated on a Test		Ever Run Away from Home	
R^2	0.232		0.057		0.094	
Intercept	0.045		0.844		0.036	
Predictor Variables						
Sex	0.044[a] (0.023)[b] 1.897[c]	0.156[d]	−0.108 (0.023) 4.582	−0.137	0.000 (0.022) 0.000	0.000
Disobedience to Parents	0.008 (0.017) 0.476	0.083	−0.011 (0.018) 0.774	0.062	0.021 (0.017) 1.264	0.181
Fighting with Parents	0.021 (0.017) 1.264	0.083	0.002 (0.017) 0.141	0.820	0.075 (0.016) 4.722	0.261
Anger at Parents	−0.026 (0.015) 1.743	0.040	0.015 (0.015) 1.024	0.115	0.009 (0.014) 0.547	0.196
Anger at School Officials	0.026 (0.012) 2.190	0.157	0.031 (0.012) 2.626	0.140	0.001 (0.011) 0.100	0.099
School Performance	−0.018 (0.013) 1.378	−0.097	−0.018 (0.013) 1.303	0.070	−0.038 (0.013) 2.983	0.152
Friends' Fighting	0.184 (0.013) 14.560	0.457	0.021 (0.013) 1.702	0.079	0.028 (0.012) 2.258	0.142
Friends' Vandalism (Damage to Private Property)	−0.042 (0.011) 3.714	0.062	0.005 (0.011) 0.447	0.072	0.002 (0.011) 0.173	0.093
Friends' Shoplifting	0.000 (0.013) 0.000	0.099	0.026 (0.014) 1.923	0.127	0.009 (0.013) 0.748	0.117
Friends' Alcohol Use	0.002 (0.008) 0.300	0.040	−0.005 (0.008) 0.632	0.010	0.003 (0.007) 0.458	0.064

[a]unstandardized slope (b).

[b]standard error.

[c]t value.

[d]zero order correlation coefficient.

VARIABLE CODING
Dependent Variables
    Fought with a Student
    Cheated on a Test
        0 = not in the last six months
        1 = one or more times in the last six months
    Run Away from Home
        0 = never
        1 = one or more times (lifetime)

Table 8-4 continued

Predictor Variables	
Sex	School Performance
0 = female	0 = far below average
1 = male	1 = below average
Disobedience to Parents	2 = average
Fighting with Parents	3 = above average
0 = not at all	4 = far above average
1 = a little	Friends' Delinquency: Estimates of Involvement
2 = some	Friends' Fighting with a Student
3 = a lot	Friends' Damage to Private Property
Anger at Parents	Friends' Shoplifting
Anger at School Officials	Friends' Alcohol Use
0 = never	0 = none
1 = hardly ever	1 = one or two
2 = sometimes	2 = some
3 = often	3 = most
4 = almost always	4 = all

affect these probabilities in a substantively important fashion. Girls are slightly more likely than boys to say that they have cheated during the last six months ($r = -0.089$). Although cheating is more common among high school students, the only noteworthy predictors in the high school equations are sex ($r = -0.108$) and anger at school officials. The impact of peer variables is small, and the model in Table 8-4 explains little variation in the cheating reported by these older students (less than 6 percent of the total variance). R^2 values for similar models in the junior high and elementary school data are also small, suggesting that variance in cheating is difficult to explain with the predictors available here.[2]

Overall, patterns in fifth and sixth graders' truancy are similar to those of cheating. Among the best predictors of elementary students' truancy are disobedience to parents, school performance, and friends' delinquencies such as vandalism or shoplifting. The most powerful of these (friends' shoplifting) alters the probability of reporting truancy by as much as eighteen percentage points. Girls are a bit more likely to report truancy than boys under statistical controls, although the probability difference between the two groups is quite small.

The variables most likely to affect the probabilities of seventh and eighth graders' truancy are anger at parents or school officials, friends' vandalism, and friends' alcohol use. School performance exerts a total impact that barely exceeds ten percentage points; the same is true of friends' shoplifting. Students who are "almost always" angry at school officials increase their chances of truancy by almost fifteen points over students who are "never" angry; anger at parents alters the chances of truancy by as much as twelve percent. These equations to a better job of predicting truancy than cheating: The R^2 value for truancy (in the junior high data) reaches a level of 0.23.

The configuration of variables that predict noncrime delinquency within a school context is an interesting one. In spite of strong stereotypes, girls are consistently more likely than boys to report cheating and truancy when statistical controls are applied. Actual sex differences are small, but given the popular belief that boys are more delinquent than girls, this consistency is worth noting. Active disobedience to parents increases the probability of younger respondent's cheating or truancy, but seems to have little impact on the school-related delinquency reported by older age groups. Aside from anger at parents, there are few family predictors that alter the probabilities of cheating or truancy in all three data sets.

More surprising is the poor predictive power of school experiences in these equations. Anger at school officials alters the probabilities of cheating or truancy in a consistent fashion, but other school factors that might logically affect these items do not have much predictive strength. Poor school performance tends to increase chances of cheating or truancy, but has less influence than one might expect. General school satisfaction, pressure to perform well, educational aspirations, or expectations do little to help one understand patterns in these school-related delinquencies. The strongest predictors are again measures of friends' delinquency, but their impact is smaller for high school respondents than for younger age groups.

The overall patterns noted for truancy are quite similar to those found for other minor forms of delinquency in early chapters (i.e., modest sex differences, primacy of peer predictors) and suggest that this activity that fits a leisure framework fairly well. Truancy is often a group phenomenon, and this could make peers both a necessary prerequisite for some types of truancy and an important source of reinforcement or sanctions for the activity. Poor school performance and anger at school officials are experiences that can affect the cost-benefit balance if one assumes that those who are doing poorly have less to lose from truancy than those who are doing well in school. These variables do have modest predictive power for seventh and eighth graders.

The patterns in cheating are less familiar and require some comment. Although peer variables exert some impact on the probability of cheating (mainly for younger cohorts of students), their impact is much smaller than that found for most other types of delinquency. The weak predictive power of school variables other than anger at school authorities is also puzzling. Logically, poor school performance should be related to cheating, but correlations are not strong even at the zero order level. These weak ties could be explained in several ways. Since cheating is widespread among this group of students, it may not have sufficient variation for strong patterns to appear in a correlation and regression analysis. When one considers the number of chances that students have to cheat over a six month period, performance or satisfaction may not differentiate between those who have cheated and those who have not. Similarly, if cheating is a commonplace occurrence among adolescents, the deviant experiences of peers may have relatively little impact on individual decisions to cheat; if everyone does it, peer experiences are a virtual constant and thus have little predictive power. Still, this does pose some difficulties for the leisure model that we have been applying to patterns in middle class delinquency. Cheating may be one activity that fits this model less well than most others.

NONCRIME DELINQUENCY: PEER CONFLICT

Peer conflict is a fairly common experience among students of all ages. Boys are especially likely to report that they have fought with another student or threatened to beat up someone. Among fifth and sixth graders, the best predictors of fighting are sex, feelings of anger, school performance, and friends' vandalism. The percentage impact of these variables is often impressive: boys are 27 percent more likely to report fighting than are girls (under these controls), and generalized anger can increase chances of "ever" fighting by as much as thirty-five percentage points. Students who claim that "almost all" of their friends have vandalized are 17 percent more likely to have fought frequently than those with no friends who have vandalized.

Many of these same predictors appear in the junior high equations. Sex continues to be a major factor in the incidence of fighting or threatening (differences of 37 percent and 16 percent respectively), and anger at school officials also increases the chances of peer conflict. One of the strongest predictors in these equations is friends' vandalism. The probability of fighting or threatening someone can change by as much as twenty-two percentage points depending on how many of ones' friends have damaged property.

Large sex differences in the incidence of peer conflict disappear in the high school data. Under the controls exerted here, high school boys are only about four percentage points more likely to report fighting than are girls. Anger at parents or school officials has a modest effect on probabilities, but their total influence barely exceeds 10 percent. General peer deviance (i.e., vandalism) appears to have a weaker impact in the high school equations than in those for younger students. Item-specific friends' measures alter probabilities in a meaningful fashion (e.g., estimates of friends' fighting can alter probabilities of fighting by as much as 74 percent), but the impact of other friends' items is rather small and occasionally negative (i.e., friends' vandalism).

These are familiar patterns, quite similar to those noted for the types of delinquency examined in previous chapters. This implies that these items reflect everyday sorts of peer conflict rather than predatory assault. There is little in these equations to suggest that fighting or threatening follow patterns that are markedly different from other types of leisure-based delinquency and both seem responsive to many of the important considerations in leisure decisionmaking. Peers should be useful predictors of fighting and threatening because (1) they are obvious prerequisites for the activity and (2) they are an important audience for the activity. Fighting and threatening can be part of learning mastery over peers, since they involve manipulating others (bullying and intimidation are obvious forms of manipulation) or learning how to effectively respond to others' attempts at manipulation. These types of peer conflict may also contribute to the development of status hierarchies among peers, although one must be careful not to assume that high prestige goes hand in hand with fighting or bullying. Some peers are likely to censure fighting, others to endorse it. These direct costs and benefits supplied by peers can also be an important element in decision-making.

There is some evidence that sex differences are larger for these personal conflict items than for most other forms of minor delinquency, particularly among junior high students. This would tend to support familiar assumptions that boys are more given to interpersonal aggression than girls (a difference that can be thought of as taste rather than innate aggressive drives). However, such a conclusion should be made cautiously and tempered by the fact that there are only minor sex differences for older age groups. If boys and girls have different opportunities for fighting or threatening, sex differences could appear quite apart from any sex-role-linked tendency toward personal conflict or aggression.

NONCRIME DELINQUENCY: RUNNING
AWAY FROM HOME

Running away is a common status offense, and even in this middle class sample, a good many students claim to have run away from home at some point in their lives. Students were asked to estimate the number of times they had "ever" run away from home, and this introduces more severe problems with temporal sequencing than encountered in most of the delinquency measures examined thus far.[3] Still, there are several patterns worth cautious comment.

Researchers frequently characterize running away from home as a uniquely female form of delinquency. This picture is generally drawn on the basis of official statistics that indicate that this is one offense common to girls (see, for example, Adler, 1975; Konopka, 1966; Cowie et al., 1966). In this light, associations with sex are quite interesting. There appear to be few sex differences at the zero order level, although boys are somewhat more likely to report running away. Once best predictor equations have been constructed and factors such as parent-child conflict, anger, and friends' delinquency are controlled, sex differences are virtually zero. In short, neither sex seems more likely to run away from home than the other.

Those high school students who fight with their parents are more likely to have a history of running away: respondents who fight "a lot" with their parents have a probability of reporting this item that is thirty percentage points higher than that of respondents who "never" fight. Again, it is difficult to lend a causal interpretation to this relationship since it is impossible to tell whether this fighting occurred before or after the decision to run away. Interestingly enough, running away is one form of delinquency that seems relatively unaffected by general measures of peers' deviance. This suggests (1) that the individual's peer network at the time of running away differs from current peer contacts, or (2) that peers may have relatively less to do with decisions to run away from home than with other types of delinquency. The second of these possibilities is especially attractive, since running away from home may be less of a group activity than an individual response to family experiences.

Patterns in running away are somewhat different from those generally found in this analysis and suggest that a leisure decision-making framework may be less applicable to running away than to most other forms of delinquency. The fact that family variables are relatively more important here and that peer variables are relatively less powerful may indicate that decisions to run away are made on the basis of different considerations from those common to incidental leisure activity. Family members may provide relatively more influential costs and benefits for running away as well as a set of situational prerequisites (i.e., one must have a family, presumably that one finds unsatisfactory, in order to run away from them) missing from their role in general leisure. This would increase their importance in an analysis of running away. Moreover, one does not usually run away from home with a group of friends, so that peer influences may well be less salient. In short, running away may be a more isolated form of delinquency than the others analyzed here.

CONCLUSION

We have examined several types of noncrime delinquency in order to evaluate their fit with a leisure decisionmaking model. Truancy and peer conflict show patterns that are quite similar to those noted in earlier chapters, suggesting that they may be responsive to many of the considerations likely to guide leisure choices. Cheating and running away from home conform less closely to these familiar patterns and pose more of an interpretive problem. The main difference between patterns in running away and those of other forms of noncrime delinquency lies in the relative importance of family and peer predictors. It is not surprising that family experiences have a greater impact on running away from home than on most other forms of delinquency. Although the important considerations that affect running away may be somewhat different from those affecting other forms of delinquency, the patterns suggest that choices may still be made according to the same decisionmaking principles.

Patterns in cheating shadow those noted for most other delinquency items; in other words, the difference between patterns in cheating and other delinquencies is largely one of degree. Important predictors follow the same configurations outlined earlier, but with relatively less power. This implies that a leisure perspective may be a useful way of approaching cheating, but we hesitate to make statements much stronger than this on the basis of the somewhat weak patterns noted here.

We included measures of noncrime delinquency in this analysis in order to see whether delinquent choices appear to be made according to the same (leisure) principles regardless of their alleged seriousness or potentially criminal character. The similarity between patterns of most noncrime delinquencies and those more likely to qualify as crimes suggests that this is the case, underscoring our earlier contention that delinquency is most profitably characterized as mundane and normal rather than as abnormal and unusual. This is an important advantage offered by a leisure decisionmaking approach to middle class delinquency, one that we will discuss further as we review the findings of our overall analysis.

NOTES

1. Again, the causal direction of these associations is unclear. Given the wording of these items, it is impossible to establish even

the temporal order between the variables that might provide some guide to the causal relationships involved.

2. Since limited statistical variability could account for these small correlations, we analyzed "cheating" using both a dichotomized and a full frequency distribution as the dependent variable. Regressing a full frequency measure on these same predictors did not alter the patterns: zero order correlations did not increase substantially, nor did these variables gain much predictive power. For this reason we have reported the dichotomized analysis in Tables 8-3 and 8-4. This suggests that the weak associations between peers' delinquency and cheating or school experiences and cheating is not solely due to artifacts introduced by dichotomization. Instead these may reflect substantive patterns of the type outlined in the text.

3. Obviously, there are problems in the temporal ordering of all of the items included in our analysis, but they are more severe in measures that reflect estimates of lifetime experiences instead of those in the last six months. Students were asked to estimate the number of times they had "ever" run away from home. We do not know when this happened (it could have been within the last week; it could have been years earlier), and there is no assurance that the current attributes of respondents that comprise the bulk of our predictors are identical to the attributes they had when they ran away from home. Using current attributes as predictors of past behavior is a risky business, and the risk increases as the time span between current attributes and past behavior widens. Not only do levels of association often decline as the gap increases, it becomes much more difficult to interpret the relationships which do appear. Thus, it should not be surprising that there are relatively few good predictors of running away or that they explain relatively little of the variance in this item.

Chapter Nine

Middle Class
Delinquency and
Leisure Decisionmaking

INTRODUCTION

Throughout this analysis we have assumed that one can learn a good deal about middle class delinquency by thinking of it as leisure activity rather than nascent crime. We have discussed delinquency as if it were a common leisure pursuit—"play" in the broad sense of the term—and argued that it has a good many parallels to other leisure activities. By identifying delinquency as "play" we do not mean to imply that it is whimsical or inconsequential, or that its sole purpose is entertainment. As theorists are quick to point out, play serves a number of purposes, and can help refine skills, techniques, and an awareness of social rules that are useful in a variety of contexts. Popular types of delinquency seem to have similar potential. The fact that they often take place alongside more conventional leisure activities suggests that they may be responsive to similar considerations, and that crime may indeed be an interesting form of play for many middle class adolescents. Patterns in middle class delinquency seem consistent with this interpretation. At this point it would be well to review the most important of these patterns, note their fit with basic assumptions of a leisure decisionmaking model, and discuss the general merits of a play and leisure approach to delinquency.

DELINQUENCY AND
LEISURE DECISIONMAKING

The leisure framework that we have proposed assumes that delinquent activities are chosen according to the same principles that individuals use in choosing nondelinquent activities. In other words, there is nothing inherently abnormal about delinquency. People anticipate the returns and risks involved in potentially delinquent acts, balance these against the returns and risks involved in nondelinquent acts, and choose those designed to provide the greatest utility. Resources are invested to obtain this utility, and in the case of adolescents, these resources are primarily leisure time. Leisure time can be invested in delinquent activity for several reasons. Direct consumption, production of goods for future investment or future consumption, and the development of nonmarket human capital are all potential outcomes of these investments.

The returns and risks of leisure investment are structured by *a priori* preferences (i.e., tastes), situational factors (i.e., oppor-responses (whether real or perceived) of peers, family members, and other authorities affect the probability of delinquent and nondelinquent leisure choices. Their impact should be reflected in overall patterns of delinquent activity and should allow at least partial prediction of these patterns.

The decisionmaking process by which leisure time (and other resources) is invested in legitimate and illegitimate activities is extremely complex and not easily modeled. Indeed, there are no formal models of delinquent decisionmaking in the literature, and our efforts here do not change this. Instead, we have extracted several important assumptions from current microeconomic models of crime, made some predictions on the basis of these assumptions, and examined self-report survey data in an effort to see whether behavior patterns are consistent with these predictions. To the extent that the data conform to these expectations, a utilitarian framework would seem to be a promising approach in the study of middle class delinquency.

SUMMARY OF PATTERNS IN
MIDDLE CLASS DELINQUENCY

Before assessing the overall fit between a leisure perspective and patterns in middle class delinquency, it may be helpful to summarize our findings. They create an interesting picture of the important dimensions that seem to guide leisure choices and can be related to a leisure perspective in some intriguing ways.

Family Experiences in
a Leisure Context

Despite popular assertions, family structure variables seem to play virtually no role in middle class delinquency. Broken homes, working mothers, permissive rule structures, or permissive rule enforcement techniques seldom differentiate between students who report delinquent activities and those who do not. This is consistent with expectations based on our leisure framework. Since most delinquency takes place outside the family, family members are not likely to be major structural elements of leisure based delinquency. In addition, leisure decisions are likely to be made in terms of considerations quite different from those implicit in theories of family breakdown. Breakdown is generally assumed to influence probabilities of delinquency *via* attendant individual pathology or lack of adult supervision. There is little evidence here to suggest that pathology or supervision can account for most middle class delinquency.

This does not mean that family actors are irrelevant in the process of leisure decisionmaking. Parents may provide meaningful costs or rewards for leisure choices and this influence is suggested by the consistent though modest predictive power of family conflict variables throughout this analysis. Fighting, anger, and disobedience are experiences that seem likely to reflect the rewards or sanctions that parents provide. One might also expect family members to serve as pro- or antideviant role models for adolescents, but this does not appear to be an especially powerful influence here. This is most obvious in our analysis of drug use. Siblings' drug use affects the probability of individual drug use to some extent, but parents' drug use seldom does so under statistically controlled conditions. A leisure framework led us to expect that parents would influence tastes in delinquency *via* modeling; this prediction appears somewhat misplaced. However, the absence of modeling effects is especially damaging to theories of middle class delinquency that concentrate on the alleged deterrent impact of parental role models. There is little evidence to suggest that conventional parents provide powerful deterrent role models for middle class adolescents.

The overall impact of family variables in this analysis changes with the age group under study. Their influence is greatest among younger students, but family variables seldom alter the probabilities of delinquency reported by high school students. This is again consistent with a leisure framework, although one must be careful not to make rigid assumptions about age variation on the basis of cohort data. Parents can provide direct rewards and sanctions for leisure choices, but they are not likely to be important structural elements of adolescents' leisure activities. Most leisure activities take place outside the home, and older children are likely to spend less time in home-based activities than are younger children. This means that they may spend proportionally more time in extrafamilial leisure pursuits which should reduce the overall impact of family considerations as children age.

In summary, a leisure decisionmaking approach fits well with the relationships between family experiences and middle class delinquency that appear in this analysis. Other explanations are less attractive. Theories linking parental permissiveness to middle class delinquency receive little support; assumptions about the affective or supervisory role of broken homes or employed mothers also seem unwarranted. Popular youth culture theories that rely on the existence of a generation gap (however phrased) to explain middle class delinquency encounter similar problems. While there is evidence that parent-child conflict is related to these students' delinquency it is difficult to argue that this conflict reflects youth culture values. Attitude measures that might tap youth culture concerns fail to show meaningful relationships to delinquency, nor are they systematically linked to measures of parent-child conflict. Thus, while the nature of this conflict is difficult to specify, there is little evidence to suggest that it is primarily the product of value disagreement based on a youth culture ethic. Clearly, the causal nature of the tie between conflict and delinquent behavior is difficult to unravel. Conflict may promote delinquent responses; it may also be a response to previous delinquent activity. More work is needed if one is to understand the way in which parent-child conflict can alter the relative balance of costs and benefits that accrue to potentially delinquent leisure activities.

Peers in a Leisure Context

Peer variables are the most systematic elements in this analysis, altering the probability of most forms of delinquency in substantively meaningful ways even under statistically controlled conditions. This is what a leisure model predicts, since it emphasizes the social character of leisure activities; ties to peers should affect the relative costs and benefits of deviant or nondeviant leisure choices. Most other theories also predict strong correlations between an individual's delinquency and that of his or her friends, although for somewhat different reasons. The crucial issue is an interpretive one: What is the mechanism linking peers' deviance with individual delinquency? As we noted in Chapter 2, some perspectives assume that peers exert a generalized prodelinquent impact on individuals, and that peers pressure adolescents into delinquency (e.g., subcultural theories of which youth culture perspectives are a special case; theories of peer status conflict). Others see the group nature of delinquency as an essentially spurious byproduct of similar worldviews that lead delinquent adolescents to congregate for mutual support (e.g., control theories).

A leisure decisionmaking framework need not take a rigid position on either side of this debate. Although most theorists seem to assume that peer influence is "either" peer pressure "or" spurious support, peers seem likely to influence leisure options in ways analogous to both. They can structure choices by providing direct costs and benefits for potentially delinquent decisions; they can provide support for like-minded individuals by serving as the necessary prerequisites for some forms of delinquency. (If one has some group-based activity in mind, one must seek out congenial peers before the activity is possible.) Their role as prerequisites is not strictly comparable to the argument that peers are spurious accompaniments to delinquency. Instead it stresses their role as structural elements in many types of delinquency. However, this is still a different type of impact from that which is usually thought of as peer pressure.

The best peer predictors in any of these analyses are those that measure the same type of delinquency for both friends and respondents. This suggests that peers tend to provide activity-specific rewards or costs for delinquency instead of a general prodeviant influence that endorses undifferentiated delinquency. This specificity is an argument in favor of the type of leisure framework that we outlined in Chapter 2. Our model assumes that potentially delinquent activities are chosen on a case-by-case basis and that "delinquent" is not an immutable attribute either of actors or of peer groups. Instead, we have assumed that peers are an important element guiding decisions about specific leisure options. Since the costs and benefits offered by peers should vary for different types of activities, peer influence should be rather activity-specific. This is not what most delinquency theories imply. While they are seldom as specific about the issue as one might like, most seem to assume that peer groups are "more" or "less" delinquent and that they exert a comprehensive and pervasive influence on the behavior of members. The patterns in this analysis do not support this interpretation. There is little evidence, particularly among older age groups, that peers provide a diffuse prodelinquent context for individual decisionmaking. In fact, peers are likely to sanction as well as reward delinquent choices and one must be careful not to assume that peer influence is automatically prodelinquent.

Despite the predictive power of peer variables in this analysis, considerable caution must be exercised in attaching causal interpretations to these patterns. The items are estimates of the proportion of friends who have been involved in various forms of delinquency. They predict individuals' chances of similar activities, but this predictive power still requires substantive interpretation. In order to understand why the number of delinquent peers increases individuals' chances of delinquency, one must understand why some adolescents have friends who apparently support delinquent experiences while others do not. There is little information in our data (or in most delinquency studies) that addresses this issue directly. There are, however, several accounts of associational patterns that are consistent with the leisure model we have proposed. While they are admittedly speculative, they seem worth some brief discussion here.

One explanation is that of "like seeks like"—in other words, that adolescents with similar tastes are drawn together since they can better reinforce one another. This assumes that tastes are an important component of delinquent choices and that peer groups reflect these tastes. The crucial issue here is how these tastes develop. A leisure framework is consistent with a dynamic view of this process in which peers play a major role.

Assume for a moment that young children, by virtue of age and inexperience, have rather poorly developed individual tastes about leisure activities. They also have little experiential knowledge to use when deciding among leisure options. Young children are often thrown together by factors not of their own choosing: groups are formed in school, at church, in other contexts largely in terms of accidents of where one lives, the classroom to which one is assigned, where one sits in class, and the like. Each group undergoes similar experiences that structure the environment. This determines the mix of opportunities that members encounter as well as the risks and rewards involved in taking advantage of these opportunities. Group members develop a set of expectations about what the environment is like and what activities are possible based on these common experiences. Tastes are gradually shaped as well. These expectations and tastes influence the way in which group members respond to subsequent experiences and opportunities, although not in a rigidly deterministic fashion. In other words, prior experiences are fashioned into expectations about the world and these order an individual's response to new experiences or opportunities.

Not all groups encounter the same experiences. Children's experiences also become more diverse with age. Group experiences (and members' responses to them) may diverge over time. Thus, some adolescents may come to see their world differently from others and develop somewhat different tastes. Some groups are likely to look more favorably on potentially delinquent activities than others, and this should affect choices among different leisure opportunities. Similar world views within the peer group could then be associated with similar patterns of behavior among members. This would lead to the familiar correlations between the activities of peers and those of individuals.[1]

Given longitudinal data one might test the accuracy of this account using some form of time series analysis that models behavior patterns over time. For example, autoregressive models (Kmenta, 1971:269-273) assume that actions at any point are a function of expectations and tastes carried over from previous time periods plus a (random) perturbation that is independent both of past experiences and of other perturbations. In other words, behavior is a function of earlier experiences that direct responses to current situations. Auto-regressive models also assume that the impact of earlier experiences dissipates over time and that behavior patterns are gradually shaped by new opportunities (provided these opportunities are different from those that occurred earlier). Obviously, autoregressive models make some assumptions that may not be borne out in real life; perturbations are seldom independent of one another (groups may begin to seek out environments that are reinforcing), and school children do not actually start out with the same experiences and tastes. In addition, early group formation may not be an entirely chance occurrence. For instance, parents may choose recreational opportunities for young children that reflect parents' tastes. Were this the case, children whose parents have similar tastes will be more likely to meet one another. Despite these problems, a time series approach could be a useful way of unraveling the complex interrelationships between peer group formation, the development of individual tastes, and the impact of each on individuals' delinquent choices.

Without longitudinal data it is difficult to reach a definitive conclusion about the causal role peers play in middle class delinquency. Still, basic patterns in this analysis are consistent with predictions made from a leisure decisionmaking framework. Alternative perspectives on peer impact seem less attractive. Peers do not appear to exert as general a delinquent influence as youth culture theories indicate. Neither do they have the wide-ranging impact that one expects on the basis of strain theories, where peers provide an alternative status system for those adolescents effectively locked out of adult systems. For these reasons, we would argue that a leisure approach is a useful way of accounting for peer influences on middle class delinquency. It allows peers to play a complex role in decisions about delinquent activities, and does not limit them to simply pressuring one another nor relegate them to a largely spurious position.

School Experiences in a Leisure Context

The patterns followed by school predictors are among the most interesting to appear in this analysis. Many delinquency theories indicate that school experiences such as performance or satisfaction should be important predictors of delinquency. For example, some authors have hypothesized that the unrealistic demands that teachers make can prompt students to rebel through negativistic delinquency (e.g., A.K. Cohen, 1955; Cloward and Ohlin, 1960; Stinchcombe, 1964). In a similar vein, poor articulation between current school performance and future status are thought to encourage even middle class students to search for more immediate (and potentially deviant) sources of success (e.g., Vaz, 1967; A.K. Cohen, 1967; England, 1967). However, measures of performance and satisfaction are not as powerful a set of predictors in this analysis as these perspectives imply. Although they are often correlated with delinquency at the zero order level, when controls for peers are introduced, their influence weakens and becomes less systematic.

A leisure framework offers a plausible explanation for this pattern which is analogous to our prior discussion of how tastes may develop. If leisure investments are an important factor in delinquency, delinquent activities are likely to be chosen in light of considerations that have relatively little to do with school performance or satisfaction *per se*. Instead, schools may serve as a place where peer groups form, and performance and satisfaction may be dimensions along which student groups are established. These variables do contribute to probabilities of delinquency net of peer predictors for younger students, perhaps because younger students' peer groups are still in the formative stages. Older students may belong to more stable groups organized more systematically along dimensions such as performance or satisfaction. Clearly there are other ways of interpreting these age differences in the impact of school variables. Performance and satisfaction may alter the costs for delinquency in a more direct fashion for younger children. It is also possible that some of the age differences observed here could be due to differences in the questionnaire items, although they are sufficiently systematic to suggest that these patterns are more than a methodological artifact.

These patterns underscore the importance of school actors in decisions about delinquency. This is again a primary focus of a leisure framework which stresses delinquency's social character. Peers are obviously important school actors who can influence delinquency and there is some evidence that school officials also have a role to play in the probability of delinquent activity. Anger at school officials is a frequent predictor in this analysis, although it is difficult to assign a clear causal interpretation to this relationship. Anger may be the product of earlier delinquent experiences to which school authorities are responding; it may also prompt additional delinquent activity, and it is difficult to decide between these alternatives in the absence of longitudinal data.

LEISURE DELINQUENCY AND ASSUMPTIONS IN A DECISIONMAKING APPROACH

Since the patterns in this analysis are largely consistent with predictions made on the basis of a decisionmaking framework, their fit with the assumptions underlying these predictions are worth a brief review. Although these data do not allow us to directly test the accuracy of these assumptions (such tests require a different type of data), patterns do imply that this is a useful way of approaching the study of middle class delinquency.

One of the most important assumptions underlying our leisure framework is that individuals who choose delinquent activities do so according to the same principles as those who choose nondelinquent activities. In other words, the cognitive processes underlying both types of choices are the same. This means that adolescents who choose delinquent activities are not inherently abnormal, and that individual pathology is not the driving force behind delinquency. While we have no data on actual decisionmaking processes, patterns in these data are consistent with this assumption. Measures of attitudes that should be related to various forms of individual maladjustment or psychological pathology fail to differentiate between those students with delinquent experiences and those without; measures of factors allegedly associated with prodelinquent pathologies (e.g., broken homes, etc.) fail to predict the delinquency that these middle class students report. Variables that predict delinquency seem to be the type that are important considerations in leisure choices generally, and there is little reason to think that they represent a complex of factors that are somehow unique to delinquents alone. This is not to argue that there is no such thing as individual pathology or that such pathology could never be related to delinquency. However, we would argue that for the vast majority of the population at risk (adolescents), variation in pathology does little to explain delinquent behavior. The bulk of what is usually thought of as delinquent activity is not easily dismissed by reference to models of individual illness or pathological maladjustment. Instead, a different, more everyday explanation of these behavior patterns is needed.

A second important assumption is that delinquent activities provide utility to those who choose them, just as legitimate activities do. In other words, delinquent activities are chosen for a purpose; they are not wanton or random occurrences. The fact that there are systematic patterns of any kind in self-reported delinquency is evidence that these activities are not random; the predictors of the patterns in these data suggest that they are not wanton. Perhaps the most direct indication that delinquent choices can provide utility comes from the drug attitude items presented in Chapter 5. Students agree that alcohol or marijuana can be "relaxing" or that they can facilitate social interaction. Both are forms of utility that may be gained through drug use. In addition, use patterns for these popular drugs appear strikingly similar to those found among adults. Few observers argue that adults' drug use is wanton or that it does not provide adults with some utility. The same conclusion would seem warranted in the case of middle class adolescents. Other forms of delinquency may provide similar utility. Minor theft can produce goods that are otherwise unobtainable; vandalism may produce psychic satisfactions; breaking and entering may be "fun" or "exciting." Nondelinquent activities may also provide these types of utility, underscoring the similarities between potentially deviant and nondeviant leisure choices.

A corollary to this assumption is that choices are made in order to gain utility on the basis of anticipated costs and benefits. This has been a central concern throughout our analysis, and we have argued that the best predictors of delinquent activities are those that are likely to reflect major sources of rewards or costs for these choices. These include peers, family members, and other authority figures whose responses are likely to affect the costs or benefits derived from delinquency and thus influence the probability of delinquent investments. The fact that these variables are the primary predictors in this analysis, rather than others that are related to arational drives or motivations, suggests that costs and benefits are taken into account in decisions about delinquent activity. We have obviously not measured all possible sources of costs or benefits for leisure choices. For example, there are opportunity costs for any investment decision (if one chooses to have fun through vandalism one cannot simultaneously obtain fun by going to the movies), and these are likely to influence choices in important ways. Still, it seems reasonable to conclude that many of the patterns reported here are consistent with those expected for purposive individual choices within a cost-benefit framework.

The assumption of maximization of returns on investments is difficult to evaluate with our data. We have little information about alternative (nondelinquent) investments that would allow us to comment on optimal allocation of resources. However, this assumption is less crucial to our argument at this point than the prior assumption that delinquent activities are indeed the product of purposive decisionmaking. Maximization is a difficult problem in microeconomics generally, as modifying concepts such as "satisficing" indicate. Still, there is a strong tradition in delinquency theory emphasizing the apparent expressiveness of the activity and the actors, and the simple assumption of a purposive, calculating actor is itself enough to reorient thinking about the topic.

One of the most important of our assumptions is that leisure investments provide information about the costs, benefits, and risks involved in unfamiliar delinquent and nondelinquent activities, as well as producing utility that can be directly consumed. For resources to be well invested, individuals must have a clear picture of the outcomes they can anticipate and the skills they need. This information must be learned, often through direct experience. We have argued that this learning is possible by experimenting with various forms of potentially delinquent activities. Through experimentation one can learn skills or techniques, ways of managing the situation (including negotiating the complex social interactions involved in many forms of group-based delinquency), the degree of risk, the probable responses of actors who can provide rewards or sanctions, and the type of satisfaction a potentially delinquent activity can offer. This learning process affects the probability of delinquent choices: probabilities may increase if skills improve; probabilities may increase as individuals become more adept at managing risky situations; probabilities may decline if individuals learn that they cannot obtain the type or amount of satisfaction they desire. This is obviously a complex process, which consists of subtle testing of social rules and limits.

Middle class adolescents appear to be experimenting with many forms of delinquency in ways consistent with these assumptions. Grade patterns in these data provide indirect evidence that adolescents choose many types of delinquent activities on a trial basis.

Again, we must caution that these are cohort data; nonetheless, curvilinear relationships between age and delinquency are often strong enough to suggest that younger children experiment until they are convinced that delinquency is not worth it (in which case frequency declines) or until they discover that delinquency affords sufficient utility to warrant regular patterns of involvement. Researchers often find that delinquent activity peaks in the early teen years and then declines, a pattern consistent with the idea of experimental learning outlined here. However, there are several forms of delinquency in this analysis that do not show familiar curvilinear patterns. Some of these are serious delinquencies that are reported by few students of any age. These may be sufficiently risky or unrewarding that few even consider trying them; those who do appear to do so on a short-term, experimental basis. There are other activities (i.e., drinking, marijuana use, shoplifting) whose frequency increases through early cohorts of students and then holds at high levels among older respondents. This suggests that adolescents find these activities sufficiently satisfying to justify reinvestment on a regular basis. It is interesting that the activities where experimentation seems to routinize are among the most popular forms of middle class delinquency. They are also those with the most direct analogy to common forms of adult deviance. There is no evidence to suggest that experimenting with delinquency automatically leads to greater and greater involvement or that involvement in one particular type of delinquency automatically generalizes to others (whether or not these others are potentially more serious). Instead, these students appear to be highly conventional people who reduce most of their delinquent activity once they learn the rules of proper behavior and can reliably estimate the relative risks and costs involved in both delinquent and nondelinquent activities.

Age differences in the opportunity costs for delinquent *versus* nondelinquent activities can also account for familiar curvilinear relationships between delinquency and age. The relative value of time invested in leisure varies for different people; the cost of spending two hours hanging around the recreation center may be greater for older adolescents who could invest these hours in a part-time job more easily than younger children. All other things being equal, older respondents may find that their time is worth more. This would alter the relative costs of delinquent versus nondelinquent choices, changing the nature of their leisure investments.[2]

Our final assumption has to do with the nature of the resources that adolescents invest in potentially delinquent activities. We have argued that these resources consist primarily of leisure time, giving delinquency an important leisure character. On balance, middle class adolescents have more resources tied up in time than in money, although both are available. Our analysis is consistent with the notion that time is the critical investment currency for adolescents. Respondents were asked questions designed to estimate the amount of money they have (e.g., allowances, income from part-time jobs). None of these variables is systematically related to the delinquency they report. This may not be surprising, in part because most of these forms of delinquent activity do not require much financial investment. But even those that do (e.g., marijuana use, alcohol use) are apparently not affected by the amount of money an individual has.

These are some of the most important assumptions that underlie our approach to middle class delinquency. Although we have not tested them directly, the patterns in this analysis suggest that this is a useful way of conceptualizing basic issues involved. There are additional considerations implicit in a leisure model that make it especially attractive in the study of middle class delinquency. Although we have outlined these at earlier points in our discussion, they are worth brief review in order to underscore the value of a leisure approach to delinquency.

LEISURE AS A METAPHOR
FOR DELINQUENCY

Once delinquency is phrased in terms of the investment of leisure time, it can be placed within the larger category of leisure activity. Since leisure takes many forms, some potentially delinquent, others less so, this directs attention to the parallels between delinquent and nondelinquent behavior. If both are leisure activities, they may be chosen in many of the same ways and for many of the same reasons. This gives delinquency a mundane, everyday character, and it need no longer appear abnormal, atypical, or strange. By extension, delinquent acts may be seen as purposive rather than as the product of individual aberration.

The parallels between delinquent and nondelinquent leisure also point out the fluid character of delinquency. Given the focus of popular theories, it is easy to assume that there are identifiably, consistently delinquent activities in the world and that once one has measured them, one has measured delinquency. However, the delinquent character of behavior is not inherent in the activity. It is an attribute that is negotiated and varies from one situation to another. In fact, this variably delinquent character of leisure pursuits is one of the important things that adolescents must learn if leisure time is to be optimally invested.

Once the inherently delinquent character of any activity is questioned, it is difficult to conceive of individuals as analogously delinquent. Many approaches to delinquency assume that one can cumulate experience with a number of different types of delinquent activities and use this to differentiate delinquents from nondelinquents. The underlying assumption is that there is a uniform set of factors driving individuals to behave in inherently delinquent ways (regardless of the specific behavioral forms these drives take). However, a leisure perspective challenges the idea that most delinquency can be explained by systematic variation in delinquent versus nondelinquent predispositions. Rather, attention is focused on the needs of all adolescents and variation in the environment in which they operate. It is the meshing of needs, resources, rewards, and costs that channels actions, and theories of delinquency cannot afford to limit themselves to the study of predispositions.

The important questions implicit in a leisure framework are thus somewhat different from those often asked about delinquency. Instead of asking, What are the characteristics of the delinquent that lead him or her to behave in this unique way, the important question becomes, What are the situational factors that structure choices among potentially delinquent and nondelinquent options? Analysis can then focus on different forms of leisure activity (as we have done here), attempting to identify similarities or differences in the factors that predict the probability of leisure choices. This is more than a simple rephrasing of the popular question, What makes them do it? since these predictors are variable characteristics of the situations in which individuals operate rather than characteristics inherent in individuals themselves. For example, one does not necessarily have a general weakness for peer pressure from delinquent friends. Instead, one evaluates the costs and benefits that friends may provide for a range of different leisure options, some of which are more likely to appear deviant than others. These costs and rewards vary with the type of leisure activity under consideration, and change with the contexts in which leisure choices are made.

In short, a leisure framework has some important implications for the way in which delinquency can be conceptualized (and by extension, explained). It focuses attention on potentially delinquent environments rather than innately delinquent individuals and does not assume that adolescents who have been involved in delinquency are radically different from those who have not. This allows one to include a model of individual choice in explanations of delinquency.

Actions are seen as the product of reasoned assessments of costs, benefits, and risks, and the potentially deviant character of these actions becomes one (variable) element in evaluating the potential utility to be gained from competing leisure opportunities. All of this underscores the normal, commonplace character of delinquency, an image that is consistent with the apparently minor nature of most delinquent activities as well as their widespread popularity among middle class adolescents.

FAMILIAR THEORIES OF MIDDLE CLASS DELINQUENCY

We have argued that a leisure framework frequently offers a more useful explanation for patterns in this analysis than those provided by other theories of middle class delinquency. It may be helpful to review some of the crucial predictions of these theories at this point and to note where our data are consistent with their expectations.

Subcultural theories of middle class delinquency are most often phrased in terms of the prodelinquent impact that youth culture values are thought to have on adolescent behavior. While there is some evidence that adult-child conflict has a role to play in middle class delinquency, it is difficult to make a strong case that this conflict is the product of youth culture values. Attitude items consistent with a youth culture ethic generally fail to differentiate between respondents with delinquent experiences and those without, and there is little evidence that these students have strongly unconventional world views. Youth culture theories stress the role that peers play in delinquency, but while peers are important elements in this analysis, they seldom exert the all-pervasive, undifferentiated influence that youth culture theories imply. Peer influence does not seem to generalize very far beyond the specific type of delinquent activity under study (especially for older respondents, who are the ones most likely to participate in a youth culture). This makes it difficult to argue that shared unconventional world views are the driving force behind middle class delinquency.

Strain theories of middle class delinquency focus on the potentially prodelinquent impact of blocked status mobility and resulting status frustration. Conventional measures of such strains were included in this study (i.e., occupational and educational aspirations and expectations), but we have not presented them here because they fail to predict patterns in these students' delinquency. Much of the strain literature also assumes that school experiences are an important source of status frustration since they influence individuals' perceptions of mobility chances. However, school experiences are not especially useful predictors of older students' delinquencies. This offers additional evidence that strains engendered by school failure are not promising explanations for middle class delinquency. Those students who are angry at teachers are somewhat more likely to report delinquent experiences, but once again it is difficult to assign a clear causal interpretation to this relationship. In the absence of other strain-related predictors, this anger is as difficult to link to the strains of blocked mobility as it is to a youth culture ethic.

Familiar socialization theories of middle class delinquency also fail to fit the patterns in this analysis. As noted throughout the previous chapters, measures of family structure, rules, or rule enforcement do not predict delinquency in any age group. Other familiar theories of individual pathology linked to socialization strategies also find little support. In short, the most popular explanations for middle class delinquency do not offer much insight into the delinquent activities that these students report. Obviously, many of these perspectives contain elements that are consistent with some of the patterns in our analysis, and we have not always been able to test these theories as definitively as one might wish. But when they are posed against the type of leisure framework outlined in Chapter 2, the leisure framework appears to be an especially useful way of conceptualizing middle class delinquency.

LEISURE, DECISIONMAKING, AND GENERAL DELINQUENCY

Earlier we argued that one of the problems with theories of middle class delinquency is that they tend to be explanations of a "special case" with little wider applicability. While a leisure framework is consistent with many of the patterns in this analysis, one might wonder whether it too is useful only in this special case. More specifically, one might wonder whether a leisure decisionmaking framework has anything to offer in the study of delinquency among adolescents who are not middle class. Since we lack cross-class delinquency data, our discussion of this issue must necessarily be impressionistic. Still, there are several reasons for thinking that a leisure framework could be a profitable approach to take to the study of delinquency in a variety of class contexts.

We have already noted how a leisure framework reorients thinking about middle class delinquency, changing its image from the abnormal to the mundane, stressing its reasoned rather than solely expressive character, and focusing attention on the activity itself rather than on unique attributes of the actor. These are common theoretical issues in general delinquency research and are not unique to the study of the middle class case. If anything, assumptions about the abnormality or nonutilitarian character of delinquency and delinquents are even stronger in popular accounts of lower class delinquency. The reorientation implicit in a leisure perspective would seem to be as theoretically provocative in the study of general delinquency as it is in an analysis of middle class data.

There seems to be little reason to assume *a priori* that a leisure decisionmaking model is a more accurate representation of choice processes among middle class adolescents than among those from other social strata. Popular stereotypes of lower class delinquency emphasize its allegedly violent and serious nature, making it easy to assume that it is arational or wanton. However, most self-report research indicates that the bulk of lower class delinquency is relatively minor and commonplace and that its violent, aggressive image is overdrawn. This would make a leisure framework appealing in the study of lower as well as middle strata delinquency. In fact, research indicates that there may be fewer class differences in actual delinquency than most theories predict (an issue dealt with in detail in Chapter 1). Certainly the types of delinquency reported by the middle class adolescents in this study do not appear radically different from those identified in other self-report research. If these middle class data are not strikingly unique, a leisure decisionmaking framework may have wider applicability in the study of delinquency. Even if delinquent activities of lower strata adolescents were more serious than most analyzed here (a dubious contention at best), this does not necessarily mean that these activities are chosen according to a different set of decisionmaking principles. In our analysis, serious delinquencies pattern in ways quite similar to those of less serious ones, suggesting that a decisionmaking framework can be profitably applied to both.

Perhaps the strongest argument in favor of the general applicability of a leisure approach is the fact that it does not automatically assume or require large class differences in delinquency. Class may have an influence on delinquency if it structures the costs, benefits, and risks involved, all other things being equal (i.e., tastes). It is conceivable that class has such an impact, but it is difficult to know how strong this influence might be among adolescents who lack a clear class position of their own. However, class is not the primary inequality on which a leisure decisionmaking framework focuses. Far more important in a leisure account are age variations in the costs, benefits, and risks involved in both delinquent and nondelinquent investments. Resources (especially leisure time) are differentially distributed by age). Leisure can be invested in the sort of learning which occurs in the process of maturation (e.g., nonmarket skills, the rules of social interaction), and the costs (both opportunity costs and the costs of formal sanction) and benefits for deviant and nondeviant leisure activities vary between age groups. The fact that maturational reform poses such difficult problems for most delinquency theory should be at least one indication that age and age inequality must be a basic consideration in any attempt to understand adolescent deviance. Most delinquency theories are modifications of perspectives on adult crime or deviance. This means that they focus on class as the dimension of inequality most important for understanding delinquency. Age inequality is then examined as a secondary theoretical issue. We would argue that the opposite should be the case. Useful theories of delinquency must be first of all responsive to the age inequality underlying adolescent experiences regardless of class position.

NOTES

1. As noted in Chapter 2, "tastes" are an important issue in any analysis of delinquency. In fact, most delinquency theorists have focused on the relationship between "tastes" (i.e., stable propensities to deviate) and adolescent deviance. In this narrative we have deliberately stressed the importance of other components of decisionmaking (the situational factors that can structure choices) but agree that to understand leisure choices one must understand how tastes are formed and how tastes affect individual decisionmaking.

2. "Risk" also has an impact on leisure choices, since decisions are affected by the degree to which individuals are "risk prone" or "risk aversive." Economists have applied the concepts of risk proneness and risk aversiveness to crime, although in a somewhat *ad hoc* fashion. The implications for this analysis are unclear, although the dimensions of risk may be worth pursuing in further work on leisure decisionmaking. (For a discussion of risk proneness with reference to crime see Ehrlich, 1974.)

Appendix A
Contact with Police
and Courts

INTRODUCTION

Much has been written about the way in which adolescents are processed through the juvenile justice system. Most discussions focus on the class biases that occur in this process. The overrepresentation of lower class children in official delinquency statistics or in incarcerated populations is a well-established fact that has been explained by a number of "official reaction hypotheses." Police patroling practices, discretionary juvenile justice policies, and the constraints of decisionmaking in processing all contribute to differences in the probability that adolescents will be officially identified and treated as delinquent.[1]

Although it seems clear that official treatment strategies vary by class, race, and sex, there is little detailed information about middle class adolescents' experiences within the juvenile justice system. Most research has concentrated on lower strata groups in an effort to understand important characteristics of their contact with official law enforcement agents. We asked these middle class students several questions about police and court contact in order to examine major patterns in these variables. These data have been included in an appendix because police and court contact were measured in a different way from that used for most of our other dependent variables. Respondents were asked to estimate police or court contact over their entire lifetime rather than in the last six months, and this complicates the interpretation of resulting patterns. There is no way of knowing when respondents' contact with police or courts occurred. It could have been fairly recently; it could have been years earlier. Most other variables in this study reflect a different time frame. Many are current attributes of the respondents, and there is no guarantee that current characteristics are the same as those that they possessed at the time that they were taken to a police station or appeared before a judge. Since causal issues are so difficult to resolve with data such as these, we will simply outline the basic patterns shown by these items. Age and sex distributions will be presented, along with major attitude, family, school, and peer correlates of contact with official law enforcement agents.[2]

BASIC DISTRIBUTION OF
CONTACT WITH OFFICIAL
LAW ENFORCEMENT AGENTS

Measures of self-reported contact with official law enforcement agents were included in all three questionnaires, but because of the limited number of fifth and sixth graders with such experiences, we will present data only for junior and senior high respondents. Seventh and eighth graders were asked how many times they had been taken to the police station, and high school students were asked both about how many times they had been taken to a station and how many times they had appeared before a judge. (Exact wording of these items can be found in Appendix B.) The distribution of their responses is presented in Table A-1.

The number of these students who report contact with either police or courts is somewhat surprising in light of familiar official reaction hypotheses. Given the emphasis placed on class bias in

Table A-1. Marginal Distribution of Police and Court Contact (percent)

Seventh and Eighth Graders	Number of times brought to police station	
Never	85.1	
Once	7.1	
2-3 times	4.7	
4-5 times	1.7	
6+ times	1.3	
	100	
	(819)	

High School Students	Number of times brought to police station	Number of times appeared before a judge
Never	69.7	90.8
Once	15.8	6.4
2-3 times	8.6	2.2
4-5 times	3.1	0.4
6+ times	2.7	0.4
	100	100
	(1234)	(1236)

processing, one tends to expect few middle class students to have been taken to the police station or to have appeared in court. Yet in this particular community a fair number of students are likely to have been processed through at least the initial levels of the juvenile justice system. Thirty percent of the high school students and fifteen percent of the seventh and eighth graders claim to have been taken to the police station at some point in their lives. Almost 10 percent of the high school students say that they have appeared before a judge for something they were accused of doing wrong. Several variables differentiate between those students who have had contact with police and courts and those who have not.

AGE AND SEX DISTRIBUTION
OF OFFICIAL CONTACT

Sex is one major dimension along which police or court contact varies (see coefficients in Tables 3-5 and 3-6). Boys are more likely to report contact with both police and courts than are girls. In fact, the sex differences in these items are among the highest for any of the variables examined in this analysis. The zero order correlation coefficient between sex and police contact (dichotomized into "never" versus "once or more") is 0.25 in the junior high data and 0.26 in the senior high. The coefficient between court contact and sex in the high school data is 0.18.

Since these items refer to respondents' total history of official contact it is also important to specify their relationship to grade. Older students should have a larger number of incidents to report by virtue of this history effect alone. However, the actual distribution by grade shows less linearity than one might expect. Close to 17 percent of both seventh and eighth graders say that they have been taken to the police station, while 26 percent of the ninth graders, 34 percent of the tenth graders, 32 percent of the eleventh graders, and 30 percent of the twelfth graders report police contact. There are several ways of accounting for this pattern. It may be that most police contact takes place among younger groups of students, that after tenth grade students are not especially likely to get involved with the police. Alternatively, these patterns could reflect cohort effects. Should police practices have altered over time, rates of police contact may be different for current seventh graders than for earlier cohorts. The relatively low levels of contact reported by high school seniors could also be attributed to the uniqueness of the twelfth grade sample.

OFFICIAL CONTACT AND
FAMILY BACKGROUND

Many official reaction hypotheses stress the impact that family structure can have on the way in which delinquent juveniles are processed through the juvenile justice system. Adolescents who lack strong parental sponsorship (e.g., those from single parent households, those whose parents do not make an effort to claim responsibility for controlling their children's subsequent behavior) are thought more likely than others to be officially designated as delinquent. In this analysis family structure variables do not differentiate between students who have been taken to the station or appeared in court. However, this does not necessarily mean that family structure is unrelated to official contact. Current family structure may be different from that which characterized these students' patterns at the time they were taken to the police station or appeared in court.

It is also interesting that the variables measuring parent-child conflict are not highly correlated with measures of police or court contact. These items often appear as meaningful predictors of these respondents' current delinquent behavior, but none of the coefficients between anger at parents, fighting with parents, or disobedience exceeds 0.15 in either data set. Whatever the mechanism linking conflict to current delinquent activities, it does not seem to affect rates of past official processing. This is not surprising if one expects official treatment to be an institutionally structured response outside the family, imposed by social control agents in a way that is not totally reflexive with individual activities or motives. On the other hand, these data show little evidence that official contact or treatment increases the degree of conflict between parents and children.

SCHOOL EXPERIENCES AND
OFFICIAL CONTACT

Both school satisfaction and school performance are associated with reported contact with police. Junior high students who dislike school are more likely to have been taken to the police station ($r = 0.25$), as are those who are doing poorly in school. Anger at school officials also increases the probability of reporting contact with the police. There are similar relationships between police contact and school experiences in the high school data, but school experiences do not appear to be systematically related to court appearances. These zero order associations are consistent with what one might expect on the basis of the analysis of delinquent activities reported in earlier chapters and on the basis of official reaction hypotheses that stress the role that school can have in differentiating between "good" and "bad" treatment risks. However, one must again be careful not to impose an unjustified causal ordering on these relationships. Given the temporal referents of these measures, it is impossible to tell whether poor performance and school dissatisfaction precede official police contact or whether they develop afterwards. Arguments can be made for either interpretation, and without additional information it is difficult to decide between them.

OFFICIAL CONTACT AND FRIENDSHIP GROUPS

The extent to which one's friends have been involved in delinquent activities is a major correlate of police contact. All of the friends' delinquency measures in the junior high data are positively correlated with police contact at levels greater than 0.30, and many of the coefficients in the high school data correlate at 0.20 or higher. The best of these include the number of friends who have stolen from another student, vandalized school property, stolen a bike, vandalized public property, or stolen auto accessories. However, none of these friends' items are substantively correlated with high school students' reports of court contact. Before concluding that friendship groups are an important dimension along which respondents with official police contact can be separated, it is important to note that these items are also correlated with respondents' current delinquent activities. Many of the zero order relationships between contact and friends' delinquency noted here could change once controls for respondents' delinquencies were introduced. In this light it may be helpful to outline the zero order associations between respondents' delinquent behavior and court or police experience.

DELINQUENT ACTIVITY AND OFFICIAL DELINQUENCY

Many types of current delinquency are correlated with these measures of police and court contact. Those with the highest zero order coefficients in the junior high data include liquor or marijuana use, vandalism, bike theft, shoplifting, and theft of auto parts. Actual coefficients for these variables range from 0.25 to 0.35. In the high school data, marijuana use, major vandalism, bike theft, and theft of auto accessories are all correlated with police contact at a level of 0.20 or higher.[3] Again, none of these items are meaningful correlates of court experiences among high school respondents.

The delinquency items that correlate most highly with official treatment tend to be those that are either among the more serious forms of delinquency (e.g., major vandalism, bike theft) or those about which police are likely to be most attentive (marijuana use, vandalism, auto part theft). This speaks well for the validity of our delinquency measures, since these are the delinquent activities one might expect to be most strongly correlated with police contact. However, conclusions about the ordering of relationships between official treatment and delinquent activity cannot be made on the basis of these zero order associations. It is impossible to tell whether these are the delinquent activities that characterized respondents' behavior at the time they were taken to the police station or whether these activities developed subsequent to official processing. Societal reaction theorists might order the sequence from official contact to current delinquency, stressing the impact of labeling and treatment on subsequent behavior patterns. Others willing to assume that current behavior patterns are rather similar to those at the time of police contact might favor the opposite interpretation. Unfortunately these data provide little guidance about the accuracy of either conclusion.

Still, these basic patterns are intriguing. It is interesting that there are so few correlates of court appearance in these data, while a number of variables (including delinquency items and estimates of friends' delinquency) are associated with police contact. In part this may be due to the more limited variability in court appearance, but it also suggests that the factors influencing court appearances among these middle class respondents have little to do with (1) current delinquent behavior or (2) factors generally thought to promote delinquent behavior or to structure the chances of coming into contact with the police.

NOTES

1. The literature on "official reaction" hypotheses is quite lengthy. Readers interested in an introduction to the issue may find the following references helpful: Cicourel (1968); Emerson (1969); Black and Reiss (1970); Cohn (1963); Gibbons and Griswold (1957); Garrett and Short (1975); Piliavin and Briar (1964); Terry (1967); Thornberry (1973); Chesney-Lind (1973).

2. While these items could have been used to predict police or

court contact, it is difficult to know how to properly interpret such an analysis. These delinquency items and the other measures outlined above could serve as indicators of factors that official reaction hypotheses assume to be important in official processing. However, this would require an assumption that these current characteristics were either identical to those held by the respondent at the time of official contact or that they are reliable proxies for such characteristics (i.e., that the degree of delinquent activities does not change much over time, so that students who report high levels of current involvement were also likely to have been involved in them at the time—whenever that might have been—that they came into contact with the police or courts). Such assumptions are tenuous at best, since alternative explanations seem equally attractive. Societal reaction theorists are quick to note that official treatment can have an impact on subsequent delinquent activity. Given the time frames involved in these measures, it is possible that current attributes (particularly delinquent activity) are a function of responses to official treatment. In light of these alternatives, it seems best simply to outline observable patterns and not to impose more interpretation on the data than they can support.

3. See Tables 3-5 and 3-6 for zero order correlations between official contact and delinquency measures.

 # Appendix B
The Instruments

5TH AND 6TH GRADE QUESTIONNAIRE

INSTRUCTIONS

Since this is a questionnaire, not a test, there are no right and wrong answers. Try to work through the questionnaire quickly, and if you are not sure about an answer, make the best guess you can. It is important that you try to do all of the questions, so do not spend too much time on any one.

Below are four practice questions which you should answer. As the first two questions show, sometimes you will be asked to fill in your own answer:

WHAT IS YOUR BIRTHDATE?

_____
month   day   year

WHAT KIND OF JOB DOES YOUR FATHER HAVE?

_____

Usually you will be asked to circle the number next to the **one best** answer. For example:

WHAT GRADE ARE YOU IN?
1. fourth
2. fifth
3. sixth
4. seventh

Sometimes you will be asked to circle numbers to **more than one** answer. For example:

IN YOUR HOME, WHICH OF THE FOLLOWING JOBS (IF ANY) DO YOU USUALLY HAVE TO DO? (Circle all that apply.)

1. clean your room
2. wash or dry dishes
3. ironing or laundry
4. babysit for younger brothers or sisters
5. take out garbage
6. mow the lawn, or do other yard work
7. take care of pets
8. wash a car
9. shovel snow
10. household repairs like painting or plumbing
11. clean rooms other than your own
12. set or clear the table
13. cooking
14. other (what?...)
15. none

Please try to work quickly. If none of the answers fit your feelings exactly, choose the one which comes closest. If you have any problems, raise your hand and your teacher will help you.

I. **THESE FIRST FEW QUESTIONS ARE ABOUT YOU AND YOUR FAMILY.**

1. ARE YOU A BOY OR A GIRL?

   1. boy
   2. girl

2. WHO DO YOU LIVE WITH?

   1. mother and father
   2. mother and stepfather
   3. father and stepmother
   4. mother only
   5. father only
   6. other

3. HOW MANY **OLDER** BROTHERS DO YOU HAVE?

   _____

   OLDER SISTERS ?

   _____

4. HAS YOUR **FATHER** GONE TO COLLEGE?

   1. no
   2. yes
   9. don't know

5. HAS YOUR **MOTHER** GONE TO COLLEGE?

   1. no
   2. yes
   9. don't know

6. IF YOUR MOTHER WORKS, WHAT KIND OF JOB DOES SHE HAVE?

   _____

7. IN THE PAST YEAR OR SO, HOW WELL HAVE YOU DONE IN YOUR SCHOOL WORK?

    1. far below average
    2. below average
    3. average
    4. above average
    5. far above average

8. HOW MUCH DO YOU LIKE SCHOOL?

    1. not at all
    2. a little
    3. some
    4. a lot

9. ABOUT HOW MANY DAYS LAST YEAR DID YOU STAY HOME FROM SCHOOL BECAUSE YOU WERE SICK?

    _____days

10. HAVE YOU EVER WORN GLASSES?

    1. no
    2. yes

11. HAVE YOU EVER WORN CONTACT LENSES?

    1. no
    .2. yes

12. HAVE YOU EVER WORN BRACES ON YOUR TEETH?

    1. no
    2. yes

13. HERE IS A LIST OF THINGS THAT SOME FAMILIES HAVE RULES ABOUT. CIRCLE THE KINDS OF FAMILY RULES THAT **YOU** HAVE. (Circle all that apply.)

    1. your table manners
    2. how much T.V. you can watch
    3. times you must be home at night (curfews)
    4. How often you can go out with friends.
    5. how much studying or homework you must do
    6. how you dress or wear your hair
    7. how you spend your money
    8. none of these

14. IN GENERAL, HOW DO YOUR PARENTS GET YOU TO OBEY FAMILY RULES? (Circle all that apply.)

    1. by talking with you
    2. by taking away privileges (like watching T.V. or "grounding" you)
    3. by embarrassing or making fun of you
    4. by ignoring you, not talking to you
    5. by giving you a reward for being good
    6. by hitting you
    7. by yelling at you
    8. other

15. HOW MUCH DO YOU FIGHT WITH YOUR PARENTS?

    1. not at all
    2. a little
    3. some
    4. a lot

16. HOW MUCH DO YOU DISOBEY YOUR PARENTS?

    1. not at all
    2. a little
    3. some
    4. a lot

Start
CARD
B

17. GENERALLY, ABOUT HOW MUCH SPENDING MONEY DO YOU GET EACH WEEK? (ADD UP THINGS LIKE ALLOWANCE, LUNCH MONEY, ETC.)

    1. under $1.00
    2. $1.00 to 2.99
    3. $3.00 to 4.99
    4. $5.00 to 9.99
    5. over $10.00

18. ABOUT HOW MUCH OF YOUR SPENDING MONEY IS GIVEN TO YOU BY YOUR PARENTS?

    1. none of it
    2. less than ¼
    3. about ¼
    4. about ½
    5. about ¾
    6. almost all of it

19. DO YOU HAVE A REGULAR JOB (LIKE BABYSITTING, OR A PAPER ROUTE) BESIDES THE JOBS YOU DO AT HOME?

    1. no
    2. yes

20. HERE IS A LIST OF GROUPS AND CLUBS. PLEASE CIRCLE THE ONES YOU ARE IN. (Circle all that apply.)

    1. a sports team
    2. a school group or club (like band, school newspaper, or science club)
    3. groups or clubs outside of school (like Scouts, or Campfire girls)
    4. church or temple groups (like youth groups or Hebrew school)
    5. volunteer work (like hospital work or recycling)
    6. park district programs
    7. other activities
    8. none

21. DO YOU TAKE LESSONS OUTSIDE SCHOOL TO LEARN THINGS LIKE MUSIC, ART, GYMNASTICS, OR KARATE?

    1. no
    2. yes

22. ABOUT HOW OFTEN DO YOU GO TO CHURCH OR TEMPLE SERVICES?

    1. never
    2. a few times a year
    3. about once a month
    4. a couple of times a month
    5. about once a week
    6. more than once a week

23. WOULD YOU LIKE TO GO TO CHURCH OR TEMPLE MORE, LESS, OR ABOUT THE SAME AMOUNT AS YOU DO NOW?

    1. less
    2. about the same as now
    3. more

II. THE NEXT FEW QUESTIONS ASK FOR MORE PERSONAL DETAILS ABOUT YOUR FAMILY.

1. DOES YOUR **FATHER** SMOKE CIGARETTES?

    1. no
    2. yes, sometimes
    3. yes, a lot
    9. don't know

2. DOES HE DRINK THINGS LIKE BEER, WINE, OR WHISKEY?

    1. no
    2. yes, sometimes
    3. yes, a lot
    9. don't know

3. DOES HE EVER TAKE PILLS TO LOSE WEIGHT, GO TO SLEEP, OR KEEP HIMSELF AWAKE?

    1. no
    2. yes, sometimes
    3. yes, a lot
    9. don't know

4. DOES YOUR **MOTHER** SMOKE CIGARETTES?

    1. no
    2. yes, sometimes
    3. yes, a lot
    9. don't know

5. DOES SHE DRINK THINGS LIKE BEER, WINE, OR WHISKEY?

    1. no
    2. yes, sometimes
    3. yes, a lot
    9. don't know

6. DOES SHE EVER TAKE PILLS TO LOSE WEIGHT, GO TO SLEEP, OR KEEP HERSELF AWAKE?

    1. no
    2. yes, sometimes
    3. yes, a lot
    9. don't know

7. DO EITHER OF YOUR PARENTS SMOKE MARIJUANA (grass, hash, pot)?

    1. no
    2. yes, sometimes
    3. yes, a lot
    9. don't know

8. IF YOU HAVE **BROTHERS** OR **SISTERS**, DO ANY OF THEM SMOKE CIGARETTES?

   1. no
   2. yes, sometimes
   3. yes, a lot
   8. have no brothers or sisters
   9. don't know

9. DO ANY OF THEM DRINK THINGS LIKE BEER, WINE, OR WHISKEY?

   1. no
   2. yes, sometimes
   3. yes, a lot
   8. have no brothers or sisters
   9. don't know

10. DO ANY OF THEM SMOKE MARIJUANA (pot, hash, grass)?

   1. no
   2. yes, sometime
   3. yes, a lot
   8. have no brothers or sisters
   9. don't know

11. DO ANY OF THEM USE DRUGS **OTHER THAN** MARIJUANA (like uppers, downers, pills or acid)?

   1. no
   2. yes, sometimes
   3. yes, a lot
   8. have no brothers or sisters
   9. don't know

III. **THIS SECTION ASKS MORE QUESTIONS ABOUT SMOKING CIGARETTES, DRINKING, AND USING DRUGS WITHOUT A DOCTOR'S ORDERS.**

1. HAVE YOU **EVER** TRIED ANY OF THESE THINGS? (Circle either yes or no under each question.)

   A. Wine or Beer

      1. no
      2. yes

   B. Hard Liquor (like scotch whiskey, rum, vodka)

      1. no
      2. yes

   C. Glue, Spray Cans, etc. for sniffing

      1. no
      2. yes

   D. Marijuana (grass, pot, weed, hash)

      1. no
      2. yes

   E. Other drugs (like acid, LSD, speed, uppers, downers, sleeping pills)

      1. no
      2. yes

   F. Cigarettes

      1. no
      2. yes

2. HAVE YOU USED ANY OF THESE THINGS **MORE THAN** ONCE OR TWICE THIS SCHOOL YEAR (since September)?

   A. Wine or Beer

      1. no
      2. yes

   B. Hard liquor (like scotch, whiskey, rum, vodka)

      1. no
      2. yes

   C. Glue, Spray Cans, etc. for sniffing

      1. no
      2. yes

   D. Marijuana (grass, pot, weed, hash)

      1. no
      2. yes

   E. Other drugs (like acid, LSD, speed, uppers, downers)

      1. no
      2. yes

3. IF YOU HAVE SMOKED CIGARETTES MORE THAN A FEW TIMES, WHAT ARE YOUR MOST IMPORTANT REASONS FOR SMOKING? (Circle all that apply.)

    1. I do not use cigarettes
    2. to feel good
    3. to relax
    4. because it is "cool"
    5. to feel more friendly
    6. to find out what it is like
    7. to annoy my teachers
    8. to see if I can get away with it
    9. to be liked by my friends
    10. to annoy my parents
    11. it makes me feel older
    12. other

4. HOW COMFORTABLE DO YOU FEEL WHEN TALKING ABOUT DRUGS WITH YOUR PARENTS?

    1. not comfortable at all
    2. somewhat comfortable
    3. very comfortable
    4. we never talk about drugs

START
CARD
C

_____

IV. THIS NEXT SET OF QUESTIONS IS ABOUT THE KIDS YOU HANG AROUND WITH.

1. ABOUT HOW MANY OF THE KIDS YOU HANG AROUND WITH HAVE TRIED THINGS LIKE BEER, WINE, OR WHISKEY?

    1. none
    2. one or two
    3. some
    4. most
    5. all
    9. don't know

2. ABOUT HOW MANY SMOKE CIGARETTES?

    1. none
    2. one or two
    3. some
    4. most
    5. all
    9. don't know

3. ABOUT HOW MANY HAVE TRIED MARIJUANA ? (pot, hash, grass, weed)

    1. none
    2. one or two
    3. some
    4. most
    5. all
    9. don't know

4. ABOUT HOW MANY HAVE STOLEN THINGS WORTH **MORE** THAN ABOUT FIVE DOLLARS?

    1. none
    2. one or two
    3. some
    4. most
    5. all
    9. don't know

5. ABOUT HOW MANY HAVE DAMAGED PROPERTY LIKE THROWING ROCKS AT CARS, SPRAY PAINTING WALLS, OR BREAKING WINDOWS **ON PURPOSE**?

    1. none
    2. one or two
    3. some
    4. most
    5. all
    9. don't know

V. THESE QUESTIONS ARE ABOUT OTHER THINGS SOME KIDS HAVE DONE.

1. HAVE YOU **EVER** DONE ANY OF THESE THINGS?
(Circle "no" or "yes" under each question.)

    A. TAKEN SOMETHING FROM A STORE THAT COST ABOUT $5.00 OR **LESS?**

        1. no
        2. yes

    B. TAKEN SOMETHING FROM A STORE THAT COST **MORE** THAN ABOUT $5.00?

        1. no
        2. yes

    C. DAMAGED PROPERTY (LIKE THROWING ROCKS AT CARS, BREAKING WINDOWS **ON PURPOSE**)?

        1. no
        2. yes

    D. WRITTEN THINGS OR DRAWN PICTURES ON BUILDINGS, SIGNS, FENCES, OR WALLS?

        1. no
        2. yes

    E. SKIPPED (OR "DITCHED") SCHOOL WITHOUT PERMISSION?

        1. no
        2. yes

    F. CHEATED ON A TEST AT SCHOOL?

        1. no
        2. yes

    G. STOLEN A BICYCLE?

        1. no
        2. yes

    H. BEEN IN A BIG FIGHT WITH ANOTHER STUDENT?

        1. no
        2. yes

2. HAVE YOU EVER RUN AWAY FROM HOME FOR MORE THAN A DAY?

    1. no
    2. yes

3. SINCE THE BEGINNING OF THE SCHOOL YEAR THIS SEPTEMBER, HAVE YOU DONE ANY OF THESE THINGS **MORE THAN ONCE OR TWICE?**

    A. TAKEN SOMETHING FROM A STORE THAT COST ABOUT $5.00 OR **LESS?**

        1. no
        2. yes

    B. TAKEN SOMETHING FROM A STORE THAT COST **MORE** THAN ABOUT $5.00?

        1. no
        2. yes

    C. DAMAGED PROPERTY (LIKE THROWING ROCKS AT CARS, BREAKING WINDOWS **ON PURPOSE**)?

        1. no
        2. yes

    D. WRITTEN THINGS OR DRAWN PICTURES ON BUILDINGS, SIGNS, FENCES, OR WALLS?

        1. no
        2. yes

    E. SKIPPED (OR "DITCHED") SCHOOL WITHOUT PERMISSION?

        1. no
        2. yes

    F. CHEATED ON A TEST AT SCHOOL?

        1. no
        2. yes

    G. STOLEN A BICYCLE?

        1. no
        2. yes

    H. BEEN IN A BIG FIGHT WITH ANOTHER STUDENT?

        1. no
        2. yes

4. HAVE YOU BEEN TAKEN TO THE POLICE STATION MORE THAN ONCE OR TWICE FOR DOING SOMETHING WRONG?

    1. no
    2. yes

VI. THESE LAST QUESTIONS ASK ABOUT FEELINGS YOU MAY HAVE. CIRCLE THE ANSWER THAT IS CLOSEST TO THE WAY YOU FEEL.

1. HOW OFTEN DO YOU FEEL THAT NO ONE LISTENS TO WHAT YOU SAY?

    1. never
    2. hardly ever
    3. sometimes
    4. often
    5. almost always

2. HOW OFTEN DO YOU FEEL HAPPY TO BE ALIVE?

    1. never
    2. hardly ever
    3. sometimes
    4. often
    5. almost always

3. HOW OFTEN DO YOU FEEL THAT EVERYONE'S ORDERING YOU AROUND?

    1. never
    2. hardly ever
    3. sometimes
    4. often
    5. almost always

4. HOW OFTEN DO YOU FEEL THAT NO ONE REALLY LIKES YOU?

    1. never
    2. hardly ever
    3. sometimes
    4. often
    5. almost always

5. HOW OFTEN DO YOU FEEL BORED?

    1. never
    2. hardly ever
    3. sometimes
    4. often
    5. almost always

6. HOW OFTEN ARE YOU HAPPY TO BE THE SEX YOU ARE?

    1. never
    2. hardly ever
    3. sometimes
    4. often
    5. almost always

7. HOW OFTEN ARE YOU ANGRY AT SOMEONE?

    1. never
    2. hardly ever
    3. sometimes
    4. often
    5. almost always

**THIS IS THE END OF THE QUESTIONNAIRE.
THANK YOU FOR YOUR HELP.**

7TH AND 8TH GRADE QUESTIONNAIRE

INSTRUCTIONS

Since this is a questionnaire, not a test, there are no right and wrong answers. Try to work through the questionnaire quickly, and if you are not sure about an answer, make the best estimate you can. It is important that you try to do all of the questions, so do not spend too much time on any one.

Some of the questions are about your parents. If you are living another adult (stepparent, foster parent, etc.) answer as if he or she were your real parent. If you are living with only one parent, answer for both real parents.

Please **answer** the following practice questions. As the first two examples show, sometimes you will be asked to fill in your own responses.

WHAT IS YOUR BIRTHDATE?

_____
month   day   year

WHAT KIND OF JOB DOES YOUR FATHER HAVE?

_____

Usually you will be asked to circle the number next to the **single best** answer. For example:

WHAT GRADE ARE YOU IN?

1. sixth
2. seventh
3. eighth
4. ninth

Sometimes you will be asked to circle numbers to **more than one** answer. For example:

IN YOUR HOME, WHICH OF THE FOLLOWING JOBS (IF ANY) DO YOU USUALLY HAVE TO DO? (Circle all that apply.)

1. clean your room
2. wash or dry dishes
3. ironing or laundry
4. babysit for younger brothers or sisters
5. take out garbage
6. mow the lawn, or do other yard work
7. take care of pets
8. wash a car
9. shovel snow
10. household repairs like painting or plumbing
11. clean rooms other than your own
12. set or clear the table
13. cooking
14. other (what?_____)
15. none

Please try to work quickly. If none of the answers fit your feelings exactly, choose the one which comes closest. If you have any problems, raise your hand and your teacher will help you.

I. THESE FIRST FEW QUESTIONS ARE ABOUT YOU AND YOUR FAMILY.

1. ARE YOU MALE OR FEMALE?

 1. male
 2. female

2. WITH WHOM DO YOU LIVE?

 1. mother and father
 2. mother and stepfather
 3. father and stepmother
 4. mother only
 5. father only
 6. other

3. HOW MANY **OLDER** BROTHERS DO YOU HAVE?

 _____

 OLDER SISTERS?

 _____

4. HAS YOUR **FATHER** GONE TO COLLEGE?

 1. no
 2. yes
 9. don't know

5. HAS YOUR **MOTHER** GONE TO COLLEGE?

 1. no
 2. yes
 9. don't know

6. IF YOUR MOTHER WORKS, WHAT KIND OF JOB DOES SHE HAVE?

 _____

7. OVER THE PAST YEAR OR SO, ABOUT HOW WELL HAVE YOU DONE IN YOUR SCHOOL WORK?

    1. far below average
    2. below average
    3. average
    4. above average
    5. far above average

8. HOW MUCH DO YOU LIKE SCHOOL?

    1. not at all
    2. a little
    3. some
    4. a lot

9. ABOUT HOW MANY DAYS LAST YEAR DID YOU STAY HOME FROM SCHOOL BECAUSE YOU WERE SICK?

    _____ days

10. HAVE YOU EVER WORN GLASSES?

    1. no
    2. yes

11. HAVE YOU EVER WORN CONTACT LENSES?

    1. no
    2. yes

12. HAVE YOU EVER WORN BRACES ON YOUR TEETH?

    1. no
    2. yes

13. ARE YOU UNDER PRESSURE FROM YOUR PARENTS TO GET HIGH GRADES?

    1. no
    2. yes, a little
    3. yes, some
    4. yes, a lot

14. HOW IMPORTANT ARE HIGH GRADES TO YOU?

    1. not at all important
    2. not very important
    3. somewhat important
    4. very important

15. HERE IS A LIST OF THINGS THAT SOME FAMILIES HAVE RULES ABOUT. CIRCLE THE KINDS OF FAMILY RULES THAT YOU HAVE. (Circle all that apply.)

    1. your table manners
    2. how much T.V. you can watch
    3. times you must be home at night (curfews)
    4. how often you can go out with friends
    5. how much studying or homework you must do
    6. how you dress or wear your hair
    7. how you spend your money
    8. none of these

16. IN GENERAL, HOW DO YOUR PARENTS GET YOU TO OBEY FAMILY RULES? (Circle all that apply.)

    1. by talking with you
    2. by taking away privileges (like watching T.V. or "grounding" you)
    3. by embarrassing or making fun of you
    4. by ignoring you, not paying attention to you
    5. by giving you a reward for being good
    6. by hitting you
    7. by yelling at you
    8. other (how?_____)

START
CARD
B

17. HOW MUCH DO YOU FIGHT WITH YOUR PARENTS?

    1. not at all
    2. a little
    3. some
    4. a lot

18. HOW MUCH DO YOU DISOBEY YOUR PARENTS?

    1. not at all
    2. a little
    3. some
    4. a lot

19. GENERALLY, ABOUT HOW MUCH SPENDING MONEY DO YOU GET EACH WEEK?
(Include allowance, lunch money, earnings, etc.)

    1. under $1.00
    2. $1.00 to 2.99
    3. $3.00 to 4.99
    4. $5.00 to 9.99
    5. $10.00 to 14.99
    6. $15.00 or more

20. ABOUT HOW MUCH OF YOUR SPENDING MONEY IS GIVEN TO YOU BY YOUR PARENTS?

    1. none of it
    2. less than ¼
    3. about ¼
    4. about ½
    5. about ¾
    6. almost all of it

21. DO YOU HAVE A REGULAR JOB BESIDES THE JOBS YOU DO AT HOME (LIKE A PAPER ROUTE OR BABYSITTING)?

    1. no
    2. yes

22. HERE IS A LIST OF GROUPS AND CLUBS. PLEASE CIRCLE THE ONES YOU ARE IN. (Circle all that apply.)

    1. a sports team
    2. a school group or club (like band, school newspaper, or science club)
    3. groups or clubs outside of school (like Scouts or Campfire girls)
    4. church or temple groups (like youth groups or Hebrew school)
    5. volunteer work (like hospital work or recycling)
    6. park district programs
    7. other (what? _____)
    8. none

23. DO YOU TAKE LESSONS OUTSIDE SCHOOL TO LEARN THINGS LIKE MUSIC, ART, GYMNASTICS, OR KARATE?

    1. no
    2. yes

24. ABOUT HOW OFTEN DO YOU GO TO CHURCH OR TEMPLE SERVICES?

    1. never
    2. a few times a year
    3. about once a month
    4. a couple of times a month
    5. about once a week
    6. more than once a week

25. WOULD YOU LIKE TO GO TO CHURCH OR TEMPLE MORE, LESS, OR ABOUT THE SAME AMOUNT AS YOU DO NOW?

    1. less
    2. about the same as now
    3. more

II. THE NEXT FEW QUESTIONS ASK FOR MORE PERSONAL DETAILS ABOUT YOUR FAMILY.

1. DOES YOUR FATHER SMOKE CIGARETTES?

    1. no
    2. yes, sometimes
    3. yes, a lot
    9. don't know

2. DOES HE DRINK THINGS LIKE BEER, WINE, OR WHISKEY?

    1. no
    2. yes, sometimes
    3. yes, a lot
    9. don't know

3. DOES HE EVER TAKE PILLS TO LOSE WEIGHT, GO TO SLEEP, OR KEEP HIMSELF ALERT?

    1. no
    2. yes, sometimes
    3. yes, a lot
    9. don't know

4. DOES YOUR MOTHER SMOKE CIGARETTES?

    1. no
    2. yes, sometimes
    3. yes, a lot
    9. don't know

5. DOES SHE DRINK THINGS LIKE BEER, WINE, OR WHISKEY?

    1. no
    2. yes, sometimes
    3. yes, a lot
    9. don't know

6. DOES SHE EVER TAKE PILLS TO LOSE WEIGHT, GO TO SLEEP, OR KEEP HERSELF ALERT?

    1. no
    2. yes, sometimes
    3. yes, a lot
    9. don't know

7. DO EITHER OF YOUR PARENTS SMOKE MARIJUANA (grass, pot, hash)?

    1. no
    2. yes, sometimes
    3. yes, a lot
    4. don't know

8. IF YOU HAVE BROTHERS OR SISTERS, DO ANY OF THEM SMOKE CIGARETTES?

    1. no
    2. yes, sometimes
    3. yes, a lot
    8. have no brothers or sisters
    9. don't know

9. DO ANY OF THEM DRINK THINGS LIKE BEER, WINE, OR WHISKEY?

    1. no
    2. yes, sometimes
    3. yes, a lot
    8. have no brothers or sisters
    9. don't know

10. DO ANY OF THEM SMOKE MARIJUANA?

    1. no
    2. yes, sometimes
    3. yes, a lot
    8. have no brothers or sisters
    9. don't know

II. DO ANY OF THEM USE DRUGS **OTHER THAN** MARIJUANA (like uppers, downers, pills or acid)?

    1. no
    2. yes, sometimes
    3. yes, a lot
    8. have no brothers or sisters
    9. don't know

III. **THIS SECTION ASKS MORE QUESTIONS ABOUT SMOKING CIGARETTES, DRINKING, AND USING DRUGS WITHOUT A DOCTOR'S ORDERS.**

1. ABOUT HOW MANY OF THE KIDS YOU HANG AROUND WITH SMOKE CIGARETTES?

    1. none
    2. one or two
    3. some
    4. most
    5. all
    9. don't know

2. ABOUT HOW MANY DRINK THINGS LIKE BEER, WINE OR WHISKEY?

    1. none
    2. one or two
    3. some
    4. most
    5. all
    9. don't know

3. ABOUT HOW MANY SMOKE MARIJUANA?

    1. none
    2. one or two
    3. some
    4. most
    5. all
    9. don't know

4. ABOUT HOW MANY USE DRUGS **OTHER THAN** MARIJUANA (like uppers, downers, pills or acid)?

    1. none
    2. one or two
    3. some
    4. most
    5. all
    9. don't know

5. DO YOU SMOKE CIGARETTES?

    1. no
    2. yes, sometimes
    3. yes, a lot

6. IF YOU HAVE SMOKED CIGARETTES MORE THAN A FEW TIMES, WHAT ARE YOUR MOST IMPORTANT REASONS FOR SMOKING? (Circle all that apply)

    1. I do not use cigarettes
    2. to feel good
    3. to relax
    4. because it is "cool"
    5. to feel more friendly
    6. to find out what it is like
    7. to annoy my teachers
    8. to see if I can get away with it
    9. to be liked by my friends
    10. to annoy my parents
    11. it makes me feel older
    12. other (why? _____

PLEASE CIRCLE THE BEST ANSWER
IN EACH BOX ACROSS THE PAGE.

START
CARD
C

	CIGARETTES	ALCOHOL (like wine, beer, whiskey, vodka)	MARIJUANA (like grass, hash)	
7. ABOUT HOW MANY OF THE PEOPLE YOU HANG AROUND WITH HAVE EVER EXPERIMENTED WITH	1. none 2. one or two 3. some 4. most 5. all 9. don't know	1. none 2. one or two 3. some 4. most 5. all 9. don't know	1. none 2. one or two 3. some 4. most 5. all 9. don't know	1. 2. 3. 4. 5. 9.
8. HAVE YOU EVER EXPERIMENTED WITH	1. no 2. yes	1. no 2. yes	1. no 2. yes	

	ALCOHOL (like wine, beer, whiskey, vodka)	MARIJUANA (like grass, pot, weed, hash)	INHALANTS (like aerosol spray
9. In the six months or so since school began last September, about how many times, if at all, have you used	_____ times	_____ times	_____ times

INHALANTS (like glue, freon, aerosol sprays for sniffing)

PILLS (like "uppers" "downers", pep pills, tranquilizers, diet pills, speed)

PSYCHEDELICS (like "acid", LSD, STP, DMT)

HEROIN

OTHER NARCOTICS (like cocaine, darvon)

, pot, weed,

none	1. none	1. none	1. none	1. none
one or two	2. one or two	2. one or two	2. one or two	2. one or two
some	3. some	3. some	3. some	3. some
most	4. most	4. most	4. most	4. most
all	5. all	5. all	5. all	5. all
don't know	9. don't know	9. don't know	9. don't know	9. don't know

| 1. no | 1. no | 1. no | 1. no | 1. no |
| 2. yes | 2. yes | 2. yes | 2. yes | 2. yes |

glue, freon, ys for sniffing)

PILLS (like "uppers", "downers", pep pills, tranquilizers, diet pills, speed)

PSYCHEDELICS (like "acid", LSD, STP, DMT)

HEROIN

OTHER NARCOTICS (like cocaine, darvon)

_____times   _____times   _____times   _____times

10. IF YOU HAVE HAD A DRUG EDUCATION PROGRAM IN SCHOOL, WAS IT . . .

. . . ACCURATE?

1. no
2. yes
3. had no program
9. don't know

. . . HELPFUL?

1. no
2. yes
3. had no program

. . . COMPLETE?

1. no
2. yes
3. had no program
9. don't know

. . . VALUABLE?

1. no
2. yes
3. had no program

. . . INTERESTING?

1. no
2. yes
3. had no program

11. HOW COMFORTABLE DO YOU FEEL WHEN TALKING ABOUT DRUGS WITH YOUR PARENTS?

1. not comfortable at all
2. somewhat comfortable
3. very comfortable
4. we never talk about drugs

12. WHERE DID YOU GET MOST OF YOUR KNOWLEDGE ABOUT DRUGS? (Circle all that apply.)

1. reading books and/or pamphlets
2. friends
3. parents
4. teachers in regular school classes
5. school drug education programs
6. personal use of drugs
7. T.V., radio, newspapers, etc.
8. a minister, priest or rabbi
9. a youth counselor, guidance counselor or social worker
10. a non-school drug program or drug "hot line"
11. other (where? _____)

IV. THESE NEXT FEW QUESTIONS ARE ABOUT THINGS OTHER THAN DRUGS THAT YOU AND YOUR FRIENDS MAY HAVE DONE.

1. OF THE KIDS YOU HANG AROUND WITH, ABOUT HOW MANY HAVE DAMAGED PROPERTY (LIKE THROWING ROCKS AT CARS, SPRAY PAINTING WALLS, OR BREAKING WINDOWS ON PURPOSE)?

1. none
2. one or two
3. some
4. most
5. all
9. don't know

2. ABOUT HOW MANY HAVE STOLEN THINGS WORTH **MORE** THAN ABOUT FIVE DOLLARS?

1. none
2. one or two
3. some
4. most
5. all
9. don't know

3. IN THE SIX MONTHS OR SO SINCE SCHOOL BEGAN, ABOUT HOW MANY TIMES (if ever) HAVE YOU DONE ANY OF THESE THINGS?

	never	once	2-3 times	4-5 times	more than 5 times
A. Stolen from another student	1	2	3	4	5
B. Threatened to beat up another student	1	2	3	4	5
C. Been in a serious fight with another student	1	2	3	4	5
D. Written things or drawn pictures on **school** buildings or walls	1	2	3	4	5
E. Damaged school property in a **small way** (like defacing books, kicking in lockers, breaking things in the washrooms or other places)	1	2	3	4	5
F. Done a **lot** of damage to school property (like breaking lots of windows, smashing desks and furniture)	1	2	3	4	5

START
CARD
D

4. IN THE SIX MONTHS OR SO SINCE SCHOOL BEGAN, ABOUT HOW MANY TIMES (if ever) HAVE YOU DONE ANY OF THESE THINGS?

	never	once	2-3 times	4-5 times	more than 5 times
A. Stolen a bicycle	1	2	3	4	5
B. Shoplifted merchandise worth about $5.00 or **less**	1	2	3	4	5
C. Shoplifted merchandise worth **more** than about $5.00	1	2	3	4	5
D. Broken into someone's store or home	1	2	3	4	5
E. Written things or drawn pictures on surfaces (like buildings or walls, **not** including school property)	1	2	3	4	5
F. Damaged property **other than** school property in a **small** way (like throwing eggs at cars or houses, breaking a window on purpose)	1	2	3	4	5
G. Done a **lot** of damage to property **other than** school property (like breaking lots of windows, smashing furniture)	1	2	3	4	5
H. Stolen tape decks, hub caps, or other items from automobiles	1	2	3	4	5
I. Stolen a car	1	2	3	4	5

5. IF YOU HAVE CHEATED ON ANY ASSIGNMENT OR TEST THIS SCHOOL YEAR, ABOUT HOW MANY TIMES HAVE YOU DONE SO?

_____ times

6. IF YOU HAVE "SKIPPED" OR "DITCHED" SCHOOL THIS SCHOOL YEAR, ABOUT HOW MANY TIMES HAVE YOU DONE SO?

_____ times

7. ABOUT HOW MANY TIMES, IF EVER, HAVE YOU BEEN BROUGHT TO A POLICE STATION FOR SOMETHING YOU WERE ACCUSED OF DOING?

_____ times

V. THESE FINAL QUESTIONS ASK ABOUT OPINIONS OR FEELINGS YOU MAY HAVE.

1. ABOUT HOW OFTEN DO YOU FEEL . . .

	never	hardly ever	sometimes	often	almost always
A. That no one takes you seriously	1	2	3	4	5
B. Hassled	1	2	3	4	5
C. That everybody's ordering you around	1	2	3	4	5
D. Happy to be the sex you are	1	2	3	4	5
E. That no one really likes you	1	2	3	4	5
F. Bored	1	2	3	4	5
G. Angry at your parents	1	2	3	4	5
H. Angry at a teacher or principal	1	2	3	4	5

2. PEOPLE OFTEN HAVE DIFFERENT OPINIONS ABOUT DRUGS. FOR EACH OF THE FOLLOWING DRUGS, PLEASE INDICATE WHETHER **YOU** BELIEVE EACH STATEMENT IS LARGELY TRUE, LARGELY FALSE, OR DEPENDS. IF YOU ARE NOT SURE, MAKE THE BEST GUESS YOU CAN.

	ALCOHOL	MARIJUANA	OTHER DRUGS ("uppers" "downers", acid, LSD, speed, etc.)
A. Helps a person be a part of their group	1. true 2. depends 3. false	1. true 2. depends 3. false	1. true 2. depends 3. false
B. Can be harmful or dangerous	1. true 2. depends 3. false	1. true 2. depends 3. false	1. true 2. depends 3. false
C. Makes a person feel good	1. true 2. depends 3. false	1. true 2. depends 3. false	1. true 2. depends 3. false
D. It's worth trying once or twice to find out what it's like	1. true 2. depends 3. false	1. true 2. depends 3. false	1. true 2. depends 3. false
E. Using it leads to feelings of guilt	1. true 2. depends 3. false	1. true 2. depends 3. false	1. true 2. depends 3. false
F. Difficult to get	1. true 2. depends 3. false	1. true 2. depends 3. false	1. true 2. depends 3. false

THIS IS THE END OF THE QUESTIONNAIRE.
THANK YOU FOR YOUR HELP.

HIGH SCHOOL QUESTIONNAIRE

INSTRUCTIONS

Since this is a questionnaire, not a test, there are no right and wrong answers. Try to work through the questionnaire quickly, and if you are not sure about an answer, make the best estimate you can. It is important that you try to do all of the questions, so do not spend too much time on any one.

Some of the questions are about your parents. If you are living another adult (stepparent, foster parent, etc.) answer as if he or she were your real parent. If you are living with only one parent, answer for both real parents.

Please **answer** the following practice questions. As the first two examples show, sometimes you will be asked to fill in your own responses.

WHAT IS YOUR BIRTHDATE?

_____
month   day   year

WHAT KIND OF JOB DOES YOUR FATHER HAVE?

_____

Usually you will be asked to circle the number next to the **single best** answer. For example:

WHAT GRADE ARE YOU IN?

1. ninth
2. tenth
3. eleventh
4. twelfth

Sometimes you will be asked to circle numbers to **more than one** answer. For example:

IN YOUR HOME, WHICH OF THE FOLLOWING JOBS (IF ANY) DO YOU USUALLY HAVE TO DO? (Circle all that apply.)

1. clean your room
2. wash or dry dishes
3. ironing or laundry
4. babysit for younger brothers or sisters
5. take out garbage
6. mow the lawn, or do other yard work
7. take care of pets
8. wash a car
9. shovel snow
10. household repairs like painting or plumbing
11. clean rooms other than your own
12. set or clear the table
13. cooking
14. other (what? _____)
15. none

Please try to work quickly. If none of the answers fit your feelings exactly, choose the one which comes closest. If you have any problems, raise your hand and your teacher will help you.

I. THESE FIRST FEW QUESTIONS ASK FOR GENERAL INFORMATION ABOUT YOU AND YOUR FAMILY.

1. WHAT IS YOUR SEX?

   1. male
   2. female

2. WITH WHOM DO YOU LIVE?

   1. mother and father
   2. mother and stepfather
   3. father and stepmother
   4. mother only
   5. father only
   6. other (who? _____)

3. HOW MANY **OLDER** BROTHERS DO YOU HAVE?

   OLDER SISTERS?

4. DID YOUR **FATHER** COMPLETE . . .

   high school?

   1. no
   2. yes
   9. don't know

   college?

   1. no
   2. yes
   9. don't know

   technical (vocational) school?

   1. no
   2. yes
   9. don't know

   graduate or professional school?

   1. no
   2. yes
   9. don't know

START
CARD
B

5. DID YOUR **MOTHER** COMPLETE . . .

high school?
1. no
2. yes
9. don't know
college?
1. no
2. yes
9. don't know
technical (vocational) school?
1. no
2. yes
9. don't know
graduate or professional school?
1. no
2. yes
9. don't know

6. IF YOUR MOTHER WORKS, WHAT KIND OF JOB DOES SHE HAVE?

_____

7. DO YOUR PARENTS WANT YOU TO COMPLETE . . .

high school?
1. no
2. yes
9. don't know
college?
1. no
2. yes
9. don't know
technical (vocational) school?
1. no
2. yes
9. don't know
graduate or professional school?
1. no
2. yes
9. don't know

8. WHEN YOU FINISH YOUR EDUCATION, WHAT JOB WOULD YOU LIKE TO HAVE? (If you are not sure, what job do you think you would like most?)

_____

9. HOW MUCH EDUCATION DO **YOU** WANT TO GET?

high school?
1. no
2. yes
9. don't know
college?
1. no
2. yes
9. don't know
technical (vocational) school?
1. no
2. yes
9. don't know
graduate or professional school?
1. no
2. yes
9. don't know

10. OVER THE PAST YEAR OR SO, HOW WELL HAVE YOU DONE IN YOUR SCHOOL WORK?

1. far below average
2. below average
3. average
4. above average
5. far above average

11. HOW MUCH DO YOU LIKE SCHOOL?

1. not at all
2. a little
3. some
4. a lot

12. ABOUT HOW MANY DAYS LAST YEAR DID YOU STAY HOME FROM SCHOOL BECAUSE YOU WERE SICK?

_____days

13. HAVE YOU EVER WORN GLASSES?

1. no
2. yes

14. HAVE YOU EVER WORN CONTACT LENSES?

1. no
2. yes

15. HAVE YOU EVER WORN BRACES ON YOUR TEETH?

    1. no
    2. yes

16. ARE YOU UNDER PRESSURE FROM YOUR PARENTS TO GET HIGH GRADES?

    1. no
    2. yes, a little
    3. yes, some
    4. yes, a lot

17. FOR WHICH OF THE FOLLOWING ARE THERE FAMILY RULES THAT APPLY TO YOU? (Circle all that apply.)

    1. your table manners
    2. the amount of T.V. you can watch
    3. Curfews (both week-end and week-day)
    4. the number of week nights you can go out with friends
    5. studying or homework for school
    6. the way you dress or wear your hair
    7. accounting for the use of your money
    8. none of these

18. IN GENERAL, HOW DO YOU YOUR PARENTS ENFORCE FAMILY RULES? (Circle all that apply.)

    1. by reasoning with you
    2. by taking away privileges (like "grounding" you, etc.)
    3. by embarrassing or ridiculing you
    4. by ignoring you
    5. by rewarding you for good behavior
    6. by hitting or striking you
    7. by yelling at you
    8. other (how? _____)

19. HOW MUCH DO YOU FIGHT WITH YOUR PARENTS?

    1. not at all
    2. a little
    3. some
    4. a lot

20. HOW MUCH DO YOU DISOBEY YOUR PARENTS?

    1. not at all
    2. a little
    3. some
    4. a lot

21. WHAT KIND OF WORK DO YOU DO OUTSIDE YOUR HOME? (Circle all that apply.)

    1. I don't work outside my home
    2. full-time work in the summer
    3. part-time in the summer
    4. full-time during the school year
    5. part-time during the school year

22. GENERALLY, ABOUT HOW MUCH SPENDING MONEY DO YOU GET EACH WEEK? (Include rarfare, lunch money, allowance, earnings, etc.)

    1. under $1.00
    2. $1.00 to $2.99
    3. $3.00 to $4.99
    4. $5.00 to $9.99
    5. $10.00 to $14.99
    6. $15.00 to $19.99
    7. over $20.00

23. ABOUT HOW MUCH OF YOUR SPENDING MONEY IS GIVEN TO YOU BY YOUR PARENTS?

    1. none of it
    2. less than ¼
    3. about ¼
    4. about ½
    5. about ¾
    6. almost all of it

24. IN WHICH OF THE FOLLOWING ACTIVITIES ARE YOU CURRENTLY INVOLVED? (Circle all that apply.)

    1. a sports team
    2. a school-sponsored activity (like band, student government, newspaper, etc.)
    3. organizations or clubs outside school (like Scouts, etc.)
    4. religious sponsored activities (like youth groups, Hebrew school, etc.)
    5. volunteer work (like hospital work, recycling projects, etc.)
    6. park district programs
    7. other activities (what?_____)
    8. none

25. DO YOU TAKE LESSONS OUTSIDE SCHOOL TO LEARN THINGS LIKE MUSIC, ART, GYMNASTICS, OR KARATE?

    1. no
    2. yes

26. HOW FREQUENTLY DO YOU ATTEND RELIGIOUS SERVICES?

    1. never
    2. a few times a year
    3. about once a month
    4. a couple times a month
    5. about once a week
    6. more than once a week

27. WOULD YOU LIKE TO ATTEND RELIGIOUS SERVICES MORE, LESS, OR ABOUT THE SAME AMOUNT AS YOU DO NOW?

    1. less
    2. about the same as now
    3. more

II. THE NEXT FEW QUESTIONS ASK FOR MORE PERSONAL DETAILS ABOUT YOUR FAMILY.

1. DOES YOUR FATHER SMOKE CIGARETTES?

    1. no
    2. yes, sometimes
    3. yes, a lot
    9. don't know

2. DOES HE DRINK (for example, beer, wine, whiskey, etc.)?

    1. no
    2. yes, sometimes
    3. yes, a lot
    9. don't know

3. DOES HE EVER TAKE DIET PILLS, SLEEPING PILLS, OR STIMULANTS TO KEEP HIMSELF ALERT?

    1. no
    2. yes, sometimes
    3. yes, a lot
    9. don't know

4. DOES YOUR MOTHER SMOKE CIGARETTES?

    1. no
    2. yes, sometimes
    3. yes, a lot
    9. don't know

5. DOES SHE DRINK?

    1. no
    2. yes, sometimes
    3. yes, a lot
    9. don't know

6. DOES SHE EVER TAKE DIET PILLS, SLEEPING PILLS, OR STIMULANTS TO KEEP HERSELF ALERT?

    1. no
    2. yes, sometimes
    3. yes, a lot
    9. don't know

7. DO EITHER OF YOUR PARENTS SMOKE MARIJUANA (grass, hash, pot)?

    1. no
    2. yes, sometimes
    3. yes, a lot
    9. don't know

8. IF YOU HAVE BROTHERS OR SISTERS, DO ANY OF THEM SMOKE CIGARETTES?

    1. no
    2. yes, sometimes
    3. yes, a lot
    8. have no brothers or sisters
    9. don't know

9. DO ANY OF THEM DRINK?

    1. no
    2. yes, sometimes
    3. yes, a lot
    8. have no brothers or sisters
    9. don't know

10. DO ANY OF THEM SMOKE MARIJUANA?

    1. no
    2. yes, sometimes
    3. yes, a lot
    8. have no brothers or sisters
    9. don't know

11. DO ANY OF THEM USE DRUGS OTHER THAN MARIJUANA (for example, uppers, downers, pills, acid, etc.)?

    1. no
    2. yes, sometimes
    3. yes, a lot
    8. have no brothers or sisters
    9. don't know

III. **THIS SECTION ASKS MORE QUESTIONS ABOUT SMOKING CIGARETTES, DRINKING, AND USING DRUGS WITHOUT A DOCTOR'S PRESCRIPTION.**

PLEASE CIRCLE THE BEST ANSWER IN EACH BOX ACROSS THE PAGE.

START CARD C

	ALCOHOL (wine, beer, whiskey, gin, rum, etc.)	INHALANTS (glue, freon, aerosols, etc.)	MARIJUANA OR HASHISH (grass, weed, hash, etc.)	PSYC...
1. ABOUT HOW MANY OF THE PEOPLE YOU HANG AROUND WITH HAVE EVER EXPERIMENTED WITH . . .	1. none 2. one or two 3. some 4. most 5. all 9. don't know	1. none 2. one or two 3. some 4. most 5. all 9. don't know	1. none 2. one or two 3. some 4. most 5. all 9. don't know	1. none 2. one or two 3. some 4. most 5. all 9. don't know
2. HAVE YOU EVER EXPERIMENTED WITH . . .	1. no 2. yes	1. no 2. yes	1. no 2. yes	1. no 2. yes
3. IN THE SIX MONTHS OR SO SINCE SCHOOL BEGAN IN SEPTEMBER, ABOUT HOW MANY TIMES (IF AT ALL) HAVE YOU USED . . .	..........times	..........times	..........times	..........times
4. ABOUT HOW MANY OF THE PEOPLE YOU HANG AROUND WITH **REGULARLY** USE (at least once a month) . . .	1. none 2. one or two 3. some 4. most 5. all 9. don't know	1. none 2. one or two 3. some 4. most 5. all 9. don't know	1. none 2. one or two 3. some 4. most 5. all 9. don't know	1. none 2. one or two 3. some 4. most 5. all 9. don't know
5. ABOUT HOW MANY OF THE PEOPLE YOU HANG AROUND WITH **HEAVILY** USE (at least once a week) . . .	1. none 2. one or two 3. some 4. most 5. all 9. don't know	1. none 2. one or two 3. some 4. most 5. all 9. don't know	1. none 2. one or two 3. some 4. most 5. all 9. don't know	1. none 2. one or two 3. some 4. most 5. all 9. don't know

	...EDELICS (acid, LSD, mescaline, ...TP, DMT, etc)	COCAINE	"UPPERS" (pep pills, diet pills, bennies, dexies, speed, methedrine, meth, etc.)	"DOWNERS" (goofballs, blues, yellows, reds, seconal, nembutal, quaaludes, librium, tranquilizers, etc.)	HEROIN	OTHER NARCOTICS (opium, morphine, methadone, darvon, etc.)
	1. none 2. one or two 3. some 4. most 5. all 9. don't know	1. none 2. one or two 3. some 4. most 5. all 9. don't know	1. none 2. one or two 3. some 4. most 5. all 9. don't know	1. none 2. one or two 3. some 4. most 5. all 9. don't know	1. none 2. one or two 3. some 4. most 5. all 9. don't know	1. none 2. one or two 3. some 4. most 5. all 9. don't know
	1. no 2. yes	1. no 2. yes	1. no 2. yes	1. no 2. yes	1. no 2. yes	
	.........times	.........times	.........times	.........times	.........times	
	1. none 2. one or two 3. some 4. most 5. all 9. don't know	1. none 2. one or two 3. some 4. most 5. all 9. don't know	1. none 2. one or two 3. some 4. most 5. all 9. don't know	1. none 2. one or two 3. some 4. most 5. all 9. don't know	1. none 2. one or two 3. some 4. most 5. all 9. don't know	1. none 2. one or two 3. some 4. most 5. all 9. don't know
	1. none 2. one or two 3. some 4. most 5. all 9. don't know	1. none 2. one or two 3. some 4. most 5. all 9. don't know	1. none 2. one or two 3. some 4. most 5. all 9. don't know	1. none 2. one or two 3. some 4. most 5. all 9. don't know	1. none 2. one or two 3. some 4. most 5. all 9. don't know	1. none 2. one or two 3. some 4. most 5. all 9. don't know

START
CARD D

6. IF YOU USE DRUGS (excluding alcohol)
WHEN ARE YOU LIKELY TO DO SO? (Circle all that apply.)

1. don't use drugs
2. parties and dances
3. studying for important exams or tests
4. at a small gathering of friends
5. when alone with someone of the opposite sex
6. concerts, movies, etc.
7. before participation in sports
8. on dates
9. before going to sleep
10. when there's nothing else to do
11. other (when? _____)

7. ABOUT HOW MANY OF THE PEOPLE YOU HANG AROUND WITH SMOKE CIGARETTES?

1. none
2. one or two
3. some
4. most
5. all
9. don't know

8. CURRENTLY, ABOUT HOW MANY CIGARETTES DO YOU SMOKE A DAY?

1. none
2. less than a couple a day
3. a couple a day
4. half a pack a day
5. a pack a day
6. over a pack a day

9. IF YOU DRINK SOCIALLY, ON THE AVERAGE, HOW MUCH DO YOU DRINK?

1. don't drink
2. not much
3. enough to relax
4. enough to get high
5. enough to get drunk

10. IN THE SIX MONTHS OR SO SINCE THIS SCHOOL YEAR BEGAN, ABOUT HOW OFTEN HAVE YOU BEEN DRINKING?

1. never
2. less than once a month
3. once or twice a month
4. once or twice a week (mostly weekends)
5. several days a week (week days)
6. every day

11. IF YOU DRINK ALCOHOL, **WHEN** ARE YOU LIKELY TO DO SO? (Circle all that apply.)

1. don't drink alcohol
2. on religious occasions (communion, passover, etc.)
3. parties or dances
4. studying for important exams or tests
5. at a small gathering of friends
6. when alone with someone of the opposite sex
7. concerts, movies, etc.
8. before participation in sports
9. on dates
10. before going to sleep
11. when there's nothing else to do
12. other (when? _____)

12. WHERE DID YOU GET MOST OF YOUR KNOWLEDGE ABOUT DRUGS? (Circle all that apply.)

1. reading books and/or pamphlets
2. friends
3. parents
4. teachers in regular school classes
5. school drug education programs
6. personal use of drugs
7. T.V., radio, newspapers, etc.
8. a minister, priest or rabbi
9. a youth counselor, guidance counselor or social worker
10. a non-school drug program or drug "hot line"
11. other (where? _____)

13. HOW COMFORTABLE DO YOU FEEL WHEN TALKING ABOUT DRUGS WITH YOUR PARENTS?

1. not comfortable at all
2. somewhat comfortable
3. very comfortable
4. we never talk about drugs

14. IF YOU HAVE HAD A DRUG EDUCATION PROGRAM IN SCHOOL, WAS IT . . .

. . . ACCURATE?

1. no
2. yes
3. had no program
9. don't know

. . . HELPFUL?

1. no
2. yes
3. had no program

. . . COMPLETE?

1. no
2. yes
3. had no program
9. don't know

. . . VALUABLE?

1. no
2. yes
3. had no program

. . . INTERESTING?

1. no
2. yes
3. had no program

IV. **THESE NEXT FEW QUESTIONS ARE ABOUT THINGS OTHER THAN DRUGS THAT YOU AND YOUR FRIENDS MAY HAVE DONE.**

1. OF THE PEOPLE YOU HANG AROUND WITH, ABOUT HOW MANY (IF ANY) HAVE EVER DONE THESE THINGS?

	none	one or two	some	most	all
A. Stolen **school** property	1	2	3	4	5
B. Stolen from another student	1	2	3	4	5
C. Been in a serious fight with another student	1	2	3	4	5
D. Written political slogans, obscenities, or drawn other graffitti on surfaces like **school** buildings or walls	1	2	3	4	5
E. Damaged **school** property in a **small** way (defacing books kicking in lockers, breaking things in the washrooms or other facilities, etc.)	1	2	3	4	5
F. Done a **lot** of damage to **school** property (breaking lots of windows, smashing desks and furniture, etc.)	1	2	3	4	5

START
CARD
E

2. IN THE SIX MONTHS OR SO SINCE THIS SCHOOL YEAR BEGAN, ABOUT HOW MANY TIMES (IF EVER) HAVE YOU DONE THESE THINGS?

	never	once	2-3 times	4-5 times	more than 5 times
A. Stolen school property	1	2	3	4	5
B. Stolen from another student	1	2	3	4	5
C. Been in a serious fight with another student	1	2	3	4	5
D. Written political slogans, obscenities or drawn other graffitti on surfaces like school buildings or walls.	1	2	3	4	5
E. Damaged school property in a small way (defacing books kicking in lockers, breaking things in the washrooms or other facilities, etc.)	1	2	3	4	5
F. Done a lot of damage to school property (breaking lots of windows, smashing desks and furniture, etc.)	1	2	3	4	5

3. OF THE PEOPLE YOU HANG AROUND WITH, ABOUT HOW MANY (IF ANY) HAVE EVER DONE THESE THINGS?

	none	one or two	some	most	all
A. Stolen a bicycle	1	2	3	4	5
B. Shoplifted merchandise worth about $5.00 or less	1	2	3	4	5
C. Shoplifted merchandise worth more than about $5.00	1	2	3	4	5
D. Broken into a store or someone's home	1	2	3	4	5
E. Damaged private property (like throwing eggs at a car or house, breaking windows, smashing furniture, etc.)	1	2	3	4	5
F. Damaged public property except a school (like breaking windows, smashing furniture, etc.)	1	2	3	4	5
G. Stolen tape decks, hub caps, or other items from automobiles.	1	2	3	4	5
H. Stolen a car.	1	2	3	4	5

4. IN THE SIX MONTHS OR SO SINCE THE BEGINNING OF THIS SCHOOL YEAR, ABOUT HOW MANY TIMES (IF EVER) HAVE YOU DONE THESE THINGS?

	never	once	2-3 times	4-5 times	more than 5 times
A. Stolen a bicycle	1	2	3	4	5
B. Shoplifted merchandise worth about $5.00 or less	1	2	3	4	5
C. Shoplifted merchandise worth more than about $5.00	1	2	3	4	5
D. Broken into a store or someone's home	1	2	3	4	5
E. Damaged private property (like throwing eggs at a car or house, breaking windows, smashing furniture, etc.)	1	2	3	4	5
F. Damaged public property except a school (like breaking windows, smashing furniture, etc.)	1	2	3	4	5
G. Stolen tape decks, hub caps, or other items from automobiles.	1	2	3	4	5
H. Stolen a car	1	2	3	4	5

5. IF YOU HAVE CHEATED ON ANY ASSIGNMENT OR TEST THIS SCHOOL YEAR, ABOUT HOW MANY TIMES HAVE YOU DONE SO?

_____ times

6. ABOUT HOW MANY TIMES, IF EVER, HAVE YOU BEEN BROUGHT TO A POLICE STATION FOR SOMETHING YOU WERE ACCUSED OF DOING?

_____ times

7. HOW MANY TIMES, IF EVER, HAVE YOU APPEARED BEFORE A JUDGE FOR SOMETHING YOU WERE ACCUSED OF DOING?

_____ times

8. HAVE YOU EVER RUN AWAY FROM HOME FOR MORE THAN A DAY?

1. yes
2. no

9. IF YOU HAVE RUN AWAY FROM HOME, HOW MANY TIMES HAVE YOU DONE SO?

_____ times

V. THE FOLLOWING QUESTIONS ARE ABOUT FEELINGS AND OPINIONS YOU MAY HAVE.

1. ABOUT HOW OFTEN DO YOU FEEL . . .

	never	hardly ever	sometimes	often	almost always
A. That no one takes you seriously	1	2	3	4	5
B. That nothing you do makes any difference	1	2	3	4	5
C. That everyone's ordering you around	1	2	3	4	5
D. Happy to be the sex you are	1	2	3	4	5
E. That no one really likes you	1	2	3	4	5
F. Hassled	1	2	3	4	5
G. Bored	1	2	3	4	5
H. Optimistic about your future	1	2	3	4	5
I. Angry at your parents	1	2	3	4	5
J. Worried about your future	1	2	3	4	5
K. Angry at a teacher or principal	1	2	3	4	5

START
CARD
  F

2. PEOPLE OFTEN HAVE DIFFERENT
   OPINIONS ABOUT DRUG USE.
   FOR EACH OF THE FOLLOWING
   DRUGS, PLEASE INDICATE
   WHETHER YOU BELIEVE EACH
   STATEMENT IS LARGELY TRUE,
   LARGELY FALSE, OR WHETHER
   IT DEPENDS. IF YOU ARE NOT
   SURE, MAKE THE BEST ESTIMATE
   YOU CAN.

	ALCOHOL	MARIJUANA	PSYCHEDELICS (acid, LSD, etc.)	"UPPERS"	"DOWNERS"	HARD DRUGS (heroin, cocaine, etc.)
A. Relaxing	1. true 2. depends 3. false	1. true 2. depends 3. false	1. true 2. depends 3. false	1. true 2. depends 3. false	1. true 2. depends 3. false	1. true 2. depends 3. false
B. Physically addictive	1. true 2. depends 3. false	1. true 2. depends 3. false	1. true 2. depends 3. false	1. true 2. depends 3. false	1. true 2. depends 3. false	1. true 2. depends 3. false
C. Increases sensitivity to oneself and to one's surroundings	1. true 2. depends 3. false	1. true 2. depends 3. false	1. true 2. depends 3. false	1. true 2. depends 3. false	1. true 2. depends 3. false	1. true 2. depends 3. false
D. Helps a person be part of their group	1. true 2. depends 3. false	1. true 2. depends 3. false	1. true 2. depends 3. false	1. true 2. depends 3. false	1. true 2. depends 3. false	1. true 2. depends 3. false
E. Heightens physical pleasures	1. true 2. depends 3. false	1. true 2. depends 3. false	1. true 2. depends 3. false	1. true 2. depends 3. false	1. true 2. depends 3. false	1. true 2. depends 3. false
F. Difficult to get	1. true 2. depends 3. false	1. true 2. depends 3. false	1. true 2. depends 3. false	1. true 2. depends 3. false	1. true 2. depends 3. false	1. true 2. depends 3. false
G. Can be harmful or dangerous	1. true 2. depends 3. false	1. true 2. depends 3. false	1. true 2. depends 3. false	1. true 2. depends 3. false	1. true 2. depends 3. false	1. true 2. depends 3. false
H. Makes a person feel good	1. true 2. depends 3. false	1. true 2. depends 3. false	1. true 2. depends 3. false	1. true 2. depends 3. false	1. true 2. depends 3. false	1. true 2. depends 3. false
I. It's worth trying once or twice to find out what it's like	1. true 2. depends 3. false	1. true 2. depends 3. false	1. true 2. depends 3. false	1. true 2. depends 3. false	1. true 2. depends 3. false	1. true 2. depends 3. false
J. Using it leads to feelings of guilt	1. true 2. depends 3. false	1. true 2. depends 3. false	1. true 2. depends 3. false	1. true 2. depends 3. false	1. true 2. depends 3. false	1. true 2. depends 3. false

THIS IS THE END OF THE QUESTIONNAIRE.

THANK YOU FOR YOUR HELP.

Appendix C
Marginal Distributions
of Major Predictors

MARGINAL DISTRIBUTION OF ATTITUDE PREDICTORS (percent)

Fifth and Sixth Graders	Feelings of Anger
never	2.1
hardly ever	20.6
sometimes	52.9
often	16.3
almost always	8.0
	100
	(748)[a]

Seventh and Eighth Graders	Anger at Parents	Anger at School Officials
never	6.9	4.9
hardly ever	28.4	21.1
sometimes	42.7	36.4
often	15.9	20.4
almost always	6.0	17.1
	100	100
	(812)	(818)

High School Students	Anger at Parents	Anger at School Officials
never	4.1	4.7
hardly ever	30.2	31.5
sometimes	40.1	38.1
often	18.6	17.2
almost always	7.0	8.5
	100	100
	(1,219)	(1,224)

[a]Total number of students given in parentheses.

MARGINAL DISTRIBUTION OF SCHOOL
PREDICTORS (percent)

School Satisfaction	Fifth and Sixth Graders	Seventh and Eighth Graders	High School Students
not at all	3.9	10.1	10.1
a little	19.6	24.0	23.0
some	46.2	50.6	46.8
a lot	30.3	15.3	20.0
	100	100	100
	(749)	(838)	(1,237)

School Performance	Fifth and Sixth Graders	Seventh and Eighth Graders	High School Students
far below average	0.4	0.8	1.6
below average	4.0	5.5	6.8
average	35.3	37.0	39.0
above average	48.3	47.4	40.7
far above average	12.0	9.3	11.9
	100	100	100
	(748)	(838)	(1,230)

Parental Pressure to Get Good Grades		Seventh and Eighth Graders	High School Students
no		38.0	25.8
a little		34.6	36.7
some		16.1	23.3
a lot		11.3	14.3
		100	100
		(839)	(1,233)

MARGINAL DISTRIBUTION OF FAMILY
PREDICTORS (percent)

Fighting with Parents	*Fifth and Sixth Graders*	*Seventh and Eighth Graders*	*High School Students*
not at all	29.7	22.3	16.5
a little	54.4	50.0	51.0
some	12.4	21.0	23.3
a lot	3.5	6.8	9.1
	100	100	100
	(746)	(840)	(1,235)

Disobedience to Parents	*Fifth and Sixth Graders*	*Seventh and Eighth Graders*	*High School Students*
not at all	13.4	9.3	9.5
a little	66.4	61.8	58.0
some	15.9	23.8	26.6
a lot	4.3	5.1	5.9
	100	100	100
	(745)	(840)	(1,237)

Siblings' Alcohol Use	*Fifth and Sixth Graders*	*Seventh and Eighth Graders*	*High School Students*
no	65.2	45.5	28.6
sometimes	26.0	40.8	52.2
a lot	4.3	8.6	15.6
no siblings	4.4	0.4	0.7
don't know		4.8	1.9
	100	100	100
	(745)	(838)	(1,234)

Siblings' Marijuana Use	Fifth and Sixth Graders	Seventh and Eighth Graders	High School Students
no	86.7	62.6	50.2
sometimes	6.3	20.0	26.5
a lot	1.6	6.6	14.0
no siblings	4.4	0.2	0.7
don't know		10.6	8.5
	100	100	100
	(728)	(834)	(1,233)

Amount of Spending Money Weekly	Fifth and Sixth Graders
under $1	35.0
$1.00 to $2.99	46.2
$3.00 to $4.99	12.2
$5.00 to $9.99	4.1
over $10.00	2.5
	100
	(729)

MARGINAL DISTRIBUTION OF FRIENDS' DELINQUENCY PREDICTORS (percent)

Fifth, Sixth, Seventh, and Eighth Graders

	Friends' Alcohol Use		Friends' Marijuana Use		Friends' Cigarette Use	
	Fifth and Sixth Graders	*Seventh and Eighth Graders*	*Fifth and Sixth Graders*	*Seventh and Eighth Graders*	*Fifth and Sixth Graders*	*Seventh and Eighth Graders*
none	28.4	23.0	69.1	44.7	49.5	23.5
one or two	26.7	20.5	11.0	16.4	20.8	23.9
some	12.8	24.9	1.7	14.1	11.7	25.2
most	9.6	16.7	1.3	7.5	5.0	18.4
all	4.1	6.0	0.7	4.8	1.9	4.3
don't know	18.3	8.8	16.1	12.5	11.3	4.8
	100 (749)	100 (838)	100 (745)	100 (837)	100 (746)	100 (838)

	Friends' "Other" Drug Use	Friend's Shoplifting		Friends' Vandalism	
	Seventh and Eighth Graders	*Fifth and Sixth Graders*	*Seventh and Eighth Graders*	*Fifth and Sixth Graders*	*Seventh and Eighth Graders*
none	58.7	59.0	39.2	50.9	30.6
one or two	12.0	16.6	24.1	21.5	24.0
some	8.0	3.2	15.8	6.7	21.3
most	1.9	1.3	7.4	2.4	11.3
all	0.8	0.8	2.9	1.2	4.8
don't know	18.6	19.0	10.6	17.3	7.9
	100 (840)	100 (746)	100 (837)	100 (745)	100 (832)

High School Students

	Friends' Alcohol Use	Friends' Marijuana Use	Friends' Cigarette Use	Friends' Amphetamine Use
none	15.5	25.5	12.4	65.3
one or two	13.3	14.1	18.9	12.3
some	18.4	17.4	31.4	8.4
most	26.2	19.7	28.6	1.9
all	23.4	18.8	7.6	1.5
don't know	3.2	4.5	1.1	10.6
	100 (1,236)	100 (1,231)	100 (1,237)	100 (1,232)

	Friends' Barbiturate Use	Friends' Psychedelic Use
none	69.5	64.4
one or two	10.6	14.1
some	6.0	8.2
most	1.2	2.4
all	1.2	1.2
don't know	11.5	9.6
	100 (1,232)	100 (1,232)

	Friends' Theft from School	Friends' Theft from a Student	Friends' Fighting with a Student	Friends' Bike Theft
none	39.0	38.6	45.7	68.2
one or two	35.3	35.6	33.2	23.4
some	18.2	18.2	14.7	6.3
most	5.0	5.2	4.6	1.7
all	2.4	2.5	1.7	0.4
	100 (1,228)	100 (1,221)	100 (1,207)	100 (1,225)

	Friends' Minor Shoplifting	Friends' Major Shoplifting	Friends' Breaking and Entering	Friends' Theft of Auto Accessories
none	19.5	45.8	79.4	72.5
one or two	38.6	32.0	15.1	18.9
some	25.7	16.3	3.9	6.3
most	10.8	3.6	0.9	1.4
all	5.3	2.3	0.7	0.9
	100 (1,224)	100 (1,216)	100 (1,216)	100 (1,224)

	Friends' Auto Theft	Friends' School Defacement	Friends' Minor School Damage	Friends' Major School Damage
none	90.2	52.6	42.7	79.6
one or two	8.8	25.5	30.4	13.8
some	0.6	14.0	15.4	5.4
most	0.2	5.4	7.7	0.9
all	0.2	2.5	3.8	0.7
	100 (1,226)	100 (1,222)	100 (1,224)	100 (1,230)

	Friends' Damage to Private Property		Friends' Damage to Public Property
none	34.4		69.9
one or two	31.6		21.1
some	19.1		6.1
most	9.5		1.7
all	5.4		1.1
	100 (1,227)		100 (1,221)

Bibliography

Adler, F. 1975. *Sisters in Crime.* New York: McGraw-Hill.

Akers, R.L. 1964. "Socio-Economic Status and Delinquent Behavior: A Retest." *Journal of Research in Crime and Delinquency* I:38-46.

Ausubel, D.P. 1958. *Drug Addiction.* New York: Random House.

Becker, G.S. 1965. "A Theory of the Allocation of Time." *Economic Journal* 75 (September):494-517.

_____. 1974. "Crime and Punishment: An Economic Approach." In *Essays in the Economics of Crime and Punishment,* ed. G.S. Becker and W.M. Landes. New York: Columbia University Press.

Berk, R.A., and M. Brewer. 1978. "Feet of Clay in Hobnail Boots: An Assessment of Statistical Inference in Applied Research." In *Evaluation Studies Review Annual,* vol. 3. Beverly Hills: Sage Publications.

Berk, R.A., and N.C. Jurik. 1979. "Life At the Margin: An Introductory Review of Some Microeconomic Models with Sociological Applications." Unpublished manuscript, Social Process Research Institute, Santa Barbara, California.

Bernard, J. 1967. "Teen-age Culture: An Overview." In *Middle Class Juvenile Delinquency,* ed. E.W. Vaz. New York: Harper and Row.

Black, D.J. 1970. "Production of Crime Rates." *American Sociological Review* 35 (August):733-48.

Black, D.J., and A.J. Reiss. 1970. "Police Control of Juveniles." *American Sociological Review* 35 (February):63-67.

Block, M.K., and J.M. Heineke. 1975. "A Labor Theoretic Analysis of the Criminal Choice." *American Economics Review* 65(3):314-25.

Bohlke, R.H. 1961. "Social Mobility, Stratification Inconsistency and Middle Class Delinquency." *Social Problems* 8 (Spring):351-63.

Bowles, S., and H. Gintis. 1976. *Schooling in Capitalist America: Educational Reform and the Contradictions of Economic Life.* New York: Basic Books.

Box, S., and J. Ford. 1971. "The Facts Don't Fit: On the Relationship Between Social Class and Criminal Behavior." *The Sociological Review* 19 (February): 31-52.

Bronfenbrenner, U. 1968. "Socialization and Social Class Through Time and Space." In *Readings in Social Psychology*, ed. E.E. Maccoby et al. New York: Holt, Rinehart, and Winston.

Bull, C.N. 1973. "The Non-Cumulative Nature of Leisure Research." *Society and Leisure* 5(1):189-91.

Cameroun, M.D. 1964. *The Booster and the Snitch: Department Store Shoplifting*. Glencoe, Ill.: The Free Press.

Casparis, J., and E.W. Vaz. 1974. "Social Class and Self-Reported Delinquent Acts Among Swiss Boys." *International Journal of Comparative Sociology* 14(1-2):47-58.

Chesney-Lind, M. 1973. "Judicial Enforcement and the Female Sex Role: The Family Court and the Female Delinquent." *Issues in Criminology* 8 (Fall): 51-69.

Cicourel, A.V. 1968. *The Social Organization of Juvenile Justice*. New York: Wiley.

Clark, J.P., and L.L. Tifft. 1966. "Polygraph and Interview Validation of Self-Reported Deviant Behavior." *American Sociological Review* 31:516:23.

Clark, J.P., and E.P. Wenninger. 1962. "Socioeconomic Class and Area as Correlates of Illegal Behavior Among Juveniles." *American Sociological Review* 27 (December):826-34.

Cloward, R.A. 1959. "Illegitimate Means, Anomie, and Deviant Behavior." *American Sociological Review* 24 (April):168-79.

Cloward, R.A., and L. Ohlin. 1960. *Delinquency and Opportunity: A Theory of Delinquent Gangs*. Chicago: The Free Press.

Cohn, Y. 1963. "Criteria for the Probation Officer's Recommendation to the Juvenile Court." *Crime and Delinquency* 9:262-75.

Cohen, A.K. 1955. *Delinquent Boys: The Culture of the Gang*. Glencoe, Ill.: The Free Press.

_____. 1965. "The Sociology of the Deviant Act: Anomie Theory and Beyond." *American Sociological Review* 30 (February):5-14.

_____. 1967. "Middle Class Delinquency and the Social Structure." In *Middle Class Delinquency*, ed. E.W. Vaz, pp. 207-21. New York: Harper and Row.

Cohen, S. 1968. "The Politics of Vandalism." *The Nation* 11(207):497-500.

_____. 1972. "Breaking Out, Smashing Up, and the Social Context of Aspiration." In *Youth at the Beginning of the 70's*, ed. B. Riven. London: Markham.

_____. 1973. "Property Destruction: Motives and Meanings." In *Vandalism*, ed. C. Ward. New York: Van Nostrand Reinhold.

Coleman, J. 1961. *The Adolescent Society*. New York: The Free Press.

_____. 1965. *Adolescents and the Schools*. New York: Basic Books.

_____. 1967. "Athletics in High School." In *Middle Class Juvenile Delinquency*, ed. E.W. Vaz. New York: Harper and Row.

Cowie, J., V. Cowie and E. Slater. 1968. *Delinquency in Girls*. London: Heinemann.

Davis, A., and R.J. Havighurst. 1946. "Social Class and Color Differences in Childrearing." *American Sociological Review* 11:698-710.

de Grazia, S. 1962. *Of Time, Work, and Leisure.* New York: 20th Century Fund.

Dentler, R.A., and L.J. Monroe. 1961. "Social Correlates of Early Adolescent Theft." *American Sociological Review* 26:723-43.

Downes, D. 1966. *The Delinquent Solution.* London: Routledge and Kegan Paul.

Dumagedier, J. 1974. *Sociology of Leisure.* New York: Elsevier.

Ehrlich, I. 1974. "Participation in Illegitimate Activities: An Economic Analysis." In *Essays in the Economics of Crime and Punishment,* ed. G.S. Becker and W.M. Landes. New York: Columbia University Press.

_____. 1975. "The Deterrent Effects of Capital Punishment: A Question of Life and Death." *The American Economics Review* 63(3):397-417.

_____. 1977. "Capital Punishment and Deterrence: Some Further Thoughts and Additional Evidence." *Journal of Political Economy* 85(4):741-88.

Emerson, R.M. 1969. *Judging Delinquents: Context and Process in Juvenile Court.* Chicago: Aldine.

Empey, L.T., and M.L. Erickson. 1966. "Hidden Delinquency and Social Status." *Social Forces* 44 (June):546-54.

England, R.W. 1967. "A Theory of Middle Class Juvenile Delinquency." In *Middle Class Juvenile Delinquency,* ed. E.W. Vaz. New York: Harper and Row.

Erickson, M.L. 1972. "The Changing Relationship Between Official and Self-Reported Measures of Delinquency: An Exploratory-Predictive Study." *Journal of Criminal Law, Criminology, and Police Science* 63 3 (September): 388-95.

Erickson, M.L., and L.T. Empey, 1963. "Court Records, Undetected Delinquency, and Decision-Making." *Journal of Criminal Law, Criminology, and Police Science* 54(4):456-59.

Erlanger, H.S. 1974. "Social Class and Corporal Punishment in Childrearing: A Reassessment." *American Sociological Review* 39:68-85.

Flacks, R. 1970. "Social and Cultural Meanings of Student Revolt: Some Informal Comparative Observations." *Social Problems* 17(3):329-68.

_____. 1971. *Youth and Social Change.* Chicago: Markham.

Fleisher, B. 1966. *The Economics of Delinquency.* Chicago: Quadrangle Books.

Friedenberg, E.Z. 1965. *Coming of Age in America: Growth and Acquiescence.* New York: Random House.

_____. 1971. "The High School as A Focus of Student Unrest," *Annals of the American Academy of Political and Social Sciences* 395:117-26.

Gans, H. 1964. *The Urban Villagers.* Glencoe, Ill.: The Free Press.

Garrett, M., and J.F. Short. 1975. "Social Class and Delinquency: Predictions and Outcomes of Police-Juvenile Encounters." *Social Problems* 22:368-83.

Gibbons, D., and M. Griswold. 1957. "Sex Differences Among Juvenile Court Referrals." *Sociology and Social Research* 42:106-10.

Glueck, S., and E. Glueck. 1962. *Family Environment and Delinquency.* London: Routledge and Kegan Paul.

Gold, M. 1966. "Undetected Delinquent Behavior." *Journal of Research in Crime and Delinquency* 4 (January):28-42.

_____. 1969. "Juvenile Delinquency as a Symptom of Alienation." *Journal of Social Issues* 25:121-35.

_____. 1970. *Delinquent Behavior in an American City.* Belmont, Ca.: Brooks-Cole Inc.

Goodman, L. 1972. "A Modified Multiple Regression Approach to the Analysis of Dichotomous Variables." *American Sociological Review* 37:28-45.

Goodman, P. 1960. *Growing Up Absurd.* New York: Random House.

Grizzle, J.E.; C.F. Starmer; and G.G. Koch. 1969. "Analysis of Categorical Data by Linear Models." *Biometrics* 25:489-504.

Harry, J. 1974. "Social Class and Delinquency: One More Time." *The Sociological Quarterly* 15 (Spring):294-301.

Hendin, H. 1975. *The Age of Sensation.* New York: McGraw-Hill.

Hennessy, M.; P. Richards; and R.A. Berk. 1978. "Broken Homes and Middle Class Delinquency: A Reassessment." *Criminology* 15 4 (February):505-28.

Hindelang, M. 1971. "Age, Sex, and the Versatility of Delinquent Involvement." *Social Problems* 18 (Spring):522-35.

Hirschi, T. 1969. *Causes of Delinquency.* Berkeley: The University of California Press.

Hirschi, T., and H. Selvin. 1967. *Delinquency Research: An Appraisal of Analytic Methods.* New York: The Free Press.

Jensen, G., and R. Eve. 1976. "Sex Differences in Delinquency: An Examination of Popular Sociological Explanations." *Criminology* 13 4 (February):427-48.

Johnston, J. 1972. *Econometric Methods.* New York: McGraw-Hill.

Johnston, L. 1973. *Drugs and American Youth.* Ann Arbor: Institute for Social Research, The University of Michigan.

Kandel, D. 1974. "Inter and Intra-Generational Influences of Adolescent Marijuana Use." *Journal of Social Issues* 30:107-36.

Kaplan, M. 1960. *Leisure in America.* New York: Wiley.

Kelley, D. 1975. "Status Origins, Track Position, and Delinquent Involvement: A Self-Report Analysis." *The Sociological Quarterly* 16 (Spring):264-71.

Kenniston, K. 1968a. *Young Radicals.* New York: Harcourt, Brace, Jovanovitch.

_____. 1968b. "Heads and Seekers: Drugs on Campus, Counter Cultures, and American Society." *The American Scholar* 38 (Winter):97-112.

Kitsuse, J.I., and A.V. Cicourel. 1963. "A Note on the Uses of Official Statistics." *Social Problems.* 11:131-39.

Klein, D. 1973. "The Etiology of Female Crime: A Review of the Literature." *Issues in Criminology* 8(2):3-31.

Kmenta, J. 1971. *Elements of Econometrics.* New York: Macmillan.

Kohn, M. 1969. *Class and Conformity: A Study in Values.* Homewood, Ill.: The Dorsey Press.

Konopka, G. 1966. *The Adolescent Girl in Conflict.* Englewood Cliffs, N.J.: Prentice-Hall.

Kratcoski, P., and J. Kratcoski, 1975. "Changing Patterns in the Delinquent Activities of Boys and Girls: A Self-Reported Delinquency Analysis." *Adolescence* 10 37 (Spring):83-91.

Krohn, M.; G. Waldo; and T. Chircos. 1974. "Self-Reported Delinquency: A Comparison of Structured Interview and Self Administered Checklists." *Journal of Criminal Law and Criminology* 64(4):545-53.

Kvaraceus, W.C. 1944. "Juvenile Delinquency and Social Class." *Journal of Educational Sociology* 18 (September):51-54.

Lippman, H.S. 1952. "Vandalism as an Outlet for Aggression." *Federal Probation* 28(1):5-6.

Liazos, A. 1974. "Class Oppression: The Functions of Juvenile Justice." *Insurgent Sociologist* 1:2-24.

Luschen, G. 1973. "Some Critical Remarks Concerning the Sociology of Leisure." *Society and Leisure* 5(1):165-75.

Madison, A. 1970. *Vandalism: The Not So Senseless Crime.* New York: Seabury Press.

Mahler, F. 1974. "Play and Counter-Play: On the Educational Ambivalence of Play or its Utilization to Counter the Negative Effects of Play." *International Review of Sport Sociology* 9(1):105-115.

Mannheim, H. 1952. "The Problem of Vandalism in Great Britain." *Federal Probation* 28(1):14-15.

Martin, J. 1961. *Juvenile Vandalism.* Springfield, Ill.: Charles C. Thomas.

Marwell, G. 1966. "Adolescent Powerlessness and Delinquent Behavior." *Social Problems* 14(1):35-47.

Mathieson, D., and P. Passell. 1976. "Homicide and Robbery in New York City: An Economic Model." *The Journal of Legal Studies* V(1):83-98.

Matza, D. 1964. *Delinquency and Drift.* New York: Wiley.

Merton, R.K. 1957. *Social Theory and Social Structure.* Glencoe, Ill.: The Free Press.

Meyerhoff, H.L., and B.G. Meyerhoff. 1964. "Field Observation of Middle Class 'Gangs'." *Social Forces* 42 (March):328-36.

Miller, W.B. 1958. "Lower Class Culture as a Generating Milieu of Gang Delinquency." *Journal of Social Issues* 14(3):1-19.

Nerlove, M. and S. Press. 1973. "Univariate and Multivariate Log-linear and Logistic Models." Rand Corporation Tech. Report R-1306-EDA/NIH. Santa Monica, Ca.

Nye, F.I. 1958. *Family Relationships and Delinquent Behavior.* New York: Wiley.

Nye, F.I., and J.F. Short. 1957. "Scaling Delinquent Behavior." *American Sociological Review* 22:328.

Nye, F.I.; J.F. Short; and V.J. Olsen. 1958. "Socioeconomic Status and Delinquent Behavior." *American Journal of Sociology* (January):381-89.

Parker, S. 1971. *The Future of Work and Leisure.* London: McGibbon and Ken.

Parsons, T. 1959. "The School Class as a Social System." *Harvard Educational Review* 29(4):297-318.

Passell, P., and J.B. Taylor. 1977. "The Deterrent Effect of Capital Punishment: Another View." *The American Economics Review* 67(3):445-58.

Phillips, L.; H.L. Votey; and J. Howell. 1976. "Handguns and Homicide: Minimizing Losses and the Costs of Control." *The Journal of Legal Studies* V(2):463-78.

Piliavin, I., and S. Briar. 1964. "Police Encounters with Juveniles." *American Journal of Sociology* 70:206-14.

Platt, A. 1969. *The Child Savers: The Invention of Delinquency.* Chicago: University of Chicago Press.

Polk, C.K. 1969. "Class, Strain, and Rebellion Among Adolescents." *Social Problems* 17:214-24.

Quinney, R. 1965. "Is Criminal Behavior Deviant Behavior?" *British Journal of Criminology* 5 (April):132-42.

———. 1970. *The Social Reality of Crime.* Boston: Little, Brown & Co.

———. 1975. *Criminology: Analysis and Critique of Crime in America.* Boston: Little, Brown & Co.

Reilly, M., ed. 1974. *Play as Exploratory Learning.* Beverly Hills, Ca.: Sage Publications.

Reiss, A.J., and A.L. Rhodes. 1961. "The Distribution of Delinquency in the Social Class Structure." *American Sociological Review* 26 (October):720-32.

Richards, P. 1976. "Patterns of Middle Class Vandalism: A Case Study of Suburban Adolescents." Ph.D. dissertation, Northwestern University, Evanston, Ill.

Schwendinger, H., and J. Schwendinger. 1978. "Marginal Youth and Social Policy." In *The Children of Ishmael,* eds. B. Kinsberg and J. Austin, Palo Alto, Ca.: Mayfield.

Scott, J.W., and E.W. Vaz. 1967. "A Perspective on Middle Class Delinquency." In *Middle Class Juvenile Delinquency,* ed. E. Vaz. New York: Harper and Row.

Sears, R.; E. Maccoby; and H. Levin. 1957. *Patterns of Childrearing.* Evanston, Ill.: Row, Peterson & Co.

Shalloo, J.P. 1952. "Vandalism: Whose Responsibility?" *Federal Probation* 28:(1):6-7.

Shaw, C. 1931. *The National History of a Delinquent Career.* Chicago: University of Chicago Press.

———. 1966. *The Jack Roller: A Delinquent Boy's Own Story.* Chicago: University of Chicago Press.

Shaw, C. et al. 1929. *Delinquency Areas.* Chicago: University of Chicago Press.

Shaw, C., and H. McKay. 1942. *Juvenile Delinquency and Urban Areas.* Chicago: University of Chicago Press.

Short, J.R., and F.I. Nye. 1957. "Reported Behavior as a Criterion of Deviant Behavior." *Social Problems* 5:207-13.

———. 1958. "Extent of Unrecorded Juvenile Delinquency: Tentative Conclusions." *Journal of Criminal Law, Criminology, and Police Science* 49:296-302.

Sjoquist, D.L. 1973. "Property Crime and Economic Behavior: Some Empirical Results." *American Economics Review* 63(3):439-46.

Spilerman, S. 1976. "Structural Characteristics of Cities and the Severity of Racial Disorders." *American Sociological Review* 41, 5 (October):771-92.

Stigler, G.S. 1970. "The Optimum Enforcement of Laws." *Journal of Political Economy* 78(3):526-36.

Stinchcombe, A. 1964. *Rebellion in a High School.* Chicago: Quadrangle Books.

Suchman, E. 1968. "The 'Hang Loose' Ethic and the Spirit of Drug Use." *Journal of Health and Social Behavior* 9 (June):146-55.

Sudman, S., and N. Bradburn. 1974. *Response Effects in Surveys: A Review and Synthesis.* Chicago: Aldine.

Taylor, L., and I. Taylor, eds. 1973. *Politics and Deviance.* Hammondsworth: Penguin.

Taylor, I.; P. Walton; and J. Young. 1973. *The New Criminology: For a Social Theory of Deviance.* New York: Harper and Row.

Terry, R.M. 1967. "Discrimination in the Handling of Juvenile Offenders by Social Control Agencies." *Journal of Research in Crime and Delinquency* 4:218-30.

Thornberry, T. 1973. "Race, Socioeconomic Status, and Sentencing in the Juvenile Justice System." *Journal of Criminal Law and Criminology* 64:90-98.

Thrasher, F.M. 1963. *The Gang: A Study of 1,313 Gangs in Chicago.* Chicago: University of Chicago Press.

Tittle, C., and W. Villamez. 1977. "Social Class and Criminality." *Social Forces* 56 2 (December):474-501.

Turk, A. 1966. "Conflict and Criminality." *American Sociological Review* 31:338-52.

_____. 1969. *Criminality and the Legal Order.* Chicago: Rand MacNally.

Turner, R. 1974. "The Theme of Contemporary Social Movements." In *The Sociology of Dissent,* ed. R.S. Denisoff. New York: Harcourt, Brace, Jovanovich.

Vaz, E.W. 1965. "Middle Class Adolescents: Self-Reported Delinquency and Youth Culture Activities." *Canadian Review of Sociology and Anthropology* 2 1:52-69.

_____, ed. 1967. *Middle Class Juvenile Delinquency.* New York: Harper and Row.

_____. 1969. "Delinquency and the Youth Culture: Upper and Middle Class Boys." *Journal of Criminal Law, Criminology, and Police Science* 60(1):33-46.

Vold, G. 1958. *Theoretical Criminology.* New York: Oxford University Press.

Voss, H. 1966. "Socioeconomic Status and Reported Delinquent Behavior." *Social Problems* 13 (Winter):314-324.

Wade, A. 1967. "Social Processes in the Act of Juvenile Vandalism." In *Criminal Behavior Systems,* ed. M. Clinard and R. Quinney. New York: Holt, Rinehart and Winston.

Ward, C., ed. 1973. *Vandalism.* New York: Van Nostrand Reinhold.

Watson, P. 1974. "Choice of Estimation Procedure for Models of Binary Choice: Some Statistical and Empirical Evidence." *Regional and Urban Economics* 4:187-200.

Weil, A., and N. Zinberg. 1970. "A Comparison of Marijuana Users and Non-Users." *Nature* 226 (Spring):119-23.

Williams, J.R., and M. Gold. 1972. "From Delinquent Behavior to Official Delinquency." *Social Problems* 20(2):209-29.

Winch, R.F., and D.T. Campbell. 1969. "Proof? No, Evidence? Yes. The Significance of Tests of Significance." *American Journal of Sociology* 4(2):140-43.

Wise, N. 1967. "Juvenile Delinquency Among Middle Class Girls." In *Juvenile Delinquency,* ed. R. Giallombardo. New York: Wiley.

Wolfgang, M.; R. Figlio; and T. Sellin. 1972. *Delinquency in A Birth Cohort.* Chicago: University of Chicago Press.

Index

About the Authors

Pamela Richards is Assistant Professor of Sociology at the University of Florida. Her interest in juvenile delinquency stems from a concern with the broader issues of deviance and age inequality. She has written on a number of delinquency topics including vandalism, sex differences in adolescent deviance, and family structure and middle class delinquency. Her current work deals with the perceived severity and certainty of criminal sanctions.

Richard A. Berk is Professor of Sociology at the University of California at Santa Barbara. He has published widely in the fields of collective behavior and evaluation research, but his most recent work has been in the sociology of law. Perhaps his best known book is *A Measure of Justice: An Empirical Study of Changes in the California Penal Code, 1955-1971*. He also routinely consults in a wide range of litigation where social science data are particularly relevant.

Brenda Forster is a sociologist with degrees in nursing and mental health. She has published research on topics as diverse as the effect of iced water on oral temperature, nursing student's reaction to the crying patient, classroom techniques for teaching ethics to health professionals, environmental benefits assessment in economic impact studies, administrative roles and procedures in faculty evaluation, and a causal model of family health care. She is currently developing a criminology program for students interested in law, law enforcement, criminal case work and corrections. Both her research and teaching are aimed at integrating theoretical perspectives with pragmatic applications.